*With*
# Concerts of Prayer
*Christians Join for Spiritual Awakening
and World Evangelization*

*With*
# Concerts of Prayer
*Christians Join for Spiritual Awakening
and World Evangelization*

# David
# Bryant

*Foreword by J. Edwin Orr*

A Division of GL Publications
Ventura, California, U.S.A.

The translation of all Regal books is under the direction of GLINT. GLINT provides technical help for the adaptation, translation and publishing of books for millions of people worldwide. For information regarding translation contact: GLINT, P.O. Box 6688, Ventura, California 93006.

Grateful appreciation is expressed to all those who granted permission to include their copyrighted material:

In chapter 1, Bruce Larson is quoted from *Between Peril and Promise* by James R. and Elizabeth Newby. Used by permission of Thomas Nelson Publishers.

The Hallesby quote in chapter 2 is reprinted by permission from *Prayer* by O. Hallesby copyright © Augsburg Publishing House.

In chapter 5, Richard Halverson is quoted from *Between Peril and Promise* by James R. and Elizabeth Newby. Used by permission of Thomas Nelson Publishers.

In chapter 7, the quote from "Engaging the World" by Donald W. Dayton is reprinted with permission from *Sojourners*, P.O. Box 29272, Washington, D.C. 20017.

Scripture quotations in this publication are from the *New International Version*, Holy Bible. Copyright © 1973 and 1978 by New York International Bible Society. Used by permission.

Published by Regal Books
A Division of GL Publications
Ventura, California 93006
Printed in U.S.A.

**Library of Congress Cataloging in Publication Data**

Bryant, David, 1945–
    With concerts of prayer.

    Bibliography: p.
    1. Prayer.   2. Spiritual life.   I. Title.
BV210.2.B77    1984                    248.3'2                    84-17916
ISBN 0-8307-0975-4

TO MY PARENTS,
Howard and Virginia Bryant,
who have covered my
life with a concert
of prayer since the
day we entered
the Kingdom together.

# ACKNOWLEDGMENTS

I've had the undeserved privilege to work for over eight years within the expanding ministry of Inter-Varsity Christian Fellowship. I want to thank President James McLeish and many staff and students for their creative efforts to grapple with and implement the ideas in this book. It has resulted in deeper, sharper thinking on my part.

I acknowledge a special debt to John Kyle, IVCF missions director, who has been mentor, guide, father and friend—all in one—over these years. Graciously God allowed us to find in each other reflections of common dreams and visions that will not be silent.

I'm also indebted to friends on the National Prayer Committee and the Lausanne Intercession Advisory Group, and to thousands in churches who've responded to my Concert of Prayer Seminars. They have provided vital input into this book both by suggestions and faithful examples.

To my secretary, Joy Mykytiuk, as well as Kathy Dobbins, Neil Bartlett and all my colleagues at Inter-Varsity Missions, my deepest thanks for hard labor and encouraging prayers. The same goes for Bill Greig and my friends at Regal Books.

Finally, to Robyne I can only say: "You *still* walk with me as one . . . in the gap. But even more so, now that we've been walking shoulder-to-shoulder with concerts of prayer. I couldn't imagine taking these steps without you."

# CONTENTS

# FOREWORD

At the time of the Lausanne Congress on Evangelism, the subject of revival or spiritual awakening had a very low priority. There was much emphasis upon church expansion techniques and social objectives, and very little upon dynamics.

Some of us who sought to correct this state of affairs planned a conference at Oxford that same year. Dr. F. Donald Coggan, Archbishop of Canterbury, Canon Max Warren of Westminster, and a number of other denominational leaders who had held the highest offices of their denominations sponsored the effort. Dr. Billy Graham provided the fares of many Third World leaders who lacked the funds to come to Europe again.

Since then, various leading church historians, professors of missions and evangelism, missionaries, evangelists, pastors and laymen have attended and made significant contributions to the general knowledge of the field.

It was on such an occasion that I had the pleasure and privilege of some days of fellowship with David Bryant, a staff worker with Inter-Varsity Christian Fellowship. His appetite for information about the outpourings of the Spirit, and the days of the right hand of the Almighty, was insatiable. No mere hobby was this, but a burning desire to see another visitation from above.

Ten years after the conference was begun at Oxford, we met again at the International Prayer Congress in Seoul, Korea, where his preaching on the subject was prophetic. Not only so, but Bryant's writings on the subject have had the profoundest influence upon the spread of concerts of prayer throughout the Christian world, a project to which he devotes his time and energy.

This present volume combines the historical with the practical interest, not only calling to mind the wonderful works of God, as the Psalmist has told us to do, but also offering sound advice on how to promote concerts of prayer. And rightly, he links the obligation of intercession to the greatest of all gospel objectives, world evangelization.

After 50 years of ministry trying to encourage people to undertake such a needed project, I can only rejoice that God is raising up younger men to carry out His declared purposes.


—J. Edwin Orr

# INTRODUCTION
## In the Gap Again!

"I looked for a man among them who would build up the wall and stand before me in the gap on behalf of the land so I would not have to destroy it, but I found none" (Ezek. 22:30, *NIV*).

There are billions on our planet who know nothing of Christ and have no one like them, near them, to tell them about Him. I call this the great "gap of opportunity." Christ is standing in the gap and we are called to join Him there. And all who are born again into God's Kingdom have been given a place somewhere in the gap—the gap between God's purposes for the whole earth and the fulfillment of those purposes; between the finished work of Christ and the testimony to that work among all the peoples of the earth.

Through Ezekiel, God is saying that we may stand in the gap on behalf of those who are in desperate straits and become involved in rebuilding their relationship with Him (the wall) so that He may turn away His wrath. If we assume such a ministry on behalf of the world's unreached, we will find every facet of our Christian life, whether in personal quiet time or worship or career decisions, molded and reshaped by the tragic and urgent needs of the gap. I would call such a person a "world Christian."

A few months ago, something curious happened to me: the Father brought me again to Ezekiel 22:30 and showed me something I had not seen there before: while God does call for someone to stand in the gap, He actually calls that person to stand "*before me* in the gap." Literally, in Hebrew, the phrase reads, "stand before my face" in the gap. Throughout Scripture, this expression refers almost exclusively to prayer. In other words, God is calling us to stand in the gap primarily as people of prayer.

A tremendous missionary outreach from South India by the Friends Missionary Prayer Band (FMPB)—involving some 20,000 lay Christians in more than 500 weekly prayer bands—was a result of concerted, sustained prayer on the part of thousands. Most of their prayer bands meet once a week to fast and pray all night for the missionaries that are sent out from their midst. However, they pray not only for the missionaries who minister to the unreached peoples of India, but also for revival in the churches of India—and God is answering them on both fronts. Theirs is a movement of prayer for the world, targeted on spiritual awakening and resulting in the harvesting of hundreds into the Kingdom who, before the FMPBers had prayed, had no opportunity to respond.

They are standing in the gap before God's face. No other explanation is possible, in view of their limited resources, for the amazing impact the FMPB had had on India in the past 20 years. They are involved in "concerts of prayer."

*Concerts of Prayer,* therefore, takes us the next step beyond *In the Gap* in a manner to reflect the overlooked component of *how* we stand in Ezekiel's gap of opportunity. And how do we stand in the gap? We stand with concerts of prayer.

Calling prayer a "concert" comes from Jesus' promise in Matthew 18:19,20: "I tell you that if two of you on earth agree about anything you ask for, it will be done for you by my Father in heaven. For where two or three come together in my name, there am I with them." The word "agree" is the Greek word *sumphōneō* and literally means "to sound together." We get our word symphony from this Greek word—hence, when we "agree about anything we ask for," we are praying in symphony, in concert to God.

When you think of a local concert of prayer gathering, think of an orchestra. In a symphony orchestra, you have one conductor and many instruments blending together in harmony to play a composition consisting of central themes and variations.

So it is with each concert of prayer. We are orchestrated by Christ. Even with differences in our understanding of God's heart, in our verbal expressions in prayer, and in our personalities (like different instruments), we are still united by the same score (visions and promises), with the same great needs for revival and world evangelization.

I did not originate the term "concerts of prayer." It has been used of prayer movements of general awakenings over the past 300 years. George Whitefield, the great preacher of awakening in the early 1700s, encouraged "concerts of prayer."

And Jonathan Edwards, in response to reports of prayer concerts in Scotland, called on Christians, who had already been touched by the general awakenings in the 1730s and 1740s, to continue uniting in concerts until God completed the work which He had begun. Edwards wrote—in his volume *A Humble Attempt to Promote Explicit Agreement and Visible Union of God's People in Extraordinary Prayer for the Revival of Religion and the Advancement of Christ's Kingdom on Earth* (that is the title, not the table of contents!):

> I would ask, whether they object against any such thing, as a visible agreement of God's people, in the coming of Christ's Kingdom? Whether such a thing being visible, would not be much for the public honor of God's name? And whether it would not tend to Christians' assistance, and encouragement in the duty, and also to their mutual comfort, by a manifestation of that union which is amiable to Christ and Christians and to promote a Christian union among professing Christians in general?

Historian J. Edwin Orr observes that succeeding generations took Edwards very seriously:

> The concerts of prayer for revival in the 1780s in Great Britain and in the 1790s in the United States, and the renewed concert of prayer in both countries in 1815 and in several European realms besides, was

clearly demonstrated to be the prime factor in motivating and equipping Christians for service in a
worldwide movement which totally eclipsed the military might of the nations at the Battle of Waterloo.[1]

Clearly then, concerts of prayer is a generic term and,
therefore, quite useful for us today. Our use of the term does
not imply the establishment of a new program or organization.
Rather, it pinpoints the possibility of a new beginning for the
whole Church.

As I step once more into Ezekiel 22 for a study of concerts of
prayer, I want to describe for you the impact on the world which
a movement of prayer could have and call all of us to unite
together, ready for all that God will do as a result.

Part I looks at the priority of concerted prayer. We will pursue biblical, historical, and contemporary examples of prayer
movements. We will also establish some of the distinctives of
"concerts of prayer."

We will highlight the target for concerts of prayer—spiritual
awakening. Considering the challenges and opportunities before
the Church today nothing less will do.

But is there hope for a spiritual awakening in our generation?
We will examine that question. Defining the divine pattern in
both Scripture and history, facing the desperate necessity for a
new work of God in the Church and the world today, and reviewing up-to-date evidence of the Lord's dramatic preparations for
spiritual awakening should fill us with great expectations about
all God can do in answer to a movement of united prayer.

Finally, Part I will focus on the people God equips to set the
pace for concerted prayer—who help all of us get to the threshold of God's new day. You may very well get to the threshold of
God's new day. You may very well discover that *you* are one of
them!

Part II presents very practical steps to take to be strategically involved in sustaining the concerted prayer efforts which
God is raising up. We will consider the critical steps of repentance, unity among believers, and personal daily preparations to
keep up with all we are asking God to do. What are the characteristics of those who spearhead a movement of prayer in a

church or on a campus or within a community? We'll find out. In what workable ways can these individuals help mobilize, organize, and guide concerts of prayer? You will be thrilled with the possibilities! The focus of this book is specifically on corporate prayer—the mobilization of corporate prayer.

Today, God continues to look for "a man [or woman] among them who would build up the wall and stand before me [my face] in the gap on behalf of the land" (Ezek. 22:30). In one sense He has already found that person—the Lord Jesus Christ, the one whose sacrifice by death has bridged the greatest gap of all: the infinite gap created by our sin. No one but Christ could have done that. Based on His sacrifice, the risen Lord continues in a ministry of unceasing intercession as He keeps on saving to the uttermost those who come to God through Him, because He always lives to intercede for them (Heb. 7:24-25).

But in another sense God wants all of us to become a company of priests unto Him, joining our Lord Jesus in His great ministry of intercession and, in so doing, filling up the other gap in the advance of His Kingdom.

Will you join me in the gap as a man or woman of prayer? Could we work together to assist a God-given *movement* of united prayer for spiritual awakening and world evangelization? I'd like that very much. And the time for it has come.

# PART I
# THE PRIORITY OF A MOVEMENT OF PRAYER FOR THE WORLD

# 1
# ORDINARY PEOPLE AT THE THRESHOLD

We *ordinary people* cannot fit our lives into pre-formed, Styrofoam boxes. We cannot manage life as well as we would like, at least not in our secret places. We cannot get all the strings tied; it won't wrap up the way we want it. For us, survival is often the biggest success story we dare hope for.

Ordinary people feel too tired a lot. They come to church and listen to words about a grace that has made life all right at the core. But they are often so muzzled by self-pity, so shackled by anger, and so paralyzed by their own real hurts that they cannot find the extra reserve of power to open their hearts to the reality of Jesus Christ and the fact of his grace. God needs to open the door.

The surprise is that God does give us the gift. Sometimes. And sometimes we accept it.[1]

I must confess, Lewis Smedes, who wrote these words, has *me* figured out pretty well. I am an ordinary person! How about you? From God's perspective, of course, anyone created and redeemed by Him can hardly be called "ordinary." Yet, in our day-to-day routine we often feel very ordinary, don't we?

But Smedes also puts his finger on the other, often extraordinary, dimension of who we are. He calls our attention to the unusual, the surprising, the miraculous ways God invades our lives. Listen as he goes on!

> Sometimes people are sure that everything is all wrong and they are tired of trying to make it right. *Then God comes* quietly to tell them that he is around them, above them, under them, in them, and ahead of them, and that with this surrounding shield of strong love, they are going to be all right.
>
> Sometimes people are in the grip of anger that chokes their hearts, stifles their joy, and smothers every intimate relationship. *Then God comes* in to break the chain of anger and liberate an ordinary person for a new try at love.
>
> Sometimes people live in quiet terror of their own death. *Then God comes* in to give them a reason for being very glad to be alive just for today.
>
> Sometimes people brood over a depressing memory of some rotten thing they did and cannot forget or forgive themselves for. *Then God comes* in to open their hearts to receive the gifts of other ordinary people's forgiveness and so come to forgive themselves.
>
> Sometimes ordinary people wrap themselves like mummies in the suffocating sackcloth of their own self-hatred; and God comes to open their eyes to the extraordinary wonder of their great worth.[2]

Many Christian leaders today believe that God is preparing to do what Smedes describes but on a broader, more intense, more earth-shaking scale than any of us have ever known. A whole host of ordinary people are currently poised at the threshold of an extraordinary work of God in the life of His whole Church. And the world is waiting!

## A TALE FOR ORDINARY PEOPLE
On the visual display of my mental terminal occurs a repeat-

ing drama—a vision of sorts as vivid as if it actually happened a moment ago. I see myself standing at the far end of a darkened hallway lined with many doors. All are shut and locked, but one. Light penetrates the hallway through a partially opened door at the far end. Curious, I want to find out more.

Gradually, I walk down the hallway toward the light. The closer I get to the door, the more brilliant and delightful the light appears to be. I even begin to feel its warmth. It almost dances.

But when I reach the threshold I find neither courage nor freedom to fling the door open and burst into the radiant room beyond. Awe and fear mingle with anticipation. I hesitate to knock, yet I know if I do, an invitation to enter eventually will come.

I knock deliberately and boldly, compelled by the conviction that until there is an answer I have little else to live for, as the hallway behind me promises little worth seeking.

My video-vision continues; I'm knocking more rapidly now. Gradually I realize I am not alone. Others are quietly rising out of the shadows of the hallway to join me. We form a litany of knuckles-on-wood, as we reflect the little light that already greets us.

More come forth. We knock together now, harder and harder, almost in a frenzy! Our knocking attracts still others, until the threshold is crowded with determined people from the shadows who, having seen something of the light, desire to step inside, into the full radiance of it.

My eyes glance for a moment back down the hallway. Suddenly my heart leaps! It strikes me that when the door finally does swing open to us and we are able to move into the glorious treasures that lie beyond, the blessing will not be for us alone. The light into which we step will, at the same moment, pour beyond us to the far ends of the hallway, dispelling any dimness that remains. And how many of those locked doors will those dazzling rays pierce, penetrating the rooms like a laser, driving out of them the even greater darkness there and calling many from the icy shadows of death.

What does it all mean? From the first moment I recorded these pictures, the interpretation was obvious. The knocking on the door is prayer. The light coming through the crack in the door is the "light of the knowledge of the glory of God in the face of Christ" (2 Cor. 4:6). The hallway represents the Church today, much of which survives in the twilight zone of all that God originally intended for us, in us, and through us. The sealed side-rooms symbolize enclaves and even whole nations, where Christ is not known.

The locked doors, waiting to be overcome by grace and truth, include structures and powers, injustices and crises, cultures and languages, persuasions old and new, that raise formidable barriers against the advancement of the Kingdom.

Those who gather at the threshold with me are members of the Lord's company—ordinary people who, already drawn to the light and benefiting from it, are hungry to know the fullness of Christ in their lives and to see the fulfillment of His purposes among the nations. The flinging wide of the central door is "spiritual awakening." It is not so much our taking more of Christ into the Church as it is Christ inviting us into more of Himself and His Kingdom. But once the door is fully open, it releases more of the intense light of the gospel and its power into the Church and thus among all peoples.

The chorus of knockers represents the current development of concerted prayer for spiritual awakening. It also describes the critical dimension of such a movement where those who are determined are seeking to enter wholly and obediently in His light gather others to join in the search. They're unwilling to stop knocking until God swings open the door into the brilliant immensity of Christ's global cause. In fact, the door on which we knock is Jesus Christ Himself ("whatever you ask in *my* name"); He is the end of our search, He is also the way in.

What a strategic place for "ordinary people" to be—standing on the threshold of a new work of God in all our lives and throughout the earth. You see, this drama goes far beyond expanding individual spiritual experiences. It's possible for a whole generation of God's praying people to be surprised (Smede's word) by Him.

## SEISMOLOGISTS TESTING FOR THE EXTRAORDINARY

Once we gather at the threshold, however, our initial experience may feel more like being caught in the middle. There's enough darkness in the hallway that we don't want to go back, and there's such promising light before us that we only want to go forward. But we can't move beyond the door that's ajar until *God* takes us on together. That's where the Church seems to be right now. We can neither go backward or forward, so we must go down corporately—on our knees—in prayer, at the threshold of God's new work in our midst. And there we must wait in hope for something to break loose.

In a parallel way, many social analysts recognize that the world at large is united in a mood of wonder and fearful transition between eras, a time of parenthesis. Though some call this a moment of fashionable pessimism, when we're weary with the past but disenchanted about the future, John Naisbitt, in his best-seller *Megatrends,* disagrees. Ours is really a time full of promise, he writes, when the world senses itself to be on the threshold of earthshaking possibilities:

> Although the time between eras is uncertain, it is a great and yeasty time, filled with opportunity. If we can learn to make uncertainty our friend, we can achieve much more than in stable eras.
>
> In stable eras, everything has a name and everything knows its place, and we can leverage very little.
>
> But in the time of the parenthesis we have extraordinary leverage and influence—individually, professionally, and institutionally—if we can only get a clear sense, a clear conception, a clear vision, of the road ahead.[3]

If this is how secularists feel about our historic moment, we Christians-in-transition should be no less hopeful, but have a far greater vision of where things are headed and, even more, who is really in charge. For the threats of serious national and international upheaval—not to mention technological revolution—should never negate our anticipating a God-given era of glorious upheaval in the Church that will have national and international repercussions for Christ's Kingdom. We ordinary people need to hear this now more than ever.

Yale historian Kenneth Scott Latourette's studies of church history can help us. 'He uncovered how most significant spiritual pulsations were a direct result of surprise interventions of God's Spirit in the life of major portions of the Body of Christ. This in turn unlocked new eras in God's saving purposes among the nations. In other words, God is always on the move outward. But He intends to have His people involved with Him, determined not to let them fall asleep for long on His mission to the world. He insists on awakening us out of the twilight into new vistas of Christ's Great Commandment and His Great Commission.

Over the years this has been reinforced for me in riveting conversations with spiritual "seismologists," like Latourette. As you know, geo-seismologists measure the tremors in the earth to determine where the next major earthquake might strike. Well, spiritual seismologists are theologians, historians, missionary statesmen, and other Christian leaders working together to determine from Scripture, history, and the contemporary scene what kind of tremblings are going on in the Church today. They are looking for evidence of another great shaking in the Body of Christ. The strong consensus is that a spiritual earthquake is not far off. And when it strikes, it may comprise an unprecedented shaking of the heavens and the earth, a shaking of all nations so that the treasures of earth's people might be brought to the feet of Jesus and fill God's house with glory (Hag. 2:6-7).

Several years ago, one of these seismologists, Sam Shoemaker, confessed: "What we are feeling for, imagining, longing for, really praying for, is a worldwide awakening under the power of the Holy Spirit. This alone would be great enough to meet our needs, to use our resources, and to incorporate our little personal stores of faith in a movement greater than anything the world has ever seen."[5]

This longing has continued to increase. More recently Bruce Larson, founder of Faith-at-Work, predicted.

> God has been waiting 2,000 years for the 100
> years ahead. I really believe this. We have seen

> models through the years of what He had in mind:
> the Franciscans, the Moravians, the Wesleyans. But
> the church at large has never caught the big picture.
> I think we are in the time when there can be some
> alternative models of what the church can be, and
> then it will spread like fire. People are tired of the
> old, tired of "churchianity," tired of religion. So am I.
> I am bored with it. I hate it. I want Jesus. I want life.
> I think we are at the beginning of what God had in
> mind when he wrote the Book of Acts.[6]

In fact, we may be at the threshold of a spiritual awakening qualitatively different from any previous one. With a mature foundation laid in knowledge of Scripture, in understanding the ministry of the Holy Spirit, in commitments to Body unity, in the initiative of the laity, and in its ready heart for total world evangelization, the Church today may be more equipped for revival than in any other era.

## A FEW "READINGS" OF MY OWN

In my 21 years as a Christian, I too have become a seismologist. Though I still feel like an amateur, I sense the rightness of others' predictions. Let me describe some "readings" from my personal seismograph.

When I was a pastor I quickly realized that without a deep work of God, both in individuals and in the corporate life of our church, there would be neither the environment nor the sustaining foundation for fostering committed Christians. That's when God first helped me understand the essentiality of spiritual awakening and its prelude, concerted prayer.

As a pastor in Kent, Ohio in 1970, I was forced to God's threshold after witnessing the Kent State University shootings that fateful day in May. The trauma of that tragic incident not only sealed the mood of our country about Vietnam but, ultimately, the course of history and nations.

Our church, as a body, felt convicted. The impact we were having on the world for Christ was negligible compared to the impact of the student-national guard confrontation on the KSU campus. By fall, five men in the church joined me in seeking some answers from God. We agreed to meet for six weeks of prayer, four nights a week, two hours a night.

The first night we met, we sat there, staring at each other with half smiles as if to say, "Well, what do we do now?" None of us had ever prayed like this before. One suggested we pray through Scripture. That made sense. We chose Ephesians. And why not? Ephesians has six chapters and we were committed to meet for six weeks.

And what an unforgettable six weeks. You can't pray through Scripture like Ephesians and stay the same. Paul swept us along in God's purposes for the nations and the Church. And I believe we saw some key evidences of spiritual awakening as a result. We grew, as a congregation, in a new appreciation for world evangelization and in a desire to begin giving ourselves to whatever God would ask of us in serving Christ's global cause. This was a new experience for me, and it could have been spawned only in prayer. Previously, I had run from missions, even in seminary. In thrilling ways, God has worked through that little church over the past 15 years to bring Christ to the nations.

My understandings of united prayer at the threshold were also initially formed in 1970. Ours was certainly a movement of prayer for the world. And it sowed in me the seed that has since germinated a conviction that, when ordinary people are willing to gather at the threshold in concerted prayer for spiritual awakening, they have assumed the most effective strategy possible for the cause of Christ.

In my work at Inter-Varsity Christian Fellowship, we continue to challenge succeeding generations of students to discover God's role for them in the world mission of the Church. We're in touch with thousands of young people who have committed themselves in writing to fulfill their roles as senders and goers.

This is earth shaking! But all of us at Inter-Varsity know that there is no way these good intentions will ever be translated into the penetration of unreached peoples unless we help foster an environment in which the search, the commitment, and the new missions thrust itself are enthusiastically backed by the Church. Nothing less will do than a movement of prayer for spiritual awakening in which local churches, students, and missionaries participate together. Toward that end we have set out to encourage concerts of prayer nationwide.

Not only does the challenge of mobilizing students give me strong seismographic "readings," but my own spiritual thirst has been equally motivating. Not long ago I stood in the back pastures of a Virginia farm at 6:00 A.M., crying out to God to satisfy my longing to know Jesus in a deeper way that would make a difference for His glory throughout the world.

As I prayed, my eye caught a cow breaking out of the herd to wind her way down a little hill to the stream below me. When she came to the edge she did not pause a moment but walked straight into the middle of the stream, planted all four feet in its bed, lowered her massive head and began to drink in the cool liquid.

At that moment I found myself reasoning with God: "Father, for many years I've been pointing people to John 7, telling them that out of their innermost being could flow rivers of living water—flowing without limits, even to the ends of the earth. And I believe it!"

I continued, "But, I myself am still so thirsty; and those to whom I've spoken about your rivers feel the same thirst.

"Father, hear me. I've done what Jesus said. I admit my thirst. I have come to Him and seek no other source to quench my thirst. But how do I drink of Christ so that out of my being will flow the rivers you have promised?"

With the warming sun on my back, I sensed God's response to me: "I know you are thirsty, and I know you have turned to my Son for water. Don't be discouraged. Know this, however: I intend to leave you thirsty for a time. That's what keeps you coming to Him. But that's not the end.

"There's that group of Christians you gather with in Madison the last Thursday night of each month. You call it a concert of prayer, don't you? You've been at it for almost four years. I have good news for you! Every time you gather to seek my face, to ask me to do a new work in your lives and in the life of the Church at large, and to pray that it would result in my Son being known and loved and served among many peoples, you *are* drinking. It may not feel like it, but keep your feet planted there and keep on seeking my Kingdom, and the rivers will come."

Suddenly, the morning sun was rising in my heart as well! Now I understood.

## THRESHOLD TO THE EXTRAORDINARY

That whole conversation with the Father returned to me with force some months later as I read Maria Monson's story in her book *The Awakening*. She too was an ordinary person. Though a dedicated Norwegian missionary to China in the early part of this century, Maria wrestled for years with the thirst in her own life. She was equally burdened for what she sensed to be dryness and lifelessness in many of her missionary companions and many of the Chinese Christians around her. For years God kept her praying, then used her to make other Christians thirsty too. The results were earthshaking.

At one point, as she wondered what good any of her praying was doing, God gave her a vision of the Yangtze River. In the vision, God asked her, "How does the Great River begin?" He proceeded to show her that it was not in the smaller rivers that converged to form the Yangtze, nor in the streams and rivulets out of the foothills, but in the tiny drops that condensed on the very top of the mountains. As she looked to God to answer her prayers for rivers of living waters, He told her to look first of all for the droplets.

For Maria, the first droplet appeared soon after in the form of another woman missionary who for years had also been praying for revival in herself and among the missionaries. With joy at discovering one another, these two women began to pray together in a concert of prayer.

"The awakening has begun," they exulted, "because two have agreed in Jesus' name." That was 1926.

Then, during a time of political unrest in the interior, these women circulated in the missionary communities that formed along the coast. They challenged their colleagues to unite in prayer for spiritual awakening. Prayer bands formed—more droplets. By the time it was safe again in the interior, God had answered them powerfully.

Having experienced spiritual awakening for themselves, the missionaries returned to their compounds to gather Chinese Christians together to continue praying with them for God to do a mighty work. They did; He did. That was the beginning of what church historians call the great awakening in China, the intensity of which lasted from 1927-1935. Many would point to this "mighty river," which flowed out of Maria's earlier years of revival prayer and the ensuing movement of united prayer, as providing the spiritual infusion that has kept the Church in China so strong in recent decades. In fact, her prayers still have international repercussions as the amazing testimony of the resilient Chinese Church is sounded worldwide.

## AT THE THRESHOLD OF TOTAL WORLD EVANGELIZATION

I believe that the destiny of a movement of united prayer could result not only in a reprieve of God's stroke of judgment on the developed world, but the unleashing of spiritual power in the Church worldwide to carry the gospel forward in an unprecedented manner. This is the hope of many, such as historian Richard Lovelace—another seismologist:

> I am not insisting that every nation must experience the degree of cultural infusion which Christianity has attained in the West. But it *seems that the millions of Muslims and Chinese should gain something more than a brief glimpse* of a flare shot over another country. Has the meaning of the gospel ever yet been adequately embodied in a widespread movement of the church, displaying for any sustained period the fullness of life available in Christ? *Has the church ever been publicly revealed as the glorious bride of Christ,* without spot or wrinkle, holy and without blemish?
>
> Our study of awakening movements only turns up *what appear to be rehearsals* for some final revelation of the full splendor of God's Kingdom . . . It is *hard to believe that God will not grant the church some greater experience of wholeness* and vitality than has yet appeared in the stumbling record of her history, in order, as Ezekiel says, that Israel and the nations may know that he is the Lord.[7]

Of course, we must temper our enthusiasm over such a prospect with biblical realism. Even if what God has planned as answer to our prayers *is* a major advancement of His Kingdom worldwide, that does not mean we'll sail past suffering lost in clouds of revival bliss. If, as Samuel Zwemer remarked, "The unoccupied fields of the world must have their Calvary before they can have their Pentecost," then spiritual awakening may draw us closer to the cross than ever before. Whatever lies on the other side of the threshold, we can be sure that one way or another we ordinary people will be increasingly *consumed* with God's glory.

J. Edwin Orr has demonstrated how revival also is always a time of war between the Spirit and the devil. As God empowers His Church for a new thrust of the gospel, displacing the works of darkness and bringing nations to the obedience of faith, we can expect an increased polarization between the kingdom of darkness and the kingdom of light. This may include increased demonic activity as well as hatred, resistance and even violence of unbelievers. Certainly it will be marked by intensified efforts of our Enemy to confuse the world with counterfeit offers, such as claims we hear right now of the coming cultic "new age." All of this warfare will be costly for praying people.

God knows that you and I are ordinary people, ready to run from the pain. And still He is willing to poise us at the threshold of a new work of His Spirit. He is preparing to awaken us to the lordship of Christ as never before, not only for the future but for our own generation.

He wants to awaken us to an obedience of faith that will allow us to abandon ourselves to Christ for His global purposes; to a hope that will help us seize the victory that Christ has already won for us, to be released through us before the nations; and to a demonstration of love which will set us free with renewed willingness to lose ourselves for Christ's sake and the gospel's.

The prolific writer on prayer, Andrew Murray, nailed this home in his volume *The Key to the Missionary Problem:* only as the Church is awakened as a whole to the greatness and glory of the task entrusted to her and led to engage in it with all her heart and strength, will she ever be able to meet the challenge before her in this generation and see a great harvesting among the nations.

United prayer in search of spiritual awakening *is* the key that will open the door for ordinary people into more of Christ's unshakeable riches for all of life. As George Whitefield prayed with others at the threshold in the 1730s: "The World is now up in arms. Blessed Jesus, whilst the kings of the earth are striving to extend their dominions, do thou secretly carry on Thy kingdom in believer's hearts, till the earth be filled with the knowledge of Thee, our Lord, as the waters cover the sea!"

Maybe you find yourself where I am—thankful for all that God has shown you of Christ, His Body, and His world mission—but regretting that you haven't appreciated fully what else Scripture clearly teaches: that only as God moves in answer to the thirsting prayers of ordinary people will we see the Church adequately mobilized to spread the gospel and advance Christ's Kingdom throughout the earth. And maybe, like me, you are ready to get down to business at the threshold.

Don't despair. There are a bunch of ordinary people like us, convinced that God is preparing to answer us in royal fashion! In fact, they're waiting for us at the threshold right now.

# 2

# CONCERTED PRAYER
## The Frontline in World Evangelization

In my hometown of Madison, Wisconsin, are two prayer meetings I may attend whenever I'm not traveling. One is our concert of prayer that meets the last Thursday evening of each month. The other I attend less frequently, but it's equally fascinating though for different reasons.

As I enter the record prayer meeting, I first take off my shoes and socks, roll up my shirtsleeves and pant legs and proceed into what looks like a shower room. I climb up on tile troughs, squat down in front of a running spigot and begin to wash my legs, feet, hands, arms, and behind my ears. Then I take water into my mouth, swish it around and spit it out.

After drying off, I enter a small auditorium with bare, white walls. On the floor is a thick, tan carpet. More than a hundred men from 40 or 50 nations of the world join me. And soon they're on their hands and faces, foreheads to the ground, praying.

Do you know where I am? I'm in a mosque. It was built not long ago by voluntary contributions from hundreds of Muslim students studying at the University of Wisconsin.

No, I haven't converted to Islam, nor am I endorsing the idea that there are many roads to heaven. I attend the mosque in order to build my friendships with Muslim students so I might

win them to Christ. And while I sit among them it's much easier
to pray for them. While they are praying to Allah, I am silently
praying for them that they may discover in Christ the only way
to know the true God.

I've often been convicted by my times at the mosque, however. I've realized I'm attending a prayer meeting that has international repercussions, if only as it helps solidify bonds of universal Muslim brotherhood. I often ask myself: how many
Christians are involved in times of united prayer that have international repercussions for Christ's Kingdom? That question has
given me a new perspective on and enthusiasm for our monthly
concerts of prayer—because I see that there we really are!

## THE FORCE OF CONCERTED PRAYER

Not long ago I heard Scottish expositor Eric Alexander talk
about the apostles' ministry priority in Acts 6:4,7. He said: "The
frontline in world evangelization is the Word of God and prayer."

He's right. World evangelization demands many things of us,
but we can never get any closer to advancing the gospel among
the nations than to link our hearts around God's Word, turning
its visions and promises into concerted prayer. Revelation 5 and
8 suggest the mingled prayers of God's people, ascending
together like incense before His throne, bear directly on the out-
working of both redemption (chap. 5) and justice (chap. 8)
among the nations.

I can't fully explain *how* prayer changes things in world evangelization. It may be that prayer fits into the sovereignty of God
in the same way that time lapse photography makes a rose open
up before my eyes in 30 seconds. If the rose hadn't unfolded naturally over a previous period of two or three days, there would
be nothing on film. Similarly, as God's people unite to seek all
that He has determined to do, prayer, like the movie camera,
accelerates and intensifies the unfolding of all God has already
willed for His Kingdom. Prayer theologian O. Hallesby put it this
way:

> When God changes the divine world-economy as
> a result of man's prayers, we mean that he governs
> the world with such a degree of elasticity that he can

alter his methods as circumstances here below
require, be they good or bad. He does not alter his
kingdom plans, only the means and methods
whereby he at each moment seeks to accomplish
them.[1]

In other words, none of us is able to begin to untangle every
crisis or meet every need in the world. But through prayer we
can accelerate and intensify God's methods for extending His
Kingdom among the nations. We can do more than watch history
happen; through our prayers we *make* history together. Or, as
my friend Dick Eastman observes, in prayer we "make room for
God." After that, anything can happen!

As Senate Chaplain Richard Halverson reminds us, we have
no alternatives: "You can organize until you are exhausted; you
can plan, program, subsidize all your plans. But if you fail to
pray, it is a waste of time. Prayer is not optional for us. It is man-
datory. Not to pray is to disobey God." Or in the well-known
statement of Oswald Chambers, "Prayer does not just fit us for
the greater work. Prayer *is* the greater work."

All through his life as a South African missionary/pastor,
Andrew Murray took the same view:

> There is a *world with its needs* entirely dependent
> upon and waiting to be helped by intercession. There
> is *a God in heaven,* with his all-sufficient supply for all
> those needs, waiting to be asked. There is *a
> Church, with its wondrous calling* and its sure prom-
> ises, waiting to be roused to a sense of its wondrous
> responsibility and power. There is a world with its
> perishing millions, with *intercession its only hope.*[2]

So prayer is God's frontline way of getting things done. But it
needs to be *united* prayer. How else can we explain that the
Christian Church today is 83 million times larger than when it
first began? How else do you explain that the outward advance
of the gospel is the longest human endeavor in the history of
mankind? How else do you explain that, directly or indirectly,
the Scriptures have altered for good most major cultures on

earth today? The outstanding answer is this: again and again, in one new generation of His people after another, God has raised up pacesetters in prayer who have united to seek His will on earth, and God has answered them far beyond what they asked or thought.

Dr. A. T. Pierson said, "There has never been a spiritual awakening in any country or locality that did not begin in united prayer." J. Edwin Orr said, "History is full of exciting results as God has worked through concerted, united, sustained prayer." From his years of missionary service and reflection, Anglican missions statesman Max Warren acknowledged that "there is no understanding of the evangelical movement of the last two centuries which fails to see as its fundamental characteristic a profound preoccupation with spontaneous prayer." Many other historians as well have documented the significant frontline role of united prayer in spiritual awakening and world evangelization.

For example, take the major missions surge that surfaced during the latter part of the 1800s among college students. Known as the Student Volunteer Movement, it later gave birth to the World Christian Student Federation and went on to field almost 20,000 career missionaries in 30 years. Its brilliant leader, John R. Mott, spent years traveling the globe, investigating spiritual movements among students and churches. He found that the source of those awakenings lay in united intercessory prayer. Therefore, he continually called for prayer concerts that would tie together his worldwide collegiate fellowship. Mott himself belonged to several prayer bands, and he's remembered most by many of those who worked closest with him as a man of prayer.

When asked about the Student Volunteer Movement and its growth Mott said: "Much credit for the success of the movement must be given to the special concerts of prayer to which students in the other federation countries were devoted." Statistics made little difference to Mott if those who were preparing to go as missionaries weren't bonded at the true frontline of world evangelization before they ever boarded a ship.

## FRONTLINE PRIORITIES OF CONCERTED PRAYER

As I have studied these matters, key principles have

emerged. Unlike Luther with his 95 theses, I have only *five* to offer! But I would be delighted to nail them on the bulletin board of any campus or church in this country and return a week later (as Luther did at Wittenburg University) to discuss the issues with lay people, pastors, missionaries, or students who would desire to do so. How would you respond to them?

1. World evangelization, its fruits and its fulfillment through Christ's global Church, is from beginning to end the work of God (Col. 1:17-23).

2. Therefore, only He can awaken the Church to renewed zeal for Christ, His Kingdom, and His global cause, and create an environment that fosters Christians who are wholly dedicated to the task of world evangelization (Eph. 1:16-23).

3. The Church pursues God's work of awakening and world evangelization through united, concerted, sustained prayer, declaring our desire to see His glory revealed and acknowledging our utter dependence on Him to advance His Kingdom (Eph. 6:16-20).

4. Such a movement of united prayer focuses on the two major sweeps of Scripture: the *fullness* of Christ manifested in His Church (revival) for the advancement of His Kingdom, and the *fulfillment* of His global cause (evangelization) (Matt. 6:9-13).

5. Such a movement of united prayer is normally initiated by pioneers of faith who embrace God's redemptive purpose and set the pace for serving it through concerted prayer, encouraging many others thereby to follow (Acts 4:23-31).

I haven't engaged in large-scale debates on these five theses yet! But over several years I have had opportunity to discuss them in depth with many eager people. Let me give you a few "word pictures" that have helped others grasp the "frontline priorities" of concerted prayer described by these theses.

## Concerted Prayer: A University

In all of his efforts to see tens of thousands mobilized into missionary service among earth's totally unreached peoples, missions strategist Ralph Winter is unshakable in his priorities. "The very first and foremost strategy for reaching unreached people must be a massive, new and urgent effort simply to expand the perspectives of the people back home." That being so, there's no better place for perspective to be transformed than in the "university of prayer."

As we pray together, grounded in the Word of God and aware of the challenges of our generation, we can help each other gain a confident, intelligent, heartfelt grasp of God's promises, purposes, and procedures. My experience in united prayer has proven that praying together is as much a workshop on the ways of God as it is a ministry of intercession for the glory of God.

As I related in chapter 1, back in the early 1970s, six weeks of thoughtful prayer through Ephesians became for our church a course of study in God's Kingdom unlike anything Kent State University ever offered. With biblical and contemporary data as our prayer agenda, God permanently expanded our perspectives on both ourselves, our church, and our mission to the world.

Six years later, I was part of another prayer group in Pasadena, California, made up of pastors, educators, missionaries, lay people, and students. We gathered every Monday evening to share our findings on the needs of the Church and the world, and to present ourselves and our dreams before the Lord. That year of prayer taught me perspectives on the application of biblical principles to world evangelization that I never picked up in my previous 12 months of graduate studies in inter-cultural communications.

Even the concert of prayer in which I'm involved in Madison has turned into four years with "Christ in the school of prayer," as Andrew Murray calls it. Many insights in this book spring from the crucible of our faithful struggle together for nearly 48 months to understand the issues in revival and world evangelization, and the interplay between them both locally and worldwide, enough to pray effectively about them.

In all three "universities," I've found that both vision and faith are infectious. As we gather together, our individual perspectives infect and expand the perspectives of others. And because this is molded by prayer, the broader view that emerges motivates us to united faith for other frontline actions.

## Concerted Prayer: A Womb

It is true that God both moves us to prayer and then by prayer. Prayer is not the only thing we can do, but it is the first thing we must do if anything else worthwhile is to follow. It leads to strategic involvement.

The scope of our praying becomes the scope of God's work in us and, subsequently, the scope of our concerned obedience to the visions God births through us. By its nature, prayer feeds a new work of God before that effort becomes visible, as a baby is fed in the womb for months of growth before it is pushed out with joy (Isa. 66:7-9).

There is a very great risk in getting serious together in prayer. Not only will our prayers change the Church and the world, but they will also form the very womb in which we are changed. Through frontline prayer, we draw dangerously close to the magnificent, compassionate but reproductive heart of Christ. In concerted prayer, therefore, we enter a sort of "gestation fellowship" that will eventually stretch all of us to want to love, in practical ways, whom Christ loves—those for whom we've prayed in His name.

By its nature, then, prayer at the frontlines indicates a willingness to let go of preconceived ideas of how God might work with us. The more we pray through Scripture, the more we face the current need for spiritual awakening on our planet, the more we will want to get ready for the surprises and refreshing options God has for us that none of us expected. In concerted prayer we declare our willingness to be open to a mighty thrusting forth of the Holy Spirit into ministry, no matter how long it may take or what changes or sacrifices are required. We believe God will somehow use us, simply because He wants to answer our prayers for the Church and the world. And our praying tells Him we are willing to get involved.

Accordingly, this womb might also be called a *spawning ground* for new dreams and the teams to advance those dreams for Christ's Kingdom worldwide. Concerted prayer provides a creative environment where God's Spirit can effectively summon those He intends to send out and those He is calling to send them—something that has happened in all the concerts of prayer in which I've shared. For example, out of the one in Pasadena came, among other things, the U.S. Center for World Mission.

## Concerted Prayer: Base of Operations

In a time of war, the base of operations is the strategic camp position from which troops lunge out into the thick of battle. It is also the space station from which exploration into outer space can take place.

Concerted prayer is a base of operation that presents a united front against all the dark powers opposed to the kingdom of God: secularism, atheism, injustice, pride, greed, poverty, and hatred, as well as spiritual shallowness and unbelief in the Church. It is also a cosmic beachhead from which God begins the work to revive His Church, expand the impact of the gospel, and press history toward its glorious climax.

As the battle presses forward, a prayer band may also be regarded as a vital outpost of the Kingdom of God, unleashing new manifestations of His glory in the Church and the world. Like a space station, our prayer groups constitute launching pads for increased spiritual mobilization in renewal and world evangelization. They remain sustaining foundations that act as docking stations to undergird the missions and ministries they have launched.

In all these metaphors—whether universities, wombs, or bases—one point is clear: a call for concerted prayer is a statement that we are as devoted to the *process* in God's spiritual breakthroughs—whether learning, conceiving, sailing, or penetrating—as we are to the breakthroughs themselves. As a process, concerted prayer is as strategic as anything we'll ever do. And the process is more visible in the Church today than we've seen for a long time!

## DISTINCTIVES OF A CONCERT OF PRAYER

Concerted prayer is distinct from other prayer times in a number of ways. First, it's primarily a *movement* of prayer. It defines an effort to forge a coalition of praying people who regularly unite for a very specific agenda surrounding spiritual awakening and *world evangelization*. In concerts of prayer we work together toward consensus about all we want God to do within

His Church and His World.

A concert of prayer requires a balanced concentration on two major sweeps: (1) fullness in the Body of Christ for (2) the fulfillment of His global cause. Both sweeps create healthy tension. A concert is designed to allow us to get at fullness and fulfillment in prayer as effectively as possible. This focus of concerted prayer rises from one common concern: zeal for God's glory. Prayer for fullness and fulfillment both seek God's glory among His people as well as among the unreached.

Often when I travel I find two kinds of prayer groups: (1) those who meet regularly to pray for renewal or revival in the church; (2) those who meet regularly to pray for local outreach, world missions or global crises. Rarely does the same person participate in both groups. Frequently, neither group is aware of the other yet the focus of the one should thrive on the other; the one should drive us to the other.

Prayer for the needs of the world urges us to pray for the Church to love Christ in such a way as to meet those needs (fullness). Seeking God's blessings for the Church, however, requires that we also pray for God to bring blessing and healing to the world through the Church (fulfillment). So you see, adding fulfillment issues to fullness prayers prevents a cop-out. Coupling fullness issues to fulfillment prayers prevents a burn-out. Put both together and we will leap out into all God has for us.

What would happen if both kinds of prayer groups would gather together sometimes? What if they shared their individual agendas, learning from one another how the two fit together? What if they blended into a great symphony of intercession that touched both prongs of God's Kingdom? Concerts of prayer provide a way to preserve the distinctive focus and commitment that is so critical for spiritual awakening which dawns as a combination of God's answers to fullness and fulfillment prayers in our time.

## THE FORCE OF CONCERTED PRAYER IS WITH US

When Christians reach a point where they are convinced there are some things in the Church and in the world that God either cannot or will not do until they pray, then miracles begin to happen.

That's why the emergence of united prayer in the Church worldwide at this moment may be the first great miracle of the awakening just ahead, a sign of other miracles to come. When prayer is on the increase, then we can be sure revival is at hand.

No, I do not see swelling crowds gathering in concerted prayer—not yet. But the breadth of prayer efforts for revival across geographical, national, denominational, organizational and social lines, and the depth of the agenda surfacing in prayer groups everywhere, suggest very clearly that God is up to something extraordinary.

The German Evangelical Alliance sponsors an annual week of prayer in more than 650 cities, towns and villages of East Germany. Almost 50 percent of the 17 million citizens call themselves Christians—evidence of spiritual vitality. A few months ago, one million Christians at 5,000 locations in East and West Germany attended prayer meetings sponsored by the Alliance.

In Romania there is a great emphasis on prayer with a resulting Church growth that may be unprecedented in Eastern Europe. Renewal is to be found not only in the independent evangelical churches but also in Romania's Eastern Orthodox Church. It is not at all unusual to find Romanian pastors rising at 4:00 A.M. to spend two hours in prayer before going to work. Dr. Peter Kuzmic at Biblical Theological Institute of Zagreb, Yugoslavia, states that any analysis of church growth in Romania that fails to identify concerted prayer as the single most important reason for growth has missed the mark.

In Poland, a movement called "Oasis and the Life and Light" aims at revival among Polish Catholics. Reliable sources suggest that more than 80,000 young people are actively involved in evangelistic training. Most of all, they are united in Bible study and prayer.

In Russia, where almost 100 million claim to be Christian, the common denominator among all groups is their commitment to prayer, especially united prayer—both in clusters and by congregations—that bonds the whole Body of Christ throughout the country. There is no other explanation for the vitality and growth in the Russian Church today.

Recently the Philippine Council of Evangelical Churches sent a paper to their 5,000 member churches representing 500,000

Filipino evangelicals. Entitled "Evangelical Response to the Current Socio-political Current in the Philippines," it not only analyzed the unrest in the Philippines, describing specific actions that Christians must take socially and politically, but also called all Filipino Christians to united revival prayer.

In France, churches have been called to prayer for revival by the Retreat for Pioneer and Itinerant Evangelists. Although the number of evangelicals in France is small, the prayer summons suggests that a time of spiritual refreshing is well within the realm of possibility in France.

For some time, a prayer movement has been quietly unfolding in the Middle East. Currently there are revival prayer groups in 23 Muslim countries, and more intensive plans are being developed for the next five years.

The *Christian,* a Japanese equivalent of *Christianity Today,* recently ran a front-page story challenging the Church in Japan to engage in concerts of prayer as its only hope for evangelizing the more than 100 million Buddhists and materialists within their island country.

In Switzerland, interdenominational prayer cells continue to mushroom, often meeting in early morning. A new spirit of prayer is reported everywhere.

The growth of the Church in China is, in part, linked to a movement of concerted prayer. Over the years, thousands of Chinese house churches, the backbone of God's work there, have demonstrated concerted prayer, often under the threat of jail or death.

Out of New Zealand has come a movement of concerted prayer known as the Lydia Movement. Women gather in bands to fast and pray one day a week, interceding for revival in the Church, their community, their nation, and for missionary outreach. Currently, this movement is active in 11 nations, including the United States.

In Brazil and Argentina, as well as in parts of Central America, concerts of prayer are just now developing, while in South Africa multidenominational, multiracial concerts of prayer have sprung up, in a number of major cities including Soweto, within the last year. These monthly prayer gatherings seek a revival throughout the South African Church that would not only heal the nation but spawn a major new missions thrust into more than a hundred countries still open to South African passports.

The whole Church in Korea seems to be one big concerted prayer movement. Peter Wagner says, "I'm convinced that Korea's greatest gift to contemporary Christianity is prayer." Across the land thousands of individuals meet between 4:00 and 7:00 each morning before going off to work or household duties. In Seoul, pastor Yonggi Cho guides the largest church in the world, more than 400,000 members. Not only does he rise at 4:30 A.M. for an hour and a half of private prayer, but 15,000 of his members come together every week for concerted prayer that lasts from 10:30 P.M. on Friday to 6:00 A.M. Saturday, while the rest meet in over 20,000 prayer cells throughout the city.

In England the World Evangelization Crusade has called upon people to begin meeting in monthly concerts of prayer. One of the great signs of renewal in the British Isles is the increasing number of small groups gathered for revival prayer, a development accelerated by recent Luis Palau and Billy Graham crusades. The Graham team established thousands of "prayer triplets" in 1984—"three agree for three others," praying for revival and evangelism.

Over the past 10 years, the evangelical Church worldwide has been united informally under the umbrella of the World Evangelical Fellowship (WEF) and the Lausanne Committee on World Evangelization (LCWE). WEF called 1983 "The Year of Prayer for Revival." LCWE's objectives for the 1980s and 1990s are: (1) to help organize Christians for a variety of cooperative efforts; (2) to promote spiritual renewal as the foundation for world evangelization; (3) to measure progress in order to focus on united prayer and other resources on the completion of the task of world evangelization. In the Lausanne occasional paper titled "Evangelism and Social Responsibility" this prayer strategy is spelled out clearly for us:

> We resolve ourselves, and call upon our churches, to take much more seriously the period of intercession in public worship; to think in terms of ten or fifteen minutes rather than five; to invite lay people to share in leading, since they often have

deep insight into the world's needs; and to focus our prayers both on the evangelization of the world (closed lands, resistant peoples, missionaries, national churches, etc.) and on the quest for peace and justice in the world (places of tension and conflict, deliverance from the nuclear horror, rulers and governments, the poor and needy, etc.). We long to see every Christian congregation bowing down in humble and expectant faith before our Sovereign Lord.[3]

In the summer of 1984, the International Prayer Assembly for World Evangelization (IPA) was held in Korea to link up hundreds of prayer mobilizers from around the world by discussing the need for united prayer, by planning strategies for mobilizing national movements of prayer, and by praying together themselves for the nations.

This Lausanne Movement gathering fit strategically in the sequence of missions-related meetings the previous four years. In 1980, representatives from 100 nations gathered in Thailand as part of the Lausanne Movement to prepare global evangelistic strategies under the theme "How Shall They Hear?" This was followed five months later with the International Consultation on Frontier Missions at Edinburgh. If the Kingdom cannot come unless people hear and obey, Edinburgh stated, they would not hear unless there was a "Church for Every People [culture group] by the Year 2000." To all that, the Prayer Assembly posed its theme: "Seeking God's Face for a Movement of Prayer for the World." In other words, none of the other would transpire apart from a new outpouring of the Spirit upon the Church in answer to concerted prayer. (See the text of the IPA's "Call to Prayer," at the back of the book.)

Beyond the "evangelical world" we also see the hand of God in raising up biblical prayer. The international gathering of the World Council of Churches at Vancouver, held in the summer of 1983, showed an expanding foundation in prayer. Under the leadership of Gwen Cashmore, the new director of renewal for the WCC, a united prayer meeting was set up before the Vancouver event to pray by name for every one who would attend the assembly. During the meetings, there was an around-the-clock prayer watch that upheld every session. Even at the peace vigil, prayer became a major focus—quite unlike WCC's thrust in social issues in the past. These are signs of things to come. God is at work.

Here in our own country, God is giving the gift of prayer to the Church on a new scale. In Washington, D.C., an effort is underway to form prayer/think tanks where Christian leaders from all levels of society can gather in concerted prayer to seek God's wisdom on major national and international problems. This project, involving hundreds, walks hand-in-hand with monthly interdenominational concerts of prayer in the Washington area.

In southern California, pastors banded together to endorse and give leadership to concerts of prayer in the Los Angeles basin. Part of this was in a direct link with the summer Olympic outreach thrust of 1984. The Olympic Outreach Committee saw as its primary objective the inciting of a movement of prayer for revival and world evangelization, not only during the Olympics but long after the Olympics. The southern California concert of prayer movement, circulating monthly from one denominational church to another, desires to unite Christians in revival prayer throughout the whole San Fernando Valley, where approximately three million evangelicals live within two hours drive of each other. They even sponsor "schools of prayer" to equip people for more meaningful corporate intercession. And they anticipate as a fruit of their efforts a major new world mission thrust, focused on earth's totally unreached.

Over the past three years in Portland, Oregon, another concert of prayer movement has steadily risen. It began with a few pastors asking God for revival in their churches. Today more than a hundred pastors meet for fasting and prayer at noon every Wednesday. They gather with many of their church members each month for city-wide concerts of prayer. The effort is endorsed by every major evangelical church and parachurch organization in the city. Their goal is to have 10,000 people meeting monthly, and they are currently training more than a thousand prayer leaders to make that possible.

In preparation for the World's Fair, churches in New Orleans called for Shalom '84. It consisted of a 365-day prayer vigil, where Christians signed up for every hour of the day and night throughout the year to pray for revival and world evangelization. They exceeded their goal of over 100,000 Christians involved, with whole churches taking blocks of days and mobilizing their people to pray. And the climaxed their year by bringing hundreds together with the National Prayer Committee to foster vision and training for ongoing concerts of prayer.

A series of events in the past two years have resulted in a number of prayer concerts in Cleveland and Akron, Ohio, all of which are networked together by a daily radio program over station WCRF. "Call to Prayer" is aired three times a day to link up pray-ers, to sharpen their understanding of how to pray and to mention specific issues for which they should unite in prayer. Through seminars, over 1,000 prayer leaders have been trained and set in place on campuses, in churches and with mission groups in more than 80 cities.

In our nation's capital, an interdenominational body recently purchased Ralph Nader's old headquarters on Capitol Hill and has designated the building as the site of a 24-hour prayer watch for revival and world evangelization. Once a month those who use the building for prayer meet with others in a concert of prayer. Currently they are sending out teams around the nation to assist in the formation of a network of prayer concerts within—ultimately—all 50 state capitals.

Recently the Association of Church Missions Committees, representing local church leadership in 50 denominations, called for corporate prayer for missions within all of their member churches as a foundation for mobilizing new mission thrusts from local congregations. One church not only sponsors several weekly concerts of prayer, but also a monthly "grand concert of prayer." Nationwide, Dick Eastman's Change the World School of Prayer has trained over 200,000 church people in day-long seminars that now conclude with teaching on concerts of prayer.

Within the Catholic Church nationwide there also seems to be a new emphasis on united biblical prayer. The recently published *Catholic Prayer Group Directory* lists more than 4,600 renewal prayer groups nationwide in the Catholic Church. I know this doesn't cover all of them, because not one of the 15 prayer groups in Madison is listed!

There are increasing efforts to draw together those whom God seems to be calling into prayer leadership within the Body of Christ. Throughout the country "prayer summits" are being held to bring Christian leaders together for days of revival prayer and to make them aware of their part in a new prayer mobilization work. In 1984, the Inter-Baptist Prayer Conference Committee drew together prayer leaders from the major Baptist denominations to Columbus, Ohio, to seek renewal for themselves, their churches and the nations. In addition to all of this, we also find an upswing in churchwide and nationwide observances of "days of prayer."

Over the past 15 years alone, charismatic and noncharismatic renewal works have given birth to thousands of prayer groups where none existed before, dramatic nerve centers inside every major denomination. Some of the catalysts have formed the Fellowship of Renewal Group Leaders. Among them, Ronald Sider, of the Evangelicals for Social Action, has increasingly called for united prayer for a "peace revival" as the only hope for reversing the world's current disposition toward nuclear self-annihilation.

There is a rising emphasis on concerted prayer within missionary communities of the evangelical Church. In 1977, Dr. George Peters addressed the joint session of the Interdenominational Foreign Missions Association (IFMA) and the Evangelical Foreign Missions Association (EFMA). He did not mince words on what was desperately needed in evangelical missions strategy:

> We have become in missions so wrapped in technology and methodology that we have forgotten that missions is, number one, the releasing of divine dynamics . . . . Reaching the unreached will, first of all, mean for us, not only to lay hold of it in faith, but to develop thousands and thousands of prayer cells in America and elsewhere that will commit themselves wholeheartedly to prayer until the victory will be won . . . . We need spiritual mobilization.
>
> After six months in the Orient this year, I am deeply convinced that technology and

methodology—as good as they are—will never win
the battle. It will be won either in the power of God
in response to prayer, or we will keep on chopping
away, but the tree will not come down . . . mobilizing
thousands of people in specific prayer for specific
areas, for specific fields. This is what we must do.[4]

In 1982, a paper I delivered to Evangelical Foreign Missions
Association leaders received strong and immediate response and
has led to further consultations among missions leaders for
cooperative efforts in revival prayer toward world evangelization. In the fall of 1984, for example, leaders of the EFMA and
other major mission organizations set aside a whole night of their
annual conference for a concert of prayer, followed the next day
with training on how leaders could mobilize similar prayer
thrusts within their own agencies.

In the student world, prayer ferment is also evident. The
Campus Ministry director of Inter-Varsity Christian Fellowship
recently called for renewal within our movement, suggesting
that one of the clear evidences of renewal would be the reemer-
gence of concerted prayer. And Operation Mobilization, as a
part of their pre-field training for summer short-termers, conducts all-night "International Concerts of Prayer."

Campus Crusade for Christ has instituted a major thrust in
united prayer. They've called on all their staff in the United
States to set aside a half day a week to unite together in prayer.
Looking at it as a businessman, Bill Bright told me that this
effort was quite a stiff investment. Four hours a week times a
10,000-member staff at a minimum of $4 an hour equal millions
of dollars a year invested in united prayer alone! But as Bright
observes:

Throughout the centuries there have been great
movements of God's Spirit in revival power that
have drawn many millions into his kingdom. As I travel the world today, I sense a growing burden and
prayer for revival among the people of God. I believe
that God wants me and us as a movement to pray for
revival. It will accelerate a hundredfold everything

we are doing. To undertake such a gargantuan task
with a 'business as usual' attitude would be folly."[5]

God has since honored Crusade's resolve by giving them, in
1984, over 10,000 students actively participating in united
prayer through the newly formed National Collegiate Prayer
Alliance. The staff set the pace; their students caught the vision.

Recently leaders from Campus Crusade, Inter-Varsity, Navi-
gators, and International Students Incorporated met in Denver.
They hammered out ways to begin gathering students together
across organizational lines on individual campuses to pray for
four issues: (1) campus and (2) world evangelization, (3) revival
in the Church, and (4) restoration of righteousness in our nation.

Seminaries are getting in on the action, too. Concerted
prayer at Gordon-Conwell Theological Seminary has been
responsible for missions renewal both there and throughout
many churches over the last 10 years. Now there are efforts to
encourage their graduates to mobilize concerts of prayer in the
churches they serve throughout New England. Fuller Theological Seminary, having delineated the tremendous problems and
opportunities facing the Church in the nuclear age, went on
record to its alumni, saying, "We pledge ourselves, therefore, to
the spiritual renewal and revived vision which will empower all of
us for more effective service." For that end, they called for fervent prayer as the beginning of a new time of healing among the
nations.

Flowing out of the Edinburgh Consultation in 1980, the Theological Students for Frontier Missions has expanded to more
than 50 seminaries across the country as well as in other
nations. Their major strategy for renewing a mission's commitment among future missionaries and pastors is to raise up united
prayer watches on each campus.

As a member of the National Prayer Committee (NPC), a
group of respected prayer leaders, I have observed firsthand
many rich signs of the times. For example in our leadership of
the National Day of Prayer, we have located prayer coordinators
in more than 200 major cities of our country. It is their desire,
working with us, to encourage united prayer in their cities for
revival and world evangelization at least annually. We have seen

similar intentions related to the World Day of Prayer, with help from the National Association of Evangelicals, and the International Day of Prayer for World Evangelization, sponsored by the Lausanne Committee and endorsed by churches in our country.

Recently the NPC sponsored a Consultation on Concerts of Prayer in Washington, D.C. Top leadership from 20 denominational and 98 interdenominational organizations attended. Fully 80 percent of the interracial body declared in writing their desire to join as leaders in calling the Church to concerted prayer for spiritual awakening, as well as to encourage their individual community organizations to unite in prayer. With the assistance of the NPC, they are actively working toward that right now.

If prayer, praying people, and a movement of prayer are gifts of God, and if that movement of prayer is designed to mobilize God's people to do something about world evangelization, then this current breadth and depth of united prayer worldwide should encourage us all. And, if God is raising up a new surge of united prayer as a prelude to and foundation for all He is preparing to do among His people and to the ends of the earth, then all of God's praying people need to be in it together, and the sooner the better!

In light of the opportunities for the gospel all around us, is there any more strategic contribution any of us can make than to assist a movement of concerted prayer? And in light of the needs of the Church and the world, is there any alternative?

From a biblical perspective, what would we expect a contemporary concert of prayer movement to look like? That is the question we address in the next chapter.

# THE ANATOMY OF A MOVEMENT OF PRAYER

In the divine economy, what should concerted prayer look like? How would God define its characteristics? By what principles does He want it to operate? These are important questions which must have biblical answers.

United prayer threads its way through Scripture from Israel in the land of bondage through a variety of episodes during the rule of the judges, the Levites serving in the Tabernacle, the exiles returning to rebuild the Temple, the people waiting eagerly before the Lord along the Jordan, and the prayer band that sent out Paul and Barnabas from Antioch.

But, more than any other, one Scripture passage has had a profound historical impact in the formation of prayer movements during the last 300 years. It's Zechariah's vision of concerted prayer (Zech. 8:18-23).

I first stumbled on this passage while reading *An Humble Attempt* by the New England puritan preacher, Jonathan Edwards. Drawing from Zechariah, Edwards set forth practical principles for executing united prayer in the 1740s, to which many responded. A generation later, Edwards's classic was rediscovered by William Carey and his little prayer band. A few years later Carey took leadership in the forming of the Baptist Missionary Society. Carey's concert of prayer, endorsing the vision of Zechariah and Edwards, republished the little volume, circulating it throughout England. As a result other concerts were launched along the model the ancient prophet had outlined.

## ZECHARIAH 8: A LOOK AT THE CONTEXT

Around 520 B.C., during the reign of Darius, king of Medo-Persia, Zechariah was sent by God to encourage the 42,000 exiles who, 16 years earlier, had returned to Jerusalem to rebuild the Temple. Although these exiles were only a remnant of the total Israelite population, they were people of faith and vision. Their mission was to rebuild the Temple to establish a witness to the world that God was in the midst of His people and was available to all who would seek Him. Their mission, if you will, was to rebuild a work of concerted prayer.

But 16 years had passed since their return, and they were discouraged. Not only did they find the task of rebuilding the Temple difficult but they were opposed by foreigners who had previously inhabited the land.

The same year, Zechariah went to Jerusalem, Haggai was also sent with a simple message from God: stop building your own houses (concentrating on your own needs and plans) and come together again to work on God's house. Only then, he told them, would they truly experience God's blessings in their personal lives. God promised that He would then accomplish a mission through them that would shake the heavens and the earth, causing the Temple to become the gathering place for all people. We read in Haggai that revival finally took place; God stirred up the spirits of leaders and citizens alike and they gave themselves to His priority: rebuilding the Temple to mobilize a movement of prayer among nations.

Then Zechariah and Haggai joined to help bring God's revival work to completion. Zechariah's message was one of prayer and awakening: "'Return to me, . . . and I will return to you,' says the Lord Almighty" (Zech. 1:3).

The book divides nicely into two major sections, with the vision for our study (Zech. 8:18-23) forming the climax of the first section, as it captures the mood and momentum of all that God revealed in the previous eight chapters.

Throughout them, God leads the Israelites into nine visions.

In the first vision (chap. 1), He shows them horses on patrol over the whole earth. The nations are at ease because God is in control. Now He is free to fulfill His purposes with His people, to have mercy, to rebuild their houses, to comfort and prosper them. God is ready to choose Israel again and to express His profound love toward them. He says, "I am very *jealous* for Jerusalem and Zion" (Zech. 1:14, italics added).

In the second vision (chap. 1), Zechariah shows us four horns (representing political powers) and four craftsmen who hammer away on those horns. This is a vision of broad judgment, the details of which are spelled out even more clearly in chapters 9 and 14.

In vision three (chap. 2), a man comes forth with a measuring line. As he measures the city of Jerusalem it becomes so large that no walls can contain it. But they are protected by a fire that circles around the outside; it is the glory of God. And God promises to live among them. As a result, many nations will join with the Lord and become His people with Israel. This work will reach the ends of the earth as all mankind becomes silent before the sovereign God who has roused Himself from His holy dwelling to fulfill His purposes among the nations.

Next God turns to rebuke Satan, His archenemy (chap. 3). He does it by cleansing Joshua, the one assigned to lead all Israel into a life of prayerful fellowship with God. Joshua receives new clothes, a sign that his guilt has been removed (since he represents all of Israel). Now, as long as he walks in God's ways, he has the right of access into God's presence at all times. The blessings promised in keeping with this vision are such that Zechariah foresees the day when the Israelites will be inviting one another to sit under the blessings, like sitting under fig trees in their own backyards.

Vision five tells us how this great work is to be accomplished (chap. 4). It is not by might nor by power, but by the Lord's Spirit poured out on His people. To emphasize this, Zechariah records a lampstand (Israel) being served by two trees— representing Joshua and Zerubbabel as leaders of the nation— through whom God is bringing the new life of His Spirit into Israel. And His promise is that those who stand before the Lord of the whole earth on behalf of Israel will bring His Temple-purpose to completion with global impact.

In vision six (chap. 5), a flying scroll illustrates how God is judging and removing all remaining evil. This is emphasized even more strongly in the seventh vision in which a woman, representing evil, is put into a basket. All that has defeated Israel in the past is being rooted out. Again Israel sees both God's jealous love for her and His commitment to renew her so fully that He is intolerant of anything unholy that remains.

Vision eight (chap. 6) brings four chariots which patrol the whole earth, assuring Israel that God's sovereign rule covers all the nations. God's regent reigns over Israel and over the earth; and, in vision nine, Joshua is crowned as an illustration that God's king will go forth as a person of prayer, a priest. Furthermore, the Temple, the very place where God's people seek His face, will become the seat of His throne as well.

To summarize, God is taking new initiative toward His people, even as He had promised through the prophets long before. In doing so, He is in control, so that what He initiates for His glory will clearly come to pass. God is at work to restore, renew, and revitalize His people, reestablishing for them freedom of access into His glorious presence. As He does all of this, not only Israel but the nations at large are to be caught up in His work of redemption. The logical response is for Israel to return to Him, as people of prayer.

## ZECHARIAH'S PRAYER VISION

In chapter seven however, Zechariah is faced with a confused delegation from Bethel. Though they are part of the faithful remnant, they fear that Zechariah's message of hope may be leading them away from a traditional time of mourning and fasting.

For 70 years, the Israelites had remembered the siege and destruction of Jerusalem by fasting four whole days. The fasts commemorated their defeat with a time of mourning over the disgrace of God's name before Gentiles, of remembering unfulfilled promises, and of asking themselves if there was any future for their nation at all. In the process, however, they undermined their hope that the spiritual poverty they had incurred in defeat would ever be fully removed. So they asked, "Should we not just continue our fasts, Zechariah, despite your promising visions?"

Zechariah's response goes right to the point. He tells them how God is still very jealous in His love for Zion. God intends to return to Zion and dwell there, and the city will become known as the City of Truth (not of disgrace). Zechariah tells them: "'It may seem marvelous to the remnant of this people at this time, but will it seem marvelous to me?' declares the Lord Almighty" (Zech. 8:6). Zechariah assures them that God determines to do good to them again, to fully revive them, and they need not be afraid.

Then he unveils the most strategic thing they should do next. He calls for unity within the remnant people as they speak truth to each other and render true and sound judgment in their courts, and love one another. But then he takes them further. He gives them one more vision which is so certain that it is described as fact:

"Again the word of the Lord Almighty came to me. This is what the Lord Almighty says: 'The fasts of the fourth, fifth, seventh, and tenth months will become joyful and glad occasions and happy festivals for Judah. Therefore love truth and peace.'

"This is what the Lord Almighty says: 'Many peoples and the inhabitants of many cities will yet come, and the inhabitants of one city will go to another and say, "Let us go at once to entreat the Lord and seek the Lord Almighty. I myself am going." And many peoples and powerful nations will come to Jerusalem to seek the Lord Almighty and to entreat him.'

"This is what the Lord Almighty says: 'In those days ten men from all languages and nations will take firm hold of one Jew by the edge of his robe and say, "Let us go with you, because we have heard that God is with you"'" (Zech. 8:18-23).

In one sense, this vision gathers up and fulfills all the others that precede it; it also acts as a hinge to turn them toward God's restoring process, more vividly described in the remaining six chapters. God calls them in to prepare for concerted prayer for revival that would have international repercussions.

Zechariah describes this prayer vision in terms of its hallmarks; God's anatomy of a movement of prayer. In another sense it is also an anatomy of spiritual awakening, for such a movement is evidence that God has already begun to revitalize their faith in Him. Let's examine four hallmarks of this anatomy: the attitude, agenda, impact, and ignition for concerts of prayer.

## Hallmark: The Attitude

We hear a lot about prayer and fasting, but Zechariah calls for prayer and *feasting*! He tells the delegation from Bethel to stop fasting and start celebrating in anticipation of all the wonderful things God is preparing to do.

Their attitude was also to be marked with urgency. They were to "go at once," or as it reads in the Hebrew, "go going." This movement of prayer, set loose in dancing, was to be intense, determined, and persevering. Edwards called it "extraordinary prayer." It is prayer that presses as far as it can go, even into the very Holy of Holies.

Two other words underscore the sense of urgency. "Entreat" means literally to travail as a woman travails in the final moments in giving birth, or as a person who is deathly sick might cry for help. Zechariah also tells us to "seek" the Lord, which more accurately means to search or strive after Him.

Both words suggest that prayer brings forth into the world something that is so precious and wonderful that all other concerts must be laid aside; that the agony of interceding for God's new work must become the primary focus of our efforts. It also means that, knowing how desperate and helpless we are apart from God's work on our behalf, we strive in prayer after the only One who can deliver us from our intolerable condition. In both cases, our prayers crackle with urgency. Certainly anticipation and urgency must mark our prayer lives, especially as we gather in concerted prayer for spiritual awakening.

## Hallmark: The Agenda

And what is the objective of Zechariah's prayer movement? What are they praying about? What are they asking God to do?

In the Hebrew it says they are "seeking God," literally "seeking the face of the Lord." On the surface, it might seem one could wrap up this prayer meeting in short order! Are we only to ask God to see His face? Is that all a concert of prayer is about?

Often the Hebrew words translated in English as "seek the

Lord" or "God's presence" or "before the Lord" contain the key idea of seeking God's face. When you come right down to it, every prayer request you have ever made and every answer to prayer you have ever received is that God reveal His face. In fact, that is the bottom line of God's redeeming work throughout the ages: He's bringing the universe back before His face.

It was God's face that was turned toward Israel, as His great benediction on their wilderness mission toward the land of promise (Num. 6:22-27). The psalmist tells us that when God's face shines on His people, His salvation is made known before all the nations (Ps. 67). That's why Ezekiel was looking for someone to stand in the gap before God's face on behalf of a disobedient nation (Ezek. 22:30). Paul understood these truths well enough that when he describes the gospel treasure he was dispensing through his own apostolic ministry, he described it as the "light of the knowledge of the glory of God in the face of Christ" (2 Cor. 4:6). The book of Revelation carries us a step further, telling us that the greatest joy in the new heaven and new earth is that God's servants will look upon His face (Rev. 22:4). A prayer movement for spiritual awakening is ultimately asking God to reveal His face—His glory—to the Church and to the world.

Zechariah understood that spiritual awakening was the greatest need for the remnant even in his day, and he knew the answer was God's alone to give. So he called on them to seek God's face in prayer.

## Hallmark: The Impact

This prayer movement was not for Israel alone. Ultimately many peoples, cities, nations, and languages would get into the act. As a result of a few vulnerable exiles rebuilding a broken-down Temple and city, God would invade their midst in such a way that many strong nations would come to seek His face.

This would not be a casual turning to the Lord. The pressure would be so great that each of the pray-ers would find people grabbing hold of their clothes, refusing to let go until they were shown the way to salvation.

Some theologians suggest that evangelism in the Old Testament is centrifugal: nations come to Jerusalem to learn of God's salvation. In contrast, they see a centripetal evangelism in the

New Testament: God's people move out from Jerusalem to the ends of the earth to declare His salvation. However, Zechariah 8:23 appears to incorporate both approaches. God's glory revealed among His people would give *credibility* to His saving word and draw the nations to Him (centrifugal). But the overflow of revival would deploy many of the pray-ers out among various nations, thus making God's saving Word *accessible* worldwide (centripetal).

In the New Testament we also find this same two-edged approach to evangelism. The international Church, which was formed out of prayer in Jerusalem in the early part of Acts, succeeded as much by its testimony to the Spirit's presence, which brought the fear of the Lord on all citizens, as it did by the apostles' preaching before crowds and the Sanhedrin.

And Paul suggests, in 1 Corinthians 14, that unbelievers drawn into a local congregation in Corinth might be won to Christ as the people proclaim the message of God in unity. "He will fall down and worship God, exclaiming, 'God is really among you!'" (14:24-25). Peter assures us that, along with declaring Christ's excellencies, living together in a godly fashion will force pagans to acknowledge the goodness of our deeds and give glory to God from whom they spring (1 Pet. 2:12).

## Hallmark: The Ignition

So where does such a movement of prayer begin? Zechariah's answer is simple: from one person going to another. Those who are still seeking call others to come and seek with them. This is not a groundswell of spiritual elitism. It is not one believer going to another believer to say, "I have found a new, deep experience with God and, if you let me help you, I can show you how to find it, too." Instead, one person and then one group goes to another and says: "We sense God is preparing to do a deep and wonderful work in our generation—look at the visions Zechariah showed us—and that as He does this, all the earth will see His glory as never before. But unless He meets us as His people in a new way, to fulfill His promises and reveal Himself to us, we can do nothing.

"Because we love him so much, we're not willing to sit idly, content with the status quo. We're ready to start seeking Him, and we don't plan to quit until we find all He has for us. In fact, we have no other option. We're desperate to know Him! But we don't want to seek alone. *All* of us need to see His face together. Why don't you come, since you're as desperate as we are, and let's go seek Him together?"

There are two sides to igniting a prayer movement. "Let *us* go" means "we must not pray alone." But, "I myself am going" means "we are so convinced of the need for prayer that even if no one else goes, we will still set the pace and press on to seek God's face."

And so Zechariah's prayer movement grows. One city goes to another, which, at first, may mean nothing more than one family going to another. But soon whole communities are calling each other to revival prayer until, finally, whole nations are carried along in concerted intercession.

Someone must get it started, however. And without the determined few who initially lead the way, it is doubtful if any prayer movement of the magnitude envisioned by Zechariah could ever be hoped for.

## INTERMEDIATE FULFILLMENTS OF ZECHARIAH 8

Has Zechariah's vision ever been fleshed out? As with many prophecies, we may need to decipher both *intermediate* and *ultimate* fulfillments. Whether Zechariah 8 has reached its ultimate fulfillment is not for us to discuss here. In Zechariah's later chapters, he expands the details on his prayer movement in ways that suggest the ultimate is still ahead for us (see 12:10; 13:8-9; 10:6,9,12; 13:1; 14:6-9, 14-21). But in terms of the *principles* for any concerted prayer effort and the promises it holds out for all of us, there have certainly been intermediate fulfillments with foretastes of more to come.

In subsequent years, Israel was marked as a seeking people, and many others returned from exile to join them. Although a century later, they were contemptuously abusing their privilege of access in prayer, Malachi, while rebuking the priests, continues to hold out the promise of all nations one day offering incense to God, seeking the Lord in a Temple purged and full of God's glory.

But it is in the New Testament that Zechariah's prayer

movement assumes grander dimensions, grounded in the finished work of Christ who encompasses the force of every one of Zechariah's visions. In the New Testament we see God's Kingdom breaking through in the Church—"new Israel"—by a movement of prayer. Armin Geshwein reminds us that prayer was the organizing principle of the early Church. We cannot explain its unity or its victory in the battle against persecution and opposition apart from its prayer life. Believers counted their growth in numbers as they met for worship and prayer. It may sound incredible, but at one time not a single member of the Church anywhere on earth was not gathering in regular, concerted prayer! Geshwein remarks: "We have forgotten that when Christ built his church, he built a prayer meeting!"

Acts 2:42 bears out that the model which Jesus set with His disciples was expanded and extended throughout the New Testament Church to the heart of the Roman Empire. It became the foundation for the Gentile missionary enterprise, and was surely the context out of which the great miracle of Acts 19 took place when all Asia heard the Word of the Lord in two years.

The day of Pentecost crackles with Zechariah 8. Under Jesus' instructions, the disciples waited in concerted prayer until God sent the Spirit and gave them their next assignment. In flaming tongues God came into their midst, and all of Jerusalem knew He had revealed His glory to a little prayer band of 120. Coming from many nations under heaven, the pilgrims at Jerusalem cried without invitation: "What must we do to be saved?" And so the band mushroomed to 3,000 souls, a ratio better than 10 to one!

Intermediate expressions of Zechariah's vision were evident in the days of both Edwards and Carey. Edwards concluded that God was prepared to fulfill the prophet's vision in more ways than any had yet realized. I wonder if the Puritan's words might be prophetic for our generation:

> There shall be given much of a spirit of prayer to
> God's people, in many places, disposing them to
> come into an express agreement, unitedly to pray to
> God in an extraordinary manner, that he would
> appear for the help of his church, and in mercy to

mankind, and pour out his Spirit, revive his work and advance his spiritual kingdom in the world, as he has promised.

*This disposition to prayer, and union in it, will gradually spread more and more,* and increase to greater degrees; with which at length will gradually be introduced a revival of religion and a disposition to greater engagedness in the worship and service of God, amongst his professing people.

This being observed, will be the means of awakening others, making them sensible of the wants of their souls, and exciting in them a great concern for their spiritual and everlasting good, and putting them upon earnestly crying to God for spiritual mercies, and disposing them to join in that extraordinary seeking and serving of God. In this manner religion shall be propagated, till the awakening reaches those that are in the highest stations, and till whole nations be awakened.[1]

## "LET US GO AT ONCE!"

Surely the time has come to reestablish a movement of concerted prayer characterized by the hallmarks of grace and promise given us by Zechariah.

God is jealous. He is ready to return and work spiritual awakening among us. He is waiting to show us the face of Christ as we have not seen Him before, that together we might reveal His face before the nations. What are we do do?

One of us needs to go to the other and say, "Come, let us go at once and seek the face of the Lord." Maybe your Bible study group or Christian fellowship might go to another in your church or your campus movement and say, "Come, let us go at once." Maybe you could meet together once a quarter or once every other month or for 10 minutes after a worship service each week to spend time in prayer just for spiritual awakening. Or maybe one Sunday School class could go to another and say, "Once a month let's set aside our Sunday School lesson and gather our two classes together to spend the hour in concerted prayer for spiritual awakening."

Maybe your church could go to another and say, "Come, let us go at once." Fifty percent of the 360,000 churches in the United States average between 50 and 75 in attendance. Another 30 percent have 75 to 200 attenders, with only five percent having over 350 average attenders. So, if two or three "average" congregations would meet together once a month or once a quarter in united prayer for spiritual awakening, it would not be unmanageable in numbers and would be exhilarating in impact.

The day could come when one community would go to another and say, "Let us go at once." After all, as John Naisbitt observes in *Megatrends,* we are moving more and more toward a popular dictum: "Think globally, act locally." Could not the Body of Christ in one town approach the Body of Christ in another town to call them to act locally but think globally in a movement of prayer for spiritual awakening? In fact, this is already happening. Concerts of prayer within "sister cities" have adopted each other.

One campus group can go to another campus group at the same university and make the request, as is already happening among some of the major interdenominational campus ministries. Or a campus prayer movement at one university can contact another campus to join them in seeking God's face, as they are doing throughout New England. A campus prayer group can approach the local churches within their city and invite them to their campus once a month to join in concerted prayer for spiritual awakening as they have done in Pittsburgh. What if one mission agency approached other mission agencies, recommending that they band together to seek a new revelation of God's face within the life and mission of the church, beginning with their own agencies? Already Operation Mobilization and others are doing this in the United States.

Could it possibly come to the time when, as Zechariah suggests, one nation would go to another and say, "Come, let us seek the Lord"? Can you see Madras going to Boston, the Churches in Chicago going to Churches in Sydney, believers in Buenos Aires going to believers in Berlin, Syracuse to Soweto, Hong Kong to London, even believers in Cairo extending the invitation to believers in Jerusalem? Actually, the International

Prayer Assembly in 1984 opened the way for this kind of involvement in a fashion unique in history.

And what might ultimately result from such a global movement of prayer for the world? Again, listen to Zechariah. The ratio between unbelievers and believers, he says, is 10 to one. Today, there are about 250 million evangelicals and 2,500 million totally unreached people worldwide. That just happens to be a ratio of 10 to one! In the United States, the ratio is even better: three to one.

The prospects of Zechariah's vision repeating itself in our day with equal impact are very good, especially if spiritual awakening revolutionizes the credibility and accessibility of the evangelical movement in answer to concerted prayer.

What if God were to give spiritual awakening with such depth that every evangelical student on campuses worldwide were working with 10 international students? Or, that among Europe's 25,000 unreached villages and towns, God sent forth 25,000 revived believers? What if a revived church worldwide were given 6,000 new cross-cultural messengers from God to deploy among the 3,000 castes and tribes, two for each, in India who have little or no access to the gospel? What if we were to make it our revival prayer objective to see one revived Christian family in residence within each of the 600,000 villages of India by the year 2000?

Yes, Zechariah's message strongly applies to us today. Through him, God is saying to us all that our duty is to so believe His promises of things to come through Jesus Christ that we unite in a continual attitude of waiting, looking, longing, and seeking. Zechariah invites ordinary people like us to the threshold of spiritual awakening. He shows us that concerted prayer to that end is the frontline in world evangelization. And he makes our effort so simple—we must seek only one thing—to see the face of God.

The face of God revealed to the world—that is what we're praying toward. Church historians describe it in a metaphorical phrase: spiritual awakening. What does that term mean? Let's focus on it next.

# 4
# BEYOND THE THRESHOLD
## The Hope Toward Which We Pray

In his thoughtful book, *The Puritan Hope,* Iain Murray carefully documents 300 years of God's renewing work through the
English Reformation. Showing the strong Puritan influence on
the philosophical underpinnings of our own republic, he goes on
to outline three major convictions of these godly forefathers: (1)
a certainty that God periodically intervenes in His Church in
mighty spiritual awakenings; (2) a clear hope that the best was
yet to come, and as it came it would bring the whole planet
under the impact of the gospel; (3) a logical conclusion, therefore, that the most strategic thing they could do was to give
themselves to sustained, united prayer until God acted.

Murray, recalling the words of the great expositor, Charles
Haddon Spurgeon, concludes with an historical appeal to us that
we again gather up such a hope:

> *The fullness of Jesus is not changed, then why are our
> works so feebly done?* Happy days would begin from
> this hour *if the Church would but awake and put on
> her strength, for in her Lord all fullness dwells.*
> Oh! The Spirit of God, bring back thy Church to a

belief in the gospel! Bring back her ministers to
preach it once again with the Holy Ghost, and not
striving after wit and learning. *Then shall we see
thine arm made bare, O God, in the eyes of all the people,* and the myriads shall be brought to rally round
the throne of God and the Lamb. *The gospel must
succeed;* it shall succeed; it cannot be prevented from
succeeding; a multitude that no man can number
must be saved.[1]

## SPIRITUAL AWAKENING:
## WHAT IS IT? WHO NEEDS IT?

In fulfilling world evangelization, it may surprise you that our
first target in prayer is *not* to pray for more missionaries! How
can this be when hundreds of thousands more are needed from
the church worldwide?

In Matthew 9:35-38, Jesus instructs us to pray for "laborers" to be sent forth by the Lord of the harvest because there
are so few to work in the ripened fields. It is apparent that the
laborers Jesus had in mind were men and women who had been
awakened to the central message of His ministry: that the Kingdom of God was bearing down on their generation. God's promises through the prophets were about to take shape—and they
were to wake up, repent and believe the good news about the
Promised One, Jesus. In turn, God would "throw out" (literal
Greek meaning in 9:38) these revived ones to bring others with
them into God's awakening work among His people—to rally
God's harassed sheep back to the sovereign Shepherd they
were seeking for, to harvest the potential of God's people for
serving His Kingdom, gathering them through renewing fires
into God's eternal purposes (cf. Luke 3:16-18).

In our concern for the world, or for a new missionary thrust,
what Jesus calls us to pray for first of all, then, is spiritual awakening that begins with a few and spreads to the many, flowing
out of prayer and borne along by the preaching of God's Son. We
need laborers who gather the Church to seek a full revelation of
Jesus Himself, the One in whom God's Kingdom is coming with
mysterious but unstoppable force, first among His people and
then to the ends of the earth.

Today, there is much talk in missionary circles about the need to reach earth's "hidden people," a term that describes billions of people throughout the world who currently have little or no chance to respond to the gospel. It's a fact that should break our hearts.

But a movement of prayer must first concentrate on the hidden Person, the Lord Jesus Christ, who is often veiled in the eyes of His followers, the only ones who can reach hidden peoples. A movement of prayer for the world must first target on our own spiritual blindness. Once Christ is revealed in the midst of His Church we will be spiritually propelled into the urgent ministry given us to extend His Kingdom among the nations.

This was Paul's great burden in Colossians 1:27–2:3. He wrestled, struggled, and labored in preaching and prayer to the end that God's wonderful plan for the ages, a mystery hidden for many generations, might be fulfilled. The plan calls for Christ to be unveiled in the midst of His Church as the promise of every glorious thing to come, so that through His Church He might be manifested before all peoples.

Spiritual awakening, as a technical term used by theologians and historians, describes these extensive new movements of God's Spirit. Two current authorities on spiritual awakening, Dr. J. Edwin Orr and Dr. Richard Lovelace, can help us get a handle on this descriptive phrase.

In *The Eager Feet,* Dr. Orr summarizes:

> An Evangelical Awakening is a movement of the Holy Spirit bringing about a revival of New Testament Christianity in the Church of Christ and in its related community. Such an awakening may change in a significant way an individual only; or it may effect a larger group of believers; or it may move a congregation, or the churches in a city or district, or the whole body of believers throughout a country or a continent; or indeed the larger body of believers throughout the world. The outpouring of the Spirit effects the reviving of the Church, the awakening of the masses, and the movement of uninstructed peoples towards the Christian faith; the revived Church,

by many or by few, is moved to engage in evangelism, in teaching, and in social issues.

Such an awakening may run its course briefly, or it may last a lifetime. It may come about in various ways, though there seems to be a pattern common to all such movements throughout history.

The major marks of an Evangelical Awakening are always some repetition of the phenomena of the Acts of the Apostles, followed by the revitalizing of nominal Christians and by bringing outsiders into vital touch with the Divine Dynamic causing all such awakenings—the Spirit of God. The surest evidence of the Divine origin of any such quickening is its presentation of the evangelical message declared in the New Testament and its re-enactment of the phenomena therein the empowering of saints and conversion of sinners.[2]

In his volume, *Dynamics of Spiritual Life,* Richard Lovelace spends almost 400 pages expanding on many of the insights captured by Dr. Orr's paragraphs. But on one page he puts it simply:

Renewal, revival and awakening trace back to biblical metaphors for the infusion of spiritual life in Christian experience by the Holy Spirit (see Romans 6:4,8:2-11; Ephesians 1:17-23; 3:14-19; 5:14). Usually they are used synonymously for *broad-scale movements of the Holy Spirit's work in renewing spiritual vitality in the church and in fostering its expansion in mission and evangelism.* Reformation refers to the purifying of doctrine and structures in the church, but implies also a component of spiritual revitalization. Renewal is sometimes used to encompass revival and reformation, and also to denote "aggiornamento," the updating of the church leading to new engagement with the surrounding world.[3]

From my studies of Scripture and history and from my

extended conversations with Orr, Lovelace, and others like them, I would like to suggest my own definition of spiritual awakening:

> *Spiritual awakening:* when the Father wakes us up to see Christ's fullness in new ways, so that together we trust Him, love Him, and obey Him in new ways, so that we move with Him in new ways for the fulfillment of His global cause.

Do you recall waking up this morning? Maybe it began with the clamor of the alarm clock, followed by the pitter-patter of feet outside your bedroom. Your eyelids barely budge, however.

Still, you were half conscious of light streaming through the venetian blinds, as you caught the aroma of bacon and eggs. (Collegians: here you might substitute the smell of your roommate's dirty laundry in the closet.) As you laid there, thoughts about the day's activities and responsibilities started to press in on you until, with your eyes half open, you reached the point of no return. Enough awareness invaded your consciousness that you realized it was best to get out of bed, get into your clothes, and get on with the day. You were finally awake!

That's a picture of what happens when God gives spiritual awakening to His Church. Enough of the person of Christ, His glory, and His kingdom—as well as the great needs of His world and our responsibilities to it—invades our consciousness until we are unable to sleep any longer. We awake to get on with God's redemptive purposes for the earth. We have to get up, clothe ourselves in the Lord Jesus Christ, get out the door, and get with the day . . . with *His* day (Rom. 13:11-14). As Paul says in Ephesians 5:14, "Wake up, O sleeper, rise from the dead [sounds like 'get out of bed!'], and Christ will shine on you."

His words remind me of Isaiah 60:1-3: "Arise, shine, for your light has come, and the glory of the Lord rises upon you. See, darkness covers the earth and thick darkness is over the peoples, but the Lord rises upon you and his glory appears over you. Nations will come to your light, and kings to the brightness of your dawn."

Doesn't that sound like getting up in the morning? Jesus uses this image with the Asian churches He addresses in Revelation 2 and 3. For example, to the church at Sardis He says: "I know your deeds; you have a reputation of being alive, but you are dead. *Wake up!* Strengthen what remains and is about to die, for I have not found your deeds complete in the sight of my God" (3:1-2, italics added). And with the church at Laodicea, Jesus is so hidden to their hardened hearts that it is as if He is on the outside of the church, asking permission to enter again and to offer salve for their blind eyes.

Paul had the same concern in mind when he prayed in his Epistles. In fact, whenever God fully answers the written prayers of Paul for any church or the whole Church in any generation, revival results!

Take for example, his prayer for the Ephesians; "I keep asking that the God of our Lord Jesus Christ, the glorious Father, may give you the Spirit of wisdom and revelation, so that you may know him better. I pray also that the eyes of your heart may be enlightened that you may know the hope to which he has called you, the riches of his glorious inheritance in the saints, and his incomparably great power for us who believe" (Eph. 1:17-19). A spirit of revelation, knowing God better, our heart's eyes enlightened, a new vision of our hope, inheritance and power—this is spiritual awakening.

Spiritual awakening is both a process and an event. In a sense, the whole process of Christian growth is awakening. It's a rapid series of mini-revivals in which at any given point one can say: "I am committing all I can see of myself to all I can see of Christ for all I can see of His global cause—at this moment." Since the Spirit daily reveals to us more of Christ, of ourselves, and of God's plans for the world, *every* new insight that leads to a new act of obedience can be called spiritual awakening.

Our insistence then is on knowing Christ, knowing who we are in Christ, and knowing how best to serve His global cause. Hebrews 11:6 describes those who desire to know more of our Lord, of His plans and purposes for us and for the world as those who "earnestly seek him." Seeking and finding is an unending process, like an upward spiral.

Two words have helped me to pinpoint the distinctiveness of spiritual awakening as an event, in its more technical, biblical-historical sense: The words are "intensify" and "accelerate." In times of broader spiritual awakening, God intensifies the Church's relationship with Christ and He accelerates the advancement of Christ's Kingdom through the Church.

Using my definition, let's study spiritual awakening as an event while breaking it down into five parts:

1. When the Father wakes us up;
2. To see the fullness of Christ in new ways;
3. To trust, love, and obey Him in new ways;
4. To move with Him in new ways for the fulfillment of His global cause; and
5. Together.

## When the Father Wakes Us Up

Spiritual awakening comes at God's gracious initiative. And we are totally dependent upon Him for it. That's why we must make it our target in prayer, so that we may see Christ in new ways. Even prayer is a gift of God. As A.W. Tozer reminds us in *The Pursuit of God,* when we feel stirred to seek after Christ, "God is always previous."

Without exception, true revival is that which is only attributable to the Father. He is responsible for a heavenly invasion in the affairs of the Church, and is directly involved at every point. In spiritual awakening, He activates a bold strategy to bring us into intimacy with Himself and His redemptive mission to the nations through an unveiling of Christ's presence in our midst.

Those who have studied it suggest that the fear of the Lord is at the heart of revival. The more vividly God shows us Himself and His purposes in Christ, the more seriously we are driven to take both our fellowship with Him and our commission from Him. The Church is reintroduced to the consuming Fire from heaven and tastes His holy love with trembling obedience. The Spirit of the Lord revives our corporate sense of Christ's intimate direction of both our inward and outward life.

This was the personal experience of John and Charles Wesley and George Whitefield, preeminent preachers of the "Great Awakening." They spent extended periods of time in a prayer group of 60 Christians who met in the 1730s in London, on Fetter Lane, to pray for revival and missions. They called themselves the Fetter Lane Society.

John Wesley records in his journal how God took charge of the prayer meeting on January 1, 1739:

"About 3:00 in the morning as we were continuing instant in prayer, the power of God came mightily upon us, inasmuch as many cried out for exceeding joy and many fell to the ground. As soon as we were recovered a little from that awe and amazement at the presence of his majesty we broke out with one voice, 'We praise thee O God, we acknowledge Thee to be the Lord.'" These three preachers went on to lead the English-speaking Church on both sides of the Atlantic to seek and find a similar intensified experience of God's majestic presence.

Jonathan Edwards used similar words to describe what he saw in God-initiated awakenings in his own Northampton congregation in 1735:

> There scarcely was a single person in the town, old or young, left unconcerned about the great things of the eternal world. Those who were wont to be the vainest and loosest, and those who had been the most disposed to think and speak lightly of vital and experimental religion, were now generally subject to great awakenings. And the work of conversion was carried out in a most astonishing manner and increased more and more; souls did as it were come by flocks to Jesus Christ . . . . This work of God as it was carried on, and the number of saints multiplied, soon made a glorious alteration in the town, so that in 1735 the town seemed full of the presence of God: it never was so full of love, nor of joy, and yet so full of distress as it was then. There were remarkable tokens of God's presence in almost every house . . . . God's day was a delight. The congregation was alive in God's service, in tears while the Word was preached; some weeping for sorrow and distress, others for joy and love, others with pity and concern for the souls of their neighbors.[4]

These experiences of God's invasion prior to and during

awakening were not unique to Wesley, Whitefield, and Edwards. For example, during the 1859 revival that swept through much of the Church worldwide, we hear such descriptions as: "A sense of the gracious presence of God pervaded the entire locality." Or, "The whole community has felt the majesty of God and His presence in the land." Or again, "All seem to think they should seek salvation, feeling as if they were on the very verge of the spiritual and eternal world, and in the immediate presence of God." During the Welsh revivals in 1904, a pastor noted: "If one were asked to describe in a word the outstanding feature of those days, one would unhesitatingly reply that it was the universal, inescapable sense of the presence of God . . . . the Lord had come down! A sense of the Lord's presence was everywhere. It pervaded, nay it created the spiritual atmosphere."

Duncan Campbell, preacher during the Hebrides Revival, looked back on that 1949 event and confessed:

> *Revival is a going of God among people,* an awareness of God laying hold of the community. Here is the difference between a successful campaign and revival, in the former we may see many brought to a saving knowledge of the truth, and the church or mission experience a time of quickening, but so far as the town or district is concerned no change is visible; the world goes on its way . . . But in revival *the fear of God lays hold* upon the community, moving men and women, who until then had no concern for spiritual things, to seek after God.[5]

In our parable of the threshold, it was the light through the partially-opened door that drew any of us to knock in the first place. Yes, God is previous. He wakes us up.

## To See Christ's Fullness in New Ways

Spiritual awakening will never take us beyond Jesus. He is what awakening is all about. God does not possess anything beyond Christ to give to His people. Jesus exhausts for all of us all we can ever know of God, all we can ever receive from God, and all we can ever become for God. The Puritans said, "We can't be in union with half of Christ." In spiritual awakening, God brings us back to the whole Christ.

Unfortunately, much Church activity today is pursued with only a vague awareness of Christ in our midst. We become more devoted to our systems, programs, creeds, organizations, leaders, and even our missionary enterprises, than we do to Christ. And evangelicals are just as guilty as any.

Revival takes us in a different direction. Christ increases as all man-made concerns, even the well-intentioned ones, decrease. Spiritual awakening intensifies and accelerates that shift. God's Spirit again brings Christ to center stage. We become increasingly dissatisfied with all things short of Christ.

I'm not saying that spiritual awakening is the apprehension of heavenly mysteries by a spiritual elite; rather, it's the Body of Christ grasping all that is already ours in Him. God helps us to stop living in the land of shadows and to see that Christ is the substance of all we could ever want or hope for (Col. 2:17). Whereas, in awakening, we may feel that we accept more of Christ into us, it may be better to say that the Father invites us into more of Him, to embrace more of Him by faith.

God awakens us to the whole gospel: what Christ has done for us, what He is doing in us, and what He is prepared to do through us. A study of awakenings throughout history suggests that when one or more of these interlinking and theologically inseparable legs of the gospel is misplaced by the Church, the table totters until God reinserts the missing piece.

In the Reformation, awakening focused more on the "for" of the gospel, while in the Great Awakening more on the "in" of the gospel, and in the next awakening, God brought His people fully alive to missions and social action, as He stressed the "through" of the gospel. But in all awakenings, to one degree or another, God brings His Church to a fuller understanding of justification (for), a greater sense of personal and corporate holiness (in), and a deeper commitment to the glory of God before the eyes of the world (through).

You have probably heard the phrase "a pouring out of the Spirit" in reference to revival. Where does that fit in? Precisely at the point of revealing the fullness of Christ and the gospel.

Of course, it is possible to pray for the Spirit's outpouring and really be asking God to bless and empower only what we have previously determined to do. But in its proper and biblical use, the Spirit's outpouring results in our seeing and embracing all we have in Christ, and responding in love to all He tells us to do.

In reality, the Spirit does not come down to us at all. He came down at Pentecost and now indwells His whole Church. Awakening is more like our total cooperation with His unrelentingly glorious ministry of taking the things of Christ and declaring them to us (John 16:14). His ministry is not to speak of Himself. He wants Christ to be glorified before us and through us. "By illuminating our minds, and by softening our hard hearts, by guiding and strengthening our wills, the Spirit leads us into an increasing experience of the deliverance that Christ won for us."[6]

This work of the Spirit blossoms in awakening. The Spirit brings within our reach an apprehension of Christ comparable to the deepest needs of the Church of that particular generation and to the outward challenge to her worldwide mission.

As I think of the Spirit's work in awakening, I think of the years I lived in the San Gabriel Valley near Los Angeles. Often the smog would hang so heavy in the air that the sweeping peaks of the San Gabriel Mountains would be invisible. Then, the Santa Ana winds would sweep in from the desert and blow the dirty air out to sea. Suddenly, we were able to breathe better, and we walked down the streets with a new spring in our steps because everywhere we turned we caught the glory of the mountains that surrounded us.

In spiritual awakening, the Spirit, like the Santa Ana winds, blows through the valleys of the Church, purifying her life so that she enters into a new vision of Christ and the majestic fullness of His salvation. This inevitably transforms her involvement in His global cause in new ways—ways never before dreamed possible.

## To Trust, Love and Obey Him in New Ways

Once the Father invades our midst, giving His children new eyes to see Christ's fullness in new ways, a response emerges from the Church that can ultimately affect the whole earth and change the course of history. Whitefield wrote of his own experience in awakenings: "My understanding was enlightened, my will broken, and my affections more and more enlivened with zeal for Christ." This zeal is best expressed in three simple words: trust, love, obey.

First, we learn to *trust* Christ in new ways. Having become newly impressed with both the supremacy and sufficiency of Christ, the Holy Spirit confronts us with specifics regarding how we propose to respond to the Lordship of Jesus. In revival, He intensifies His probings: Is Christ Lord of heaven and earth? Does He stand at the climax of history? Is He the one at whose feet the nations will come out for disposal? Is He Lord of the Church? Is He Lord through the Church to fulfill His purposes for all peoples and bring all of life under the rule of His Kingdom? Is He Lord of my life? Does He have the right to my allegiance, my obedience, and my love? Am I prepared to give all to Christ, without reservations, without strings attached, and without deceit?

The spirit presses us further in revival: Do we trust Christ enough, based on all that the Spirit has shown us of Him, to take every thought, every conversation, every effort back to Him to be willing to say with Paul, "For to me, to live is Christ" (Phil. 1:21)? Do we trust Him enough to give Him full access to our needs, resources, abilities, and destiny? And are we willing to break with everything in our lives, individually and corporately, that conflicts with His Lordship?

Such a faith will not stand alone. It leads to love, and love leads to obedience. Just as faith takes on new dimensions in spiritual awakening, so love and obedience accelerate. We come to *love* Christ in new ways simply because He stops being a stranger. We have a vivid experience with Christ that springs from faith because our relationship with Him has been heightened and intensified. Some would say that awakening overwhelms us with Christ, taking us out of ourselves and into devotion to Him. After all, as Paul teaches in Galatians 5, our faith in Him will increasingly work itself out in love.

And love gives birth to *obedience*. Awakening is not only a profound new experience with Christ, it is also a time for plain "guts." When Jesus calls us to follow Him and lose our lives for

His sake and the gospel's, He is talking about sacrificial obedience. Awakening helps the Church accelerate in its knowledge of Christ which, in the original language, means to grow in our "caring" for Christ and the things of Christ. And caring changes the direction of our affections so that we willingly give Him obedience in a love that knows no limits. That is gutsy stuff!

Obedience becomes such a natural fruit because, in awakening, the Father shows us again how much He loves us in Christ. He shows us where we have come from through His gracious work and helps us to measure ourselves only by where we stand, totally accepted before Him in Christ. He shows us that we are totally loved.

Seeing the fullness of His love for us leads us in turn into a life fully pleasing to Him and full of good works, as we willingly become more fully His by everything we do (Col. 1:10-12).

I remember seeing an ad for an airlines. Under a full-page photo of an attractive young flight attendant with a magnetic smile was the caption: "If you're wondering where all this comes from, well, it comes from inside. Our people are happy. Because they love what they do and who they do it for. When people feel that way, they simply have more to give . . . . "

Just so, as God brings us to know Christ's love in new ways because we see Him in new ways, we are set free to obediently give love to others in new ways whether in the form of a smile, a bank check, a word of encouragement, or our very lives. In awakening, we encounter the heart of the universe, which is nothing less than sacrificial love, and as we obey Him He leads us to the same expression of love. As we learn to know the presence of God in all of His gifts of love, we become willing to abandon ourselves for His purposes of love.

This demonstration of faith through love and obedience is what I call "decisive devotion," a devotion that is a single-minded giving of ourselves to Christ. We trust Him and love Him so much that our thoughts, our words, our relationships, and the directions we move with Him are centered on the fulfillment of everything that is on His heart.

Throughout many of the awakenings over the past 300 years, those who led out in Christ's global cause expressed a renewed relationship to Christ that could be characterized as intensified, decisive devotion. The Moravian leader, Count Zinzendorf, declared, "I have one passion, Christ—it is he, it is he." Henry Martyn, pioneer missionary to India, said on arriving at his destination, "Now let me burn out for God." Hudson Taylor, leading a missionary advance to inland China in the 1850s, proclaimed that his love for Christ made him wish he had a thousand lives that he could give for the Chinese.

The ultimate goal of awakening is decisive devotion to Christ, manifested in three ways: (1) Our highest passion becomes Christ Himself, that we may know Him and that others may know and love Him with us; (2) our highest purpose becomes the advancement of Christ's Kingdom by the impact of the gospel, for this is how all people can join us to know and love Him for who He is; and, (3) our highest priority increasingly becomes the unreached and unliberated of the earth, who are unresponsive and unaware of the gospel and, therefore, unclaimed for Christ's Kingdom and unable to love and serve Him at all.

## To Move with Him in the Fulfillment of His Global Cause

Not long ago I spent a few hours with a group of students, praying for revival at their college. After we had prayed for two or three hours in a little chapel on campus, I gazed up at the stained glass window in front of us. Jesus was pictured standing on a multi-colored globe of the world with His arms stretched out toward us. I announced that the picture represented the precise response Jesus had for us as we prayed that day for spiritual awakening. At that very moment He was saying to us, "Here I am—standing gloriously in your midst! Now that you see me for who I really am, come to me and move with me in the fulfillment of my purposes for the whole earth."

Two words that have helped me understand the scope of spiritual awakening as portrayed in that window are "fullness" and "fulfillment." Both words are used in the definition we're exploring here. As we've seen, fullness speaks of everything that God is and offers to us in His Son. Christ is the fullness of the Godhead in bodily form, in whom we have come to fullness of life (Col. 2:9-10).

Fulfillment points *not* to personal fulfillment (except indirectly), but rather to the fulfillment of all that is on the heart of God—His work through a revived Church to bring the fullness of Christ to the attention of the nations in the advancement of His Kingdom. Without such fulfillment, revival will stagnate in the shallows of selfish ambition.

Spiritual awakening in the Church holds the promise of spiritual awakening among the nations. When God blesses us in awakening it is so that we might become a blessing to the families of the earth (Gen. 12:2-3). The more He engages us with His son, the more He wants us to move with Christ to fulfill His global cause.

It has always been that way in spiritual awakenings. David Brainerd, early American missionary to the Indians, wrote: "One morning, the cause of God appeared exceedingly precious to me. The Redeemer's Kingdom is all that is valuable in the earth, and I would not but long for the promotion of it in the world."

You may be familiar with the little booklet *My Heart, Christ's Home* by Robert Munger, an excellent statement on what it means to become a Christian. He describes conversion as Jesus standing at the door of our lives and knocking until we open the door and invite Him to come in. At that point He roams through the house of our lives, as though stepping from room to room, dealing with one area of sin or weakness after another, demonstrating that He is Lord of it all. Eventually, according to Munger, we decide to give Him the deed and the keys, making the whole house His.

That's a good description of what it means to come alive to Christ. Here's another: Christ knocks at the door, but when I open the door I see Him standing there with a backpack on! He tells me He has only a few minutes and asks if He can come in. He leads me into the living room, sits me down, pulls out a Bible and a map of the world and begins to explain His wonderful purposes for the nations and how much remains to be done. Then He tells me to get my backpack and put in it only those things I think I will need to take with me, because He is inviting me to follow Him out of my house on a journey that goes to the ends of the earth. The story ends with both of us walking out of the house, shutting the door behind us and throwing away the keys.

My version captures something of God's purposes in spiritual awakening—what it means to come alive to *more* of who Christ is. As we accept the offer to see Christ's fullness and pursue it, we submit our lives to Him at the same time to be broken and reshaped to fit wherever and however we may best serve His global cause. Does this hold similarities to the threshold parable in chapter 1? In one sense, it is the other side of that story.

If revival does not enhance His glory and advance His Kingdom throughout the earth, it needs to be questioned. Sometimes we can even shape revival into an idol and worship it as a way to achieve our own objectives or feather our own nests. How foolish we can be. Revival is no shortcut to the blessings of being a heavenly saint; rather, it opens the long road to the blessings and sufferings of being Christ's earthly servant. As Anglican missions statesman Max Warren reminds us: "Awakening is a reformation of the Church for action."

When God wakes us up to see Christ's fullness, He shows us at the same time how His glory and the cause of His Kingdom is languishing among the nations. He puts in us a zeal that drives us to pray for a revived Church that will bring forth laborers to flesh out revival on all fronts, ultimately among earth's totally unreached.

It's not surprising to me that contemporary composer/singer Keith Green, shortly before his untimely and fatal plane crash, was beginning to extend his fervent preaching on revival to include a strong dose of challenge to young people to become involved wholeheartedly in world evangelization. Like myself, he seemed to realize that, many times, awakenings naturally encompass basic phases. I see five such phases:

1. The Spirit of God raises up a movement of united prayer for revival.

2. In response to prayer, the Church receives an intensified vision of Christ's fullness.

3. As a result, the Church is led into a deep unity of love for one another and a resolve to serve the purposes of Christ together.

4. From this springs up a revitalization and a pruning of existing ministries.

5. All of this flows into an expansion of Christ's Kingdom with international repercussions.

What Green and I discovered is that, like waves washing higher and higher on a beach, spiritual awakening accelerates the impact of Christ's lordship not only in the life of the Church, but also in society, and among the nations, and at many levels.

That's why historians can write:

> A series of revivals broke out during the 1730s and 1740s which had an effect on almost every aspect of colonial religious life. The evolution of the American churches continued. They still reflected social and demographic changes, and they still had their own internal development. But the Great Awakening exerted a force which left the churches altered forever.
>
> A modern historian, Richard Bushman, has said of the colonial revival that it was "like the civil rights demonstrations, the campus disturbances, and the urban riots of the 1960's combined. All together these may approach though certainly not surpass, the Great Awakening in their impact on national life."[7]

Similarly, the awakenings in the 1790s onward resulted in the creation of scores of compassionate organizations moving on all fronts—political, social, evangelistic. The awakened Church said, "The gospel will triumph; it must triumph. It is equal to all it has to perform. And it is through us that it must be made known." The Church moved with Christ in the fulfillment of His global cause because faith became increasingly more morally oriented. God broke the Church free from the hold of mammon to the place where it became engaged in the struggles of the poor. This was true even earlier, for example, in the Wesleyan revival to dispossessed coal miners and the urban poor.

Similarly, in an awakening today we can expect the Kingdom to extend its influence as the Church moves forward in obedience. Marriages will be healed and homes restored. The crime rate will drop, often dramatically. A spirit of generosity and sacrificial giving will increase. Christian influence will be brought to bear on the media and on institutions of higher learning. Christ's lordship will be explored in many spheres: care of the environment, concern for the unemployed, the humane treatment of employees, honesty in work, and advocacy for the disadvantaged. Society will become infused with dedicated love and practical justice. Social and moral legislation will emerge as the Church gains renewed sensitivity to the poor and disenfranchised. The Church will learn to know how powerful Jesus is as she sees Him at work through her in the lives of the powerless. And peacemaking among the nations will become a growing concern of leaders in lands where spiritual awakening has flowed.

Most encouragingly, a study of the last two centuries shows an indisputable link between revivals and the growth of missionary outreach. For example, William Carey's vision for establishing a new Protestant missionary endeavor out of England came out of his prayer group for spiritual awakening. But once the vision was given and a revived Church had been rallied, Carey had to move with Christ to fulfill that vision. He went to India despite the French Revolution which threatened to engulf the whole European continent.

Others followed; between 1793 and 1834 no less than 13 British missionary societies were formed. And the first American missionaries, who emerged from general awakenings in New England—undergirded by student prayer groups for missions and revival that sprang from the "Haystack Prayer Meeting" at Williams College—actually sailed for India in 1812, the year war broke out between the United States and Britain. Hudson Taylor, whose missionary penetration of China was accelerated by the awakening of the mid-1800s, had to incorporate his missionary recruits into a ministry beseiged by the Taiping Rebellion that lasted until almost 1870. In every case, only a heightened vision of the global Christ in the midst of His Church, to which the Church could respond in active obedience, could have ever provoked such a persistent enterprise for world evangelization. This is no less true today.

When God awakens us to Himself He awakens us to the whole earth. As He shows us Christ, He also shows us His worldwide purpose in Christ, the world full of possibilities for fulfilling that purpose through Christ, and a world full of people without Christ who are currently beyond the reach of the gospel. And He affirms to us our world-sized part with Christ—individual and corporate—in serving His global cause.

No longer does the topic of missions need to make us feel that someone is asking us, in the midst of our hectic lives, to be willing to take on the whole rest of the world. Instead of the world resting on our shoulders, God shows us that in Christ it is totally on His!

And so revival provokes missionary enthusiasm as well as sustaining missionary endeavor. This is our only hope for reaching almost three billion beyond the impact of the gospel today.

## So That . . . Together

Although awakening may be an individual experience, God intends it ultimately to be corporate.

Revival accelerates our commitment to the Church because what we think of Christ and what we think of His Church go hand-in-hand. The more we love Christ and the more we see of Him in an awakened Church—that is, the more we see of Him in each other—the more we will desire to give ourselves to one another for Jesus' sake.

In revival God intensifies all the gifts already within the Body and allows them to overflow with the fullness of Christ. According to Ephesians 4, it's impossible to enter into the fullness of Christ until the spiritual gifts are set free, made available, and activated. Consider the covenant or small group that you may be a part of right now. What if God gave awakening to your group so that you were set free not only to serve one another but also to seek out a ministry together to the world around you? Would that derail what you originally envisioned for your group when it formed? Of course not. It would complete your purpose. Now expand that proposition to your local church, and to the Church at large. You see, being "together" is a critical part of both entering into awakening and bringing forth its fruits.

Awakening involves the whole Church. As the Church gets reacquainted with Christ, and begins to learn to care for each other, Jesus becomes more visible and attractive to the whole world. A Church living together in holiness and love alerts the world to the possibility that the message she proclaims is both credible and desirable, as Zechariah predicted.

It is hard to oppose the gospel when it is presented by a coalition of revived people who are decisively devoted to Jesus Christ and in love with each other, especially if the world sees that they have been firmly reconciled to each other despite major differences.

A few months ago my church in Madison sent out a couple to work in London, England, among Bengali Muslim immigrants. On the commissioning Sunday, after Russ and Phyllis had once again told of their commitment to a mission to Muslims, they shared one last challenge with us who sent them: "Thanks for your prayers, your financial support, your constant encouragement, your love. But as we go, there is one vital contribution you can make to our work across the Atlantic, without which much will be in vain. Give yourselves, as a congregation, more and more to Christ in wholehearted devotion to Him. For we are an extension among Bengalis of who you are here with Christ. We give to them what we know of Christ in your midst. So, back us by becoming totally devoted to Him."

They understood that they were calling us to revival, and they saw clearly its impact on their impact for Christ's global cause.

## CONCLUSION: GANDHI AND AWAKENING

As I sat captivated by the Academy Award-winning film *Gandhi*, I thought of revival. Why? Because I saw the life of a man who, though not committed to the King, lived out with determination many of the principles Jesus taught as basic building blocks of the Kingdom. As a result of his unyielding adherence to such principles as simplicity, humility, identity with the poor, love of enemies, and vicarious suffering, the life of this one man, Gandhi, transformed the face of India and redirected the twentieth century.

Watching the movie I thought to myself: What if God were to revive His people with renewed, decisive devotion to the King? What if the whole Church, or at least a large segment of it, would awaken to the principle of the Kingdom in uncompromising obedience in union with the King? Considering what one human sinner with a few divine truths accomplished on his own, could a revived Church leave the world the same? Would there not come forth a dramatic fulfillment of Christ's global cause that would be unstoppable? Would we not see the knowledge of the glory of Christ covering the earth "as the waters cover the sea" (Hab. 2:14)?

Spiritual awakening, then, is the strategic target for concerted prayer. Again, spiritual awakening is "when the Father wakes us up to see Christ's fullness in new ways, so that together we trust Him, love Him, and obey Him in new ways, so that we move with Him in new ways for the fulfillment of His global cause." A movement of prayer that focuses on this is never parochial; in every respect it is a movement of prayer for the world. Concerted prayer for spiritual awakening is the most critical step the church can take for the sake of the nation.

That leaves us, however, with one important question: Do we have any reason to believe that ours is a generation in which God would be pleased to grant spiritual awakening to a Church united in prayer to seek Him in it? Is there hope?

The answer to that should encourage us all.

# 5

# SPIRITUAL AWAKENING
Four Good Reasons to Look for It!

I should have guessed I was in for an unusual experience when my 747 landed in Johannesburg, South Africa. Three hundred and fifty of us were delegates to the Consultation on Careers in Frontier Missions and were looking at creative ways to reach unreached peoples. Most of the delegates were young adults who came from each of the major racial groups and classes in South Africa. Despite such diversity, a spirit of unity prevailed unlike anything we had ever seen before. We knew we were one in Christ and in the fulfillment of His global cause. It was miraculous evidence of a revival.

And the miracles continued. On the last night four major commitments were made: (1) The entire assembly expressed willingness to become men and women of prayer; (2) the same number indicated their readiness to do anything God wanted them to do in light of the world's pressing need for the gospel; (3) approximately 300 stood silently to indicate their intention to mobilize concerts of prayer—to take leadership and to be pacesetters until it happened; and (4) over 200 committed to life-time involvement in saving totally unreached peoples—more evidence of revival at hand!

But that was only part of what God had planned. Within six months, concerts of prayer were multiplying in key cities nationwide. Not large in numbers but broad in representation, they forecast the future.

Our Father is at work in South Africa through Christians joined in prayer for spiritual awakening and world evangelization. One such prayer movement can be strategic for world evangelization. When God brings revival and restores unity across all the barriers that divide South Africa, He will bring His kingdom and justice to bear with new force. This will give the gospel new credibility not only in South Africa but also in the community of nations which are watching. Such a revival will strengthen the missionary thrust of South Africans who, sharing the gospel with a unique insight, will influence social and political situations throughout the world.

What spawned such a wave of concerted prayer? God brought together these keen young adults intent on sacrificial service for Christ, and set before them an explosive panorama of where He is headed. I was given the privilege of discussing that panorama with them. God gave us all a vision of what we are to be praying toward, showing us the necessity of spiritual awakening, why to expect it and how to pray for it. For if we want to assist concerts of prayer where we live, we must grasp the vision of what we are praying toward. That will motivate and help us to endure until God answers.

There are four reasons for us to expect a spiritual awakening and to pray hopefully toward it.

*Reason #1—The Divine Pattern.* Time and again, in answer to a movement of prayer, God has awakened His people to His purposes. If He has done it before, He will do it again. We should expect and pray for it. There is hope because of who God is!

*Reason #2—The Dark Prospects.* Unless God does intervene as He has in the past, there is no answer to the crises we face as a global community. We've exhausted many of our options. We're coming to the end, and we know it. In God's economy, that's the hour to expect and pray toward spiritual awakening. It is our only genuine hope.

*Reason #3—The Disturbing Paralysis.* Considering our numbers, resources and enthusiasm, American evangelicals are not making enough of an impact for Christ on our nation and the world. Many of us are distressed by this, yet feel powerless to change it. We are growing desperate for God to break through the status quo in our service for Christ. That's precisely what

He wants us to want! From such realism can flow humility, surrender, teachableness, prayer, and ultimately revival. In dependence on Him for a new work, we can expect and pray toward
spiritual awakening. There is hope!

*Reason #4—The Dramatic Preparations.* Clearly, God is
setting the stage for a new advance of His Kingdom. He is bringing the global community to ask the questions for which the gospel is the answer. And He is providing His global Church unprecedented resources and channels for fulfilling Christ's mission
among the nations. If He is building this highway of preparations
in the desert, can it be long before all humankind sees God's glorious salvation? (Isa. 40, Luke 3.) And will that be nothing less
than spiritual awakening? There is hope!

That's the vision set loose in South Africa. Let's explore it
together here, for the evidence is substantial that we need to be
about the business of mobilizing concerted prayer now.

## Reason #1
## THE DIVINE PATTERN

With our Father, awakening and revival are a way of life.
During the least promising of times, He has always had a people
of prayer, full of faith that He would re-awaken His Church with
international repercussions. What kept them praying? They
believed: "God has done it before, surely He is willing and able
to do it again, even in our generation."

I was hit with His pattern by an experiment I recently conducted. Taking an inexpensive copy of the Bible, I worked
through it from Genesis to Revelation looking for verses on
awakening. I marked each one I found with a yellow highlighting
pen. Then I thumbed back through the pages for the results. Do
you know what? Almost half my Bible was yellow! There was
*that* much in it on God's renewing, restoring, recovering, reviving His people. And there were hundreds of other verses on His
redeeming purposes for *all* nations, often advanced as a result of
revival. I haven't prayed the same since.

I found that the Old Testament emphasizes why awakening
and restoration are necessary and why they are critically tied to
the worldwide impact of God's Kingdom. The New Testament
describes in what forms a full awakening occurs. In fact, it

records the supreme case study of one.

Surveying the past 2,000 years helps us uncover the diverse drama of this biblical pattern. It's like studying the changing shafts of light from a masterfully cut diamond. We're left with great encouragement for any movement of prayer. If God has revived His people before, He is willing and able to do it again, even in our generation. Some church historians suggest that past awakenings are like dress rehearsals for a reviving work which God is preparing to unfold today.

Let's survey some of these awakenings in Scripture and in church history.

## The Old Testament: Prototypes and Principles

*During the Patriarchs: Awakening and Covenant.* Abraham's experience, as God called him out of Babel's confusing folly of idolatry, might properly be termed an awakening. God shined on him with a promise not only to bless him (fullness) but also make him a blessing to the families of the earth (fulfillment).

Twice at Bethel, Jacob was awakened to the same covenant God. First, he saw the gates of heaven opened before him. Then he wrestled with the Lord's angel and knew that he had met God face to face.

In Joseph's day, much of the earth was given a clearer knowledge of the Creator because He was committed to reviving, physically and spiritually, His own people.

Throughout Old Testament times, God recalled for Israel these pictures of the patriarchs' awakenings, appealing to them as His promise for future recoveries.

*Around the Exodus: Awakening and Mission.* The Exodus is every bit a prototype of spiritual awakenings to come. In desperate bondage, the Israelites cried to God—a movement of prayer. In new ways, God brought His people alive to Himself and His mission before the nations (Exod. 19). The Exodus itself was designed to awaken both Israel and Egypt to the fullness of God's grace and power (Exod. 6).

Over and over throughout its wilderness wanderings, Israel's heart reached back for the security of Egypt, but each time they returned to God as He freshly revealed Himself to them (see also Ps. 106).

*Judges to David: The Ups and Downs of Awakening.* In the book of Judges, we find a 400-year account of the divine pattern. It goes like this: A new generation rises up who does not know the Lord and forsakes Him for other gods. God gives them over to their enemies. Their physical and spiritual lives are depleted until they awaken to their need to be restored to Jehovah. They cry out together to the Lord. He responds by raising up Judges who lead the people back into His ways (fullness). As a result, surrounding nations stop harassing Israel, because the fear of God is so evident in their midst (fulfillment).

*Under Solomon: A High Watermark in Awakenings.* From the text in 1 Chronicles 29:1-22, it seems the building of the Temple was a time of mighty revival. When the Temple was completed and Israel was assembled for its dedication, the cloud of God's glorious presence filled the Temple so thoroughly that no one could enter it (fullness). Solomon rose to offer a prayer of dedication, which remains one of the most significant revival prayers in Scripture. Before the whole assembly, he reviewed God's promises, then called on Him to hear the prayers of Israel (1 Kings 8). God answered so powerfully that we read of many nations sending representatives to investigate the splendor of awakening in Solomon's generation (fulfillment) (1 Kings 9.)

*Under Judah's Kings: Magnificent Moments of Awakening.* In Judah God raised up many kings to bring His bride back to life. Under King Asa for example (2 Chron. 14–15), a comprehensive movement of prayer emerged. And we are told that the pray-ers found God. "They entered into a covenant to seek the Lord, the God of their fathers, with all their heart and soul . . . . They took an oath to the Lord with loud acclamation, with shouting and with trumpets and horns. All Judah rejoiced about the oath because they had sworn it wholeheartedly. They sought God eagerly, and he was found by them [fullness]. So the Lord gave them rest on every side" (2 Chron. 15:12-15). The phrase "rest on every side" describes how other nations changed their view of God as a result (fulfillment).

*As the Exiles Return: Awakened to Rebuild.* One day God put His hand on the Persian emperor Cyrus, alerted him to the supremacy of the Lord of Israel, and through him opened a door for the exiles to return to the land and rebuild the Temple, the place of prayer for all nations. A remnant of 42,000 responded to the stirrings of the Spirit in their midst. Under Zerubbabel, Joshua, Ezra, Haggai and Zechariah, and later Nehemiah and Malachi, great revivals sprung forth. Although there were times of fear and discouragement, God kept before them the vision of His readiness to bring forth a movement of prayer that would shake the heavens and the earth (Hag. 2).

As Malachi insists, God was prepared to awaken His people once more so that all nations would call them blessed of the Lord and join to offer prayers in response to His glory.

*In the Prophets: Promises of Awakening.* In studying the prophets on awakenings, frequently used concepts have helped me group something of what they saw as the essence of revival. The themes of fullness and fulfillment are evident throughout. Let me note a few:

(1) The Image of Light: Day Has Come, Wake Up! (Mic. 7, Isa. 9)

(2) The Image of Water: Time to Drink Up! (Joel 2, Hos. 5)

(3) The Image of Fire: Time to Burn Up! (Mal. 4, Zeph. 3)

(4) The Image of Roads: Time to Come Up to the Lord! (Mic. 4, Isa. 35)

(5) Image of a Remnant: Time to Spring Up! (Jer. 31, Isa. 11)

(6) Images of Global Awakening: Time to Speak Up! (Isa. 49, Ezek. 36–37)

*Through the Psalms: Practical Experiences in Awakenings.* Before our venture into the New Testament, it's worth noting how the Psalms, beyond their hymns of praise, document the responses of many generations to spiritual awakening. This is obvious in Psalm 51, as David records his personal revival following God's judgment on his sin with Bathsheba.

However, several Psalms vividly paint perimeters of spiritual awakening for the entire nation. For example, Psalm 85:6 explores God's restoring work and cries: "Will you not revive us again, that your people may rejoice in you?" Psalm 107 sets off a litany of desperate situations when people sought a new work from God as they cried to the Lord in prayer. Precise descriptions of revival follow each time.

## The New Testament: The Ultimate Awakening

Every awakening or promise of the Old Testament finds a graphic demonstration in the first-century Church. God gave an unprecedented revival when the nucleus of awakening, Jesus Christ Himself, stepped into history.

*In the Gospels: Christ Is the Awakening.* Jesus came at a time of heightened concern for renewal in Israel. The Pharisees pursued it as laymen, and the Sadducees, as clergy. The Zealots followed more violent renewal efforts, convinced that only revolution against the Roman Empire would restore Israel. And the Essenes, a Jewish monastic order, retreated into desert caves to purify themselves for the messianic revival movement for which this remnant prayed relentlessly.

But genuine awakening was to be found in another— "Immanuel, God with us"—serving in the midst of His people to save them from their sins. Full of grace and truth, the Son became flesh and lived among them, revealing the Father in fullness, to renew them with one blessing after another (John 1).

Christ appeared to a repentant people longing to see Him, "waiting expectantly and were all wondering in their hearts" (Luke 3:15). Ready to baptize with the Holy Spirit and with fire, He strode forth, winnowing fork in hand, to clear His threshing floor and gather the wheat into His barn, while the chaff burned with unquenchable fire. Clearly His would be revival deeds!

When Jesus set out preaching He had His eye on all that the prophets had promised (Mark 1). Every hope they had offered for recovery through a mighty God-ordained revival was available to His generation, because He was the Kingdom foretold. No wonder that after successfully defying the Prince of Darkness, Jesus stepped into His hometown synagogue to announce that the Lord had anointed Him to proclaim release to the captives, sight to the blind, good news to the poor (see Luke 4). Revival was at the door.

The bottom line response in spiritual awakening is decisive devotion to Jesus Christ. Because of the seriousness of God's reviving work, Jesus spoke of this as the heart of His mission: "If anyone would come after me, he must deny himself and take up his cross and follow me. For whoever wants to save his life will lose it, but whoever loses his life for me and for the gospel will save it" (Mark 8:34). Revitalized with such devotion, His disciples took His words seriously enough to leave home and families, declaring far and wide at great personal cost, what wonders God was about to do in and through the midst of his people (Matthew 10).

But Jesus did more than just teach or demonstrate awakening. His mission was to secure the fruits of spiritual awakening for all of God's people for all time to come. And He did that by His perfect life, His death for sin and His resurrection, the greatest revival in all of history.

But there was more. Out of the Resurrection, awakening unfurled with greater intensity than ever. "After his suffering, he showed himself to these men and gave many convincing proofs that he was alive. He appeared to them over a period of forty days and spoke about the kingdom of God" (Acts 1:3). As He did at first with men and women huddled in fear, He continues to accelerate the Church's understanding of the Scriptures, so that we too become eye-witnesses to His majesty. No wonder we are given only one logical response to what we see: Preach repentance and forgiveness of sins in His name to all nations, beginning in Jerusalem. The awakening moves outward as the Church is filled with the Holy Spirit and begins to revive the nations with the life-giving power of forgiveness and reconciliation to the Father.

*During the Acts: The Church Extends the Awakening.* Pentecost became another high point in the history of spiritual awakenings. Everyone was filled with awe as many wonders and miraculous signs, frequently found to be a part of subsequent revivals, were done before the crowds. The result? Many more were added to the Church as the Word of God spread. Strengthened by the Holy Spirit, the Church continued to grow in numbers, and the presence of the Lord was felt deeply by all, not only in the Church, but beyond.

In Acts 4, during the middle of great persecution, the Church prayed for God to deepen the work of spiritual awakening, so they might preach the Word of God with boldness and the place was shaken! The awakening spread across cultural barriers as even the "half-breed" Samaritans were brought face to face the

Lord with Jesus Christ (Acts 8).

Ultimately however, the church had a grander assignment than extending awakening among the Jews. As revival harvest within the covenant people took place, God opened the way for taking awakening to the Gentile world, even to Rome itself (Acts 14:27; 26:15-23).

*Through the Letters: Pointers on Awakening.* Developed within the context of this expanding awakening, Paul and the other apostles gives us some important pointers on awakening. No wonder the Church has turned to the Epistles over centuries of revivals and found them to be helpful in interpreting and assisting God's renewing work. Let's survey a couple of their many insights.

First of all, they document God's sovereign role in bringing awakening. He causes the darkness to retreat as the true light begins to shine. Though we may feel that we are wasting away, we are being renewed daily (see 2 Cor. 4). As the Spirit ministers to us He draws from the deep things of God and reveals them to us, Spirit-to-spirit (see 1 Cor. 2).

In Paul's written prayers we find keen understanding of God's ongoing initiative in awakening. But they also treat another dimension in the pattern. They speak of our responsibility. The Epistles call us to stay awake. "The hour has come for you to wake up from your slumber, . . . put aside the deeds of darkness and put on the armor of light . . . . Clothe yourselves with the Lord Jesus Christ" (Rom. 13:11-14). There is great warning in the New Testament to those who have once been enlightened—who have known heavenly gifts, who have shared the Spirit's revelation of Christ, who have tasted the goodness of God's Word and the reviving powers of the age to come.

*In the Revelation: Climax of Awakening.* By the time Jesus appeared to John on the island of Patmos, some of the intensity of the first-century awakening had mellowed. Over the years, many of the churches born in the initial awakening had begun to cool, or to retreat, or to sidetrack into preoccupations. God's lampstands nursed flickering flames.

In Revelation, Jesus displayed an enlarged view of His purposes for history showing His Church the coming climax of an awakening in which they had already participated. He knew though, that the churches of the first century needed to be *rea*-wakened themselves. So He appeared to John to clarify who He was to those who had once known and loved Him more vividly, and to show them how His revelation to all peoples would ulti-mately lead toward the consummation of the age.

### The Historical Pattern: Episodes Abound

The divine pattern of spiritual awakening thoroughly perme-ates Scripture, so it's no surprise to find additional episodes throughout the past 2,000 years of church history. The history of revivals continues to inspire hope that even at the darkest hours God will intervene in His Church to revitalize it with a new vision of His Son. As always, this will result in fullness of life for the Church as well as new levels of the fulfillment of His pur-poses among nations.

The great monastic movements, for example, which endured over 1,500 years, frequently acted as bases of both renewal and missionary operation. Breaking with the values of their cultures, these communities developed life-styles of praise, commitment, vision, simplicity and mission.

The Reformation itself is a high watermark in Church awak-enings. It may have been the greatest revival since Pentecost. But the writings of the Puritans between 1675 and 1750 indicate that most of them expected greater works of renewal yet to come. The Puritans prayed intensely for revival, taking a long-term view of world missions, and looking at the need in their generation to lay foundations of prayer and spiritual vitality that would result in future awakenings.

At the same time as the Puritan Revival, another awakening surfaced within European Protestantism known as the Pietist movement. One of the stories bears repeating; it pulsates with the divine pattern.

Count Nicholas Ludwig von Zinzendorf lived from 1700-1760, in what today is East Germany. He studied at the Univer-sity of Halle, the great Pietist education and discipleship center, and at the University of Wittenburg, home of the Reformation. In both schools, he met with other students in prayer meetings, sometimes praying all night, as they sought God for revival. At

Halle, he, five other students, and Professor Franke formed the Order of the Mustard Seed and were responsible for sending out Protestant missionaries to India.

Four years after he graduated, political upheavals and religious persecution brought Zinzendorf together with what has since been known as the Moravian Brethren. These 200 refugees came to America from different countries, social standings and religious persuasions.

Zinzendorf and three other elders committed themselves to pray for God's intervention within their Herrnhut Community, as they called it, because of increased tensions among so diverse a group. They eventually prayed day and night for revival. On August 13, 1727, God poured out His Holy Spirit on the community. Revival came, and historians call this "the Moravian Pentecost."

Then each of 24 hours of the day was assigned to 24 men and 24 women who prayed in pairs. This God-ordained prayer vigil lasted over 100 years! As a result, the community was revived with a desire to see the worldwide Church awakened to its calling to world evangelization.

Richard Lovelace says:

> More than the Anabaptist settlements, Herrnhut turned its concerns outward to embrace the rest of the church and the world. It was organized around an urgent concern to revive professing Christendom and to reach the whole planet with the gospel. The pattern of foreign missionary effort established by the Herrnhuters included both the preaching of the Lamb and initiatives of social and cultural healing. They cared for the sick, established schools and provided for the aged, widows and orphans. Thus the main thrust of evangelical foreign missions, springing from the social concern of Hale and Hurrnhut, has rarely lacked a social dimension even when the home missionary work of evangelicals has been socially passive, as the case has often been during the twentieth century.[1]

Within 12 years the Moravians, nicknamed "the Savior's

happy people," established mission bases in the West Indies, Greenland, India, South Africa, Guinea, Ceylon and Turkey, as well as in various parts of Europe and the New World. In the first 100 years they sent out over 2,150 missionaries.

With equal zeal, they also sent out "renewal teams" to preach revival and unity in Christ to churches in many nations, with some even going to Rome to preach to the Pope! Many historians believe the Moravian movement was foundational to both the Great Awakening that swept much of the Protestant world in the 1700s and the one that emerged in the late 1700s and the early 1800s. The extensive revival of 1730 onward, involving people like the Wesleys and Whitefield, was termed the "Great Awakening" in its American expression and the "Evangelical Revival" within its English setting. It varied widely in duration throughout the English-speaking world. Some historians mark seven major surges of revival from 1730-1790 in some part of the Body of Christ.

The second awakening is staked out from 1790 onward. Prior to this revival, William Carey, called by some the father of modern missions, was part of a small prayer band in the English town of Kettering. They met monthly for almost eight years before they saw their revival prayers answered.

Carey also prayed daily over a map of the world as he worked as a shoemaker. In this environment of revival prayer he dreamed and strategized persistently to bring the gospel to the entire human race. In the ferment of the awakening that followed, his vision proved contagious. Thus the evangelical awakening, plus new possibilities offered by British freedom and mastery of the seas, set loose the British missionary enterprise with a thrust that has yet to reach its fullest extent.

William Wilberforce, member of a community that formed together for prayer and ministry in the Anglican parish of Clapham near London, spearheaded many other fruits of the second awakening. Under Wilberforce's leadership, the Clapham community turned England into a force for justice and a channel for the gospel of Christ. They led battles for judicial, penal, and industrial reform, and for the spread of popular education. Undergirding all of their efforts was a deep commitment to sacrificial living and fervent prayer. In fact they spent three hours a day in prayer; morning, noon and evening.

The third awakening surfaced noticeably in 1857 when a Manhattan businessman, Jeremiah Lamphier, sent out an invitation for people to join him at the Reformed Church consistory on Fulton Street, for a noontime prayer meeting for revival. At the first gathering, out of a population of one million, only six people showed up.

But gradually the prayer meeting spread. By 1858, New York City alone had 6,000 people involved in daily noon prayer meetings! Tens of thousands crowded into the churches for prayer in the evenings. Ten thousand a week were converted. In Chicago at the same time, almost 2,000 gathered for an hour of prayer every noon. Eventually this prayer movement spread from much of the English-speaking world to the mission fields.

In *The Fervent Prayer,* Dr. Orr says of this awakening:

> The mid-century awakenings (1858-59) revived all of the existing missionary societies and enabled them to enter other fields. The practical evangelical ecumenism of the revival was embodied in the China Inland Mission founded by Hudson Taylor in the aftermath of the British Awakening, the first of the interdenominational 'faith missions.' As in the first half of the century, practically every missionary invasion was launched by men revived or converted in the awakenings of the churches in the sending countries.[2]

Some would look at the Welsh revival in 1904 under Evan Roberts as the fountainhead for a fourth awakening. This revival was not localized in a few coal mines; it was preceded by prayer concerts all over the world. A strong surge of missionary outreach and endeavor followed. In this awakening, revival had come of age because the initiative now lay as much with churches in Asia and Africa as it did in the West.

Have we already entered into a fifth awakening? Today a consolidation of three vital movements in the Church—Pentecostal, charismatic and evangelical—appears to have unleashed a spiritual fervency in the Body of Christ that in terms of numbers is unparalleled in church history. Donald Bloesch, theologian of renewal, suggests that this diverse evangelicalism, rather than being a distinct party within the Church, is basically a *movement* of spiritual revival, serving the Church as a catalyst.

You and I are the only heirs to what those who have gone before us have found in the Lord and passed on. What will we do with this vast treasure?

Elton Trueblood suggests one response: "When a Christian expresses sadness about the church, it is always the sadness of a lover. He knows that there have been great periods and consequently, he is not willing to settle for anything less than those in his time."[3]

Shouldn't we expect God to be willing and able to revive us again? Can we settle for less? We need not, if we unite in prayer for God to repeat His pattern in our time.

## Reason #2
## THE DARK PROSPECTS

In 1983, Aleksandr Solzhenitsyn observed, "Today's world has reached a stage that, if it had been described to preceding centuries, it would have called forth the cry: 'this is apocalypse.'" In his recent best-seller, *Approaching Hoofbeats*, Billy Graham writes: "There is something ominous in the air and my bones vibrate with the horror of it."

I want to explore some current global nightmares—not to depress you but to convince you that we must cry to God in prayer. Awakenings have often occurred during the world's darkest hours. Frankly, the situation today is bad enough that there's little question God must intervene, either in judgment because our rebellion has gone too far, or in a global-sized work of grace as He rains mercy down on us all. And there is every reason to believe that if we cry for mercy, it will be ours! For if God doesn't give awakening, the world has no other hopeful prospect.

### The Unreached: Six Million Beachheads to Go

The numbers of unreached people are staggering. There are as many people in the world who have no knowledge of Christ as the number of times your heart will beat from the day you were born to the day you reach 75—at least 2.5 billion strong. This does not include, of course, the hundreds of millions of nominal Christians in the world who have yet to come to true saving faith in Christ. Nor does it include the one billion non-Christians who could be reached through regular evangelism by Christians around the world who are like them culturally, socially and linguistically. No, we're talking about 2.5 billion people who can be reached only by major new cross-cultural efforts in love and communication.

Obviously, then, the complexity of the task is just as overwhelming as the numbers involved. There are tremendous roadblocks to the gospel within the diverse human family. Throughout the world, awesome boundaries—geographical, social, economic, political, cultural, linguistic, religious, racial, generational, and even physical—cut human beings off from one another. Some estimate as many as 20,000 distinct people groupings throughout the world—some with as few as 9,000 members, like a tribe in Nigeria; others with as many as 30 million, like a caste in India—where there's no inborn evangelizing community of Christians among them. Most of the time, they're in need of outside, cross-cultural assistance if they are ever to come to Christ.

The world can be evangelized effectively only by a Church so thoroughly revived that we begin sacrificially to multiply determined, equipped, Spirit-filled, cross-cultural servants of the gospel. If we were to pray that God would give the earth one actively ministering congregation for every 1,000 people in the world—a ratio that insures adequate resources for ministry to the whole person, approximately six million new churches would be needed among non-Christians or nominal Christians by the year 2000. It would also require 600,000 additional intercultural workers from the Church worldwide. If that doesn't call for extraordinary divine intervention on behalf of the nations, I don't know what does!

Currently, however, the Protestant missionary force worldwide is about 85,000, with 8,000 concentrating directly on the unfinished work among almost three billion lives. One estimate has only 75 cross-cultural servants working throughout the 20 Arab speaking nations. Unless this response greatly improves, the prospects for the world are dark indeed.

And yet that's not the end of the nightmare. Other crises overlap the challenge of world evangelization, making things even more complicated for the advancement of Christ's Kingdom. Rapid population growth, war, suffering, disease, and hunger are prevailing conditions among earth's unreached, and they enlarge our task and strain our resources to exhaustion. As *Time* in 1984 described the continent of Africa, where millions still know little of Christ: "It vibrates with catastrophe, corruption, coups, conflicts." If God doesn't give awakening, the world has no hope. Let's briefly explore a few more nightmares that must be included on the agenda of a movement of prayer toward spiritual awakening.

## Population Explosion: Where's Your Calculator?

There are more people alive today than ever died in all of human history! Every five days, another one million people are added to our planet. At the end of 1982, the world registered its biggest 12-month population increase in history: 84 million people.

In 1983, 4.7 billion people inhabited the earth. By 1990 that number will rise to 5.3 billion; by the middle of the next century, we will have 9 billion inhabitants. Most of the growth will take place in the less developed world. Today, 10 of every 11 babies are born in the Third World. With most of the unreached currently in Africa and Asia, what will it mean to have 75 percent of our planet's people residing there within two decades?

With all of these sobering statistics staring us in the face, we realize that the Church entering the twenty-first century faces a larger number of people to be loved and reached for Jesus Christ than ever before.

## Population Implosion: Can Anyone Pry Us Apart?

"Population implosion" occurs when more and more people are jammed into smaller and smaller areas. Today there is a massive movement of our growing population from the country to the city, referred to as urbanization.

Sociologists talk of "world class cities," those that have one million people or more. The number of these cities should double by the year 2000, with almost 300 cities of one million and 70 of two million or more. As we move toward the twenty-first century, 75 percent of Third World population will live in urban settings. For the first time in history, a majority of the world's urban dwellers will be found in the Third World. These urban centers often become, in Ray Bakke's terms, "the throw away place" for an upwardly and outwardly migrating middle class, and a caldron of unfulfilled expectations and frustrations for newly arrived, usually unskilled minorities. Theodore White calls our cities "warehouses for the very poor or enclaves for the very rich."

What does this urbanization mean for evangelization and a movement of prayer for the world? For one thing, it's a fact that where the cities go, the nations go, and so goes the world. So, unless Christians successfully confront the major urban problems of our day, we will soon face unfathomable difficulties in preaching the gospel, and we'll be up against cultural and moral forces undreamed of today. Are there any hopeful prospects unless God powerfully intervenes to mobilize His Church?

## Poverty: A Brutality That Lasts and Lasts

The more settled and secure our daily experiences are, the harder it is for us to imagine the brutality of poverty that so much of the world experiences. Almost one billion people survive on a per capita income of $75 a year (I just paid that much for a summer blazer!). No wonder they spend most of their time simply worrying about survival.

In India, as many as 300 million people concentrate their limited physical energy on securing one bowl of rice each day. The number of hopelessly poor worldwide is increasing at a rate faster than total population. By the year 2000, an estimated one billion people will be among the landless, hopelessly poor.

Wherever we find it, the experience of poverty is quite similar. It adds up to a loss of dignity, sense of powerlessness, and a lack of self-determination. The poor have little freedom from fear, insecurity, terrorism, barbarianism or war.

Some experts suggest that unless something can be done to reverse the present situation, we in the West risk "the proletarian wrath," when the poor of the earth will rise up to take what they need, no matter what the cost in human life. After all, what do they have to lose? The 1979 Presidential Commission on World Hunger warned: "The most potentially explosive force in the world today is the frustrated desire of poor people to attain a decent standard of living."

Poverty is brutal and difficult to focus upon. But in the statistics, we find God's call to prayer for spiritual awakening. Where sin and its brutality abound, grace and its liberation do much more abound! God loves the poor of the earth and desires to establish Christ's Kingdom among them. That's why we find hope that such a God will not leave things in the Church or the world as they are. For the sake of the poor He will revive His church. For the sake of mankind's survival, we must seek God's powerful and just interventions.

It is critical that the Church move immediately from any passive analysis of the hungry and dispossessed. Unitedly, we must ask the Lord to awaken us to the fullness of Christ so that out of His love and our obedience to Him, we might respond with repentance, justice, and compassion to earth's poor, most of whom are also unreached.

## Technocracy: The Empire Strikes Fast!

The arena of technology presents us with a "good news-bad news" situation. The good news is that much of what's being developed can be harnessed for the furtherance of the gospel. The bad news is that much of it could create global nightmares that make *Star Wars* look like a bedtime story.

The dominance of technology, sometimes called "technocracy," can lead, for example, to increased possibilities for surveillance and control of others. We face genetic engineering, which allows us the possibility of playing God with other people's lives. When we control the genetic makeup and even the direction of a person's future, we exercise ultimate power over another human.

The information revolution—the availability of instant information—will have impact well beyond upheavals of the Industrial Revolution. Once knowledge was truth; today knowledge has become power. As a result, social scientists are predicting the emergence of a new class of citizens within every nation and sometimes including whole nations: the "information poor," those who are unable to become part of the information age. This can only exaccerbate their already desperate economic plight.

The Church must lead the way to the understanding of true biblical values and their relationship to technological powers and dangers. As the Church harnesses technology for the advance of the Kingdom, it must also have the heart to use technology to serve a world that is suffering and lost and to facilitate the obedience of faith among the nations. Surely this is what our Father would desire for us. Unless He revives the hearts of Christians to care and respond, the world is vulnerable to a technocratic empire that may strike back at us with a fury.

## Militarism: Road to Armaggedon?

Will there even *be* a world to evangelize by the year 2000? It's a sobering but valid question, posed with the greatest urgency. And the prospects are dark indeed.

The governments of the world are turning us into a massive armed camp. In 1976, world military expenditures exceeded $350 billion. Just eight years later that figure soared to more than $600 billion. At $1 million a minute, the world today spends twice as much on defense as it spends on food, and five times as much as it spends on housing.

And it isn't all just sitting in storage, either! We often think World War III will be a final nuclear blow-up. But if we use the term "world war" to mean a sustained international conflict involving large numbers of nations of the world, it's fair to say that today we are already witnessing World War III. Over 100 non-nuclear wars have been fought since 1945, involving 80 nations and killing more people than died during all of World War II. Even as I write these words, the battle between Iran and Iraq has claimed a total of 30,000 dead in one month alone.

Most thinking people would agree that this world-at-war is on a collision course with total annihilation: nuclear war. We're caught in an escalating nuclear arms race. A recent CBS documentary on the nuclear buildup entitled their findings "The Road to Armageddon."

The world's atomic arsenal holds the equivalent of over two tons of dynamite for every man, woman, and child on earth. The U.S.S.R. has the capacity to kill everybody in the world 95 times over, and the U.S. can do so 100 times over. Either could vaporize the planet in 15 minutes. Simply and frankly, modern history offers no example, as George Kennan noted, of the development by rival powers of huge armed forces that did not, in the end, lead to an outbreak of hostilities. Are we wiser than all of our ancestors? No wonder 53 percent of U.S. high schoolers list the threat of nuclear war as their greatest fear.

The prospects grow darker, however. Very soon almost any country with a "backyard plutonium kit" will be able to deal in nuclear destruction. By the end of this century, an estimated 50 nations in the world may possess atomic weapons. George Will wryly calls this "the democratization of nuclear weapons."

What if the Church does not find a convincingly renewed life under the Lord Jesus to boldly confront the fear, aggression, and insane plotting that brings forth this destruction? And what if we don't awaken to stand together as a people who genuinely demonstrate by word, deed, and policy that Christ, not the bomb, is our refuge and our Lord? I'm afraid we will have little spiritual power to preach the Good News of reconciliation with effect among the earth's unreached, even if they survive to hear us and we to tell them.

It is in this desperate situation that we find the greatest hope that God is ready to respond in mercy to a movement of prayer toward spiritual awakening. We also find every good reason in this to get about the business of praying.

## Competition: Buffeted by Seas of Doctrine

Without an awakening we face other dark prospects due to the increased intensity of ideological forces that oppose the advancement of the gospel.

For example, secularism claims, "Whatever can be accomplished through human resources is all that there is." As a world view it presents a deadly clash with the gospel. Humanism, the fruit of secularization, declares humankind to be the final authority in everything. The world's universities, which have largely surrendered active concern over the realities of spirit and of revelation, are saturated with humanism. There seems to be no strong regard for fixed truth or values. Instead there's an accommodation to many views as the special triumph of modern man.

In its studies of gospel and culture, the Lausanne Committee in 1980 published in the Willowbank Report their insights on how the secular nightmare complicates our efforts at world evangelization:

> In the 20th century West, often more sophisticated but no less horrible examples of the evils which were opposed in the 19th century still exist. Parallel to cannibalism is social injustice which "eats" the poor; to widow-strangling, the oppression of women; to infanticide, abortion; to patricide, a criminal neglect of senior citizens; to tribal wars, World War II; and to ritual prostitution, sexual promiscuity . . . . the smog of secularism has choked out for most any sense of the "holy."[4]

The Church is also buffeted by seas of *competing religions*. When it comes to the penetration of the gospel among the great world religions, the prospects seem dark indeed. For example, we've watched a great upsurge in Buddhism since World War II. There are more than 500 million Buddhists worldwide. Despite its idolatry and superstitious darkness, Hinduism is experiencing its own mass awakening. Much of this "awakening" has been carried out at great personal sacrifice on the part of workers who go forth to preach Hinduism and to the many who, out of a meager income, support those who go.

Although the percentage of Christians worldwide has declined throughout this century, that of Muslims has increased. Today in 53 countries, Muslims compose over half the population. There are almost 800 million worldwide. In the face of secularism's de-Christianizing impact, Muslims now stalk Europe, expecting Europe to be their most successful mission field. In the United States, a $5 million Islamic community, complete with mosque and prayer tower, is being constructed in northern New Mexico, mostly with oil money from Saudi Arabia. It will serve as a center for Islamic missionary activities in the United States.

It seems that the Church worldwide will shortly be engulfed
by these waves of sophisticated doctrine unless God convinces
the nations with irrefutable clarify that Jesus is Lord and that He
is in the midst of His people as the hope of the world (Colossians
1:27). Toward that miracle, concerted prayer must move; by
that hopeful vision concerted prayer will be sustained.

## The Greatest Conspiracy

Ultimately, however, we face the overwhelming nightmare
found in every generation: the condition of humankind's heart.
The fifty-dollar term theologians use is "total depravity." There
are enough dark prospects in this nightmare alone to compel a
movement of prayer.

It is not that we humans are entirely bad—we are able to
paint beautiful paintings or engage in a variety of philanthropic
works if we choose—but our desire to know God and to pursue
all of our legitimate goals in order to please Him, is, in David
Hubbard's words, stone cold. All people are lawless, rebellious,
and wicked. This rebellion goes beyond rebellious acts to rebellious intentions, attitudes, alliances, and allegiances.

But there is an added dimension to this. We are told that the
whole world of sinners lies in the hands "of the evil one" (1 John
5:19). A conspiracy is active right now against the Kingdom of
God, and its leader is alive and working feverishly on earth. The
temptations, oppressions, and persecutions we often experience in the world missionary thrust come at this point. We
aggressively operate in the whirlpool ultimately created, not by
scarcity, technology or war, but by the convergence of two diametrically opposed spiritual powers, one who knows his time is
very short and One who is assured of ultimate victory.

The more oppressive Satan makes the world's night, the
greater our hope that we in the Church are near the dawn of a
new era of spiritual awakening. Our King will not be defeated! In
a movement of prayer we rally toward His coming triumph, we
forcefully advance His Kingdom against all foes.

## Reason #3
## OUR DISTURBING PARALYSIS

Next, we turn to the wonder and mystery of the American

evangelical movement—the wonder of its potential for serving Christ's Kingdom and the mystery of its paralysis to activate spiritual dynamics that comprehensively transform our nation and the world.

We might call the latter a "paralysis of faith." It focuses on nightmares closer to home and represents the third major reason for the need of awakening. For if God doesn't revive us, the Church may have no other way out of its paralysis.

## A Visibly Thriving Enterprise

Something quite significant is definitely happening. Our God-given potential is showing. A look at the ferment in our churches proves we must be doing more than just daydreaming. In the United States at least 40 million of us—nearly one out of every five adults—are evangelicals. What difference does that make?

In general, studies conclude that evangelicals contribute more generously to the Church, understand their faith better, and are more ready to speak of it to others. American evangelicals are strongly Bible-centered in their faith, and seek to be faithful to Scripture, convinced the Bible is God's Word. Recent surveys show that 85 percent of North American protestants are absolutely certain Scripture is the "revealed word of God." Eighty-five percent of U.S. evangelicals dip into the Scriptures at least weekly, almost half every day.

If one measure of spiritual vitality is church membership, note that in 1981 church membership stood at 138,452,614, an increase of almost 4 million over 10 years before. Today there are 370,000 churches in the United States to service this growing interest. It's no surprise then, that outwardly evangelicalism appears to be a thriving enterprise.

Over the past 10 years, evangelical churches have posted record gains and have also increased political clout. They've taken on crusades as never before on a variety of issues including abortion, homosexuality, the role of women, the plight of the poor, and the reformation of national morality.

Vitality can also be seen in the growth of the charismatic renewal movement which, though a worldwide phenomenon, has its largest following in the United States. In 1980, a Gallup poll concluded that 29 million evangelicals also call themselves charismatic. The charismatic movement has penetrated every denomination, with its most significant dimension within the Roman Catholic Church.

Evangelical books now account for a third of the total domestic commercial book sales. More than 1,300 radio stations and dozens of television stations devote all or most of their time to religious broadcasting. We have multiplied what many call parachurch organizations, providing a plethora of ways for evangelicals to obey the Great Commission. Over 1,000 organizations are members of the National Religious Broadcasters, while over 30 nationwide campus ministries are seeking to penetrate both Christian and secular campuses. In responding to the world beyond our shores, the American evangelical movement has fostered over 700 overseas ministries, many of which have appeared within the past 30 years.

What are we to make of this kaleidoscope of activity and energy? Richard Lovelace calls it a "steadily increasing displacement of the works of darkness" and suggests that it may appropriately be called a revival in a biblical sense. If that's true, it leaves me with hope of more to come.

## The Paralysis of American Evangelicalism

Yet everywhere I go, in my discussions with evangelical leaders, it appears that despite all this, something is not quite right. As theologian Louis Drummond remarks on current evangelical renewal: "It simply has missed the bulk of God's people. And that is the prime problem!"

Having spent time with Senate Chaplain Richard Halverson, I understand his concern expressed in an interview with *Eternity* magazine:

> I believe we're on the threshold of something happening that is going to be as great or greater than the Reformation . . . I feel that we are a lot farther into it than we realize . . . (But) I am deeply concerned about the acculturation of evangelicals. They are infected by a very subtle worldliness— materialism and comfort in this world. I have been concerned about the pragmatism—the quantification

of everything: numbers, bigness, television success, buildings. It is as though quality has nothing to do with growth . . . with all the growing evangelicalism—the talk of spiritual awakening—our social order continues to deteriorate.[5]

In one of his last editorials for *Christianity Today,* Dr. Kenneth Kantzer concurred. Looking at the potency of evangelicalism in 1983 and beyond, he raised serious questions about the depth of its influence on our nation: "Evangelicalism is weaker now than it was fifteen years ago, or fifty years ago. The influence of evangelical faith and evangelical ethics is less. As a culture, our nation and, indeed western Europe, are moving away from biblical Christianity. Most people don't realize that one hundred years ago the mainline denominations were all evangelical."[6]

Of course, there are reasonable explanations for this paralysis. As we just saw, the immensity and complexity of reaching our world for Christ, as well as the uncertainties of the task are almost suffocating. Crushed by forces that plague our society, we freeze to our seats like passive spectators.

On top of all that, many of us are spiritually and psychologically fatigued. Ruth Graham calls the modern evangelical "packed man." We have so many options that we are paralyzed with over-choice and fatigued by trying to carry out too much, too soon, too fast, too often.

Are we unwilling to be involved more deeply in world evangelization? Or are we unable, despite all of our potential? Perhaps we're not so much weary of the work as we are weary in the work. For many, heart exhaustion has set in.

In any case, the present evangelical "revival" appears to have relatively little impact on such issues as crime, racism, poverty, militarism and the general moral climate. Let's look at some specific illustrations of this:

*Materialism Breeds Paralysis.* Evangelicals have not broken the stranglehold of materialism. Our national vision remains one of driving passion for comfort and security. It seems as if consumption has become a patriotic duty, one of our inalienable rights. Despite our strong evangelical pronouncements to the contrary, a majority of Americans continue to organize their lives around money, not God. Our standard of living often shapes our morality. The Higher Education Research Institute at UCLA found recently among our nation's college freshmen, "The decline in social concern has not been as dramatic as the increase in materialism and greed." Mother Theresa remarked to me recently, "In America you have the greatest poverty. You have poverty of spirit." She's right. And the ineffective witness of the Church is, in large measure, to blame.

*A Failure to Dignify Life.* Francis Schaeffer held that eventually every nation in every age must be judged by this test: How did it treat its people? One measure of evangelical power, then, would be our ability to impress upon our citizens a strong appreciation for the dignity inherent in every human life.

Instead, we find that life is losing dignity in many ways from abortion to nuclear proliferation. Our materialistic throwaway culture bestows the term "human" on people more on the basis of achievement than of divine endowment.

Take abortion, for example. In 1973, the U.S. Supreme Court effectively established the right to abortion on demand relevant to the well-being, primarily, of the patient. The unborn child became subject to destruction at the request of the mother. Since 1973, abortions have increasd by at least 250,000 per year—over 12 million to date or 12 times all U.S. war dead, becoming the most common medical procedure performed on adults in the United States. By 1980, one out of every four pregnancies was terminated by an abortion. That's over 4,000 every day, 177 per hour, 3 a minute, or 1 every 20 seconds.

Abortion is violence against human life not only for the unborn, but also by its proven correlation to child and wife abuse and its undermining of the significance of the family. Yet the church seems unable to reverse this growing trend of violence.

Bearing an unwanted child is fraught with anxiety and fatigue, with embarrassment, financial stresses and often a sense of utter hopelessness. Yet few churches have been willing to make the relatively small sacrifice it would take to establish crisis pregnancy centers to help mothers-to-be to cope and to become healthy and whole. What if we were devoting the resources of our mighty evangelical enterprise to solving these human problems? What if we encouraged pregnant women to choose life by meeting the needs of both the mother and her child? Spiritual awakening would fire the Church with new vision and compassion to move out to establish God's truth and grace at all levels of human dignity.

*Inadequate to Bring Forth Justice.* The evangelical movement must weigh its responsibility to bring forth justice for our citizens. We have not turned the national mood strongly enough toward compassionate, grass roots action for the poor and oppressed. The realities of the Gospel have not yet sufficiently penetrated the soul of our nation.

For example, in 1983, over 34 million Americans—almost one in seven—had an income below the poverty line. Inflation translates into decreased food-buying power for the poor and their children. Nearly 40 percent of black children are chronically hungry. This cycle of poverty and deprivation seems to spur greater violence within families, affecting both children and spouses.

Except for the Soviet Union and South Africa, the United States has the highest prison population per capita in the world—one out of every 350 Americans. And the inhabitants of our prisons come predominantly from the poor. As our prison population increases 15 times faster than our general population the poor move from ghettos into prisons that are overcrowded, understaffed, dirty and—in most cases—brutal. If 300,000 evangelical families would be revived to "adopt"—care for and pray for—each of our nation's 300,000 prisoners, we would see wonders.

In our paralysis, we've failed to sink deep roots for ministry among the urban poor. And, except for Pentecostalism's frequent efforts to seek out the underclass, many of us have pursued membership cards to the middle class. This is a sad commentary on the Church, since 50 million urban poor in North America remain mostly unchurched. At a recent urban conference, futurist Tom Sine said: "If you look at a map of where the needs in this nation are and where the Christians are, you will wind up with two different maps. Christians are holding each others' hands in the suburbs and letting the cities wither and die of neglect."

It is in the heart of God to see this changed. The plight of our poor and the purposes of our God give us reason to hope that in the midst of evangelical paralysis, He is preparing to bring the evangelical Church in North America to a decisive devotion to Christ . . . for the poor's sake as well as ours. Accordingly, we need to get down to prayer about it.

*Paralysis Within the Home.* Our families are facing unprecedented stress today. The nuclear family continues to be dismembered and attacked at such rate that if it continues at the present rate, it is estimated that not one American nuclear family will be left by the year 2008! Ours is the highest divorce rate in the industrialized world—one divorce for every 1.8 marriages.

Violence in the home is increasing. In 1983, *Time* magazine spoke of child abuse, molesting, wife beating and rape as the "private violence." Police spend one-third of their time responding to domestic violence calls. There is a definite correlation between violence in the home and increases of violence in society as a whole.

In it all, Christian paralysis is evident. With the evangelical Church itself facing as high a divorce rate in its own families as in society in general, how can the current drift toward family disintegration be challenged successfully or altered by our witness? That troubles me. Does it you?

Our paralysis in dealing effectively with the battered family should drive us with hope to seek our Father through prayer for a deep move of the Spirit to awaken us to the love, righteousness and wisdom of the Lord Jesus. For truly, things seem beyond our resources to heal, apart from a new work of God.

*Paralyzed Before the Nations.* The United States is no longer regarded by the international community as a preeminent source of virtue! We are often perceived as weak and lacking the will to act. Our friends are more cautious and critical towards us and our enemies are bolder against us. Further, many Third World nations see us as struggling not only for stability through the balance of power and constant shifting of alliances, but also pursuing imperialistic expansion and influence. Even claims that we're helping embattled friendly governments to combat terrorism and outside subversion are being translated by much of the world as an attempt to prop up weak, excessive and even repressive regimes so that we might preserve our markets abroad. Clearly, in some cases this has been true.

Surely, then, spiritual awakening in the American Church is essential for the credibility of the gospel abroad. In part, it would revitalize what is perceived abroad as a Christian culture. More importantly, it would transform the life of the Church in our nation so we become a purified Body, overcoming the entanglements of affluence, privilege, and power. And, should God give the American Church an awakening that reshapes the role of our nation among the nations, it would release the whole evangelical movement toward a mighty new surge of missionary outreach.

Consider, for example, the potential of an awakening's impact on missions by how it could transform *evangelical lifestyle*. Because North American missionaries come from the world of the rich, they are separated culturally and psychologically from those they seek to reach. Our message can be distorted by the spiritual malaise of the affluent Church from which we emerge.

Further, many believe our mission efforts come out of overabundance rather than sacrifice. The Third World often accurately sees our missionaries as greedy and as having done little to deal with the inequalities between Western Christians and Third World Christians who languish in hunger and poverty. Revival may be our only hope for breaking open new demonstrations of sacrificial love on this level. Awakening, life-style and world evangelization must come together in any future North American missionary strategy.

There's another evidence of paralysis in the American Protestant missionary thrust waiting to be reversed by revival. For many of us, missions appears to have become more of a hobby than a cause. One look at the number both of missionaries and "tent-makers" sent out in proportion to the size of our evangelical population tells us something is wrong. We are hoarding more than we're sharing, yet we have 80 percent of Christian wealth in the world and 75 percent of its formally trained Christians within the churches in our nation.

Right now many mission boards are scrambling to find personnel. The percentage of our mission force who are either short-termers or those close to retirement has dramatically increased. Over the next 10 years, by one estimate, missionaries from the United States will retire four times faster than the current rate of new recruits entering the field!

*Faltering to Reach Our Own.* How is our country responding to the impact of the Gospel? The picture here is not encouraging either.

The seventh annual survey on "Who Runs America" conducted by *U.S. News and World Report,* found that of 30 institutions regarded as having significant power in molding our culture, Christianity ranked 28th, sandwiched between the Republican Party and small business.

While the general population growth is at 11.5 percent, the growth of the Church is only at 4.1 percent. By some estimates, there are 130 million unchurched people in our country.

What does the nation think of the evangelical movement? Psychologist John White claims that "because God is not perceived by non-Christians as the power behind the success, success may be only partial and be thought of as being no different from that of other clubs and associations."[7] A.W. Tozer said, "Current evangelism has laid the altar and divided the sacrifice into parts, but now seems satisfied to count the stones and rearrange the pieces with never a care that there is not a sign of fire upon top of the lofty Carmel."[8] Our society, failing to see the sign of fire, often turns away disillusioned, skeptical, or bored. Somebody needs to wake up!

## Analysis of Paralysis

We can't avoid the facts. The evangelical movement of America is experiencing a disturbing sense of paralysis. Carl Henry wonders if we're "out of the closet but going nowhere?" This paralysis may be the greatest barrier to effective mobilization for world evangelization, as well.

The more we become aware of our paralysis, the more pressure we should sense from the Spirit to seek the face of God in a movement of prayer for spiritual awakening. And that's the beginning of a new day for all of us. It will bring us into the realms of hope described for another paralyzed generation in Isaiah 26:17-19:

As a woman with child and about to give birth
writhes and cries out in her pain, so were we in your
presence, O Lord. We were with child, we writhed
in pain, but we gave birth to wind. We have not
brought salvation to the earth; we have not given
birth to the people of the world.

But your dead will live; their bodies will rise. You
who dwell in the dust, wake up and shout for joy.
Your dew is like the dew of the morning; the earth
will give birth to her dead.

No matter how thwarted we evangelicals may feel in our
impact on society or the nations, we can still rejoice in our God-
given potential for the Kingdom—if we simply become a Church
at prayer for revival—ordinary people at the threshold.

## Reason #4
## THE DRAMATIC PREPARATIONS

Woody Allen satirizes, "Mankind is caught at a crossroads.
One road leads to hopelessness and despair, and the other leads
to total annihilation. Let us pray we have the wisdom to choose
rightly!" He's hit on one mood of our generation.

But there is another mood abroad. Others have begun to
place hope for global survival squarely in the arena of the human
spirit, in spiritual and moral renaissance. There's a growing cry
for mediators, for those with the intellectual and moral integrity
not just to model the solutions, but to help lead us into those
solutions.

It is critical that the Church ask God to break us out of our
bulwark mentality, our hardness of heart—out of our paralysis of
faith—into the versatility and power of His Kingdom. What an
hour for the Church to rediscover the fullness of Christ as Lord,
and to move with Him in the fulfillment of His global cause! He
can end hostilities between nations. He can lead cultures and
peoples into an experience of redemption and justice. He is the
one able to satisfy the basic longings of the human heart and to
quiet the fears that plague mankind. The world appears to be in
preparation to hear the message of Christ as never before!

forefront of the Church's thinking today.

Catch your breath! We have just covered a lot of ground in this chapter. But what a panorama of challenge and hope it has put before us! The time has come now for us to take the priority of concerted prayer seriously. In view of the desperate necessity and the reasons for hope, have we any other alternative but to join in a movement of prayer targeted on spiritual awakening and world evangelization?

But who is ready to set the pace? Who will lead the way to the threshold? We'll find an answer in the next chapter.

An examination of some of these preparations suggests that God is building a fireplace, brick by brick to project the heat and light of His Kingdom to the ends of the earth. But the question we need to ask is, if God is building this fireplace, can the fire of spiritual awakening be very far behind? If God is preparing the Church and the world for revival, should we not expect it to be at hand? And should we all not be praying toward it with electric hope?

## International Preparations

The world is being bonded together as never before, preparing the way for God's redemptive action on a magnificent scale.

John Naisbitt suggests that two inventions have played a key role in transforming our planet into a global city: the jet airplane and the communications satellite, with the satellite being the most important of the two. For the first time, we have the capability of instantaneous interaction. Before the close of this decade, our planet will have 1 billion telephones that are so interconnected that it will be possible to call directly to anyone else among the other 1 billion. The amount of time needed to transmit information has been reduced to seconds.

The world faces survival issues that can be addressed effectively only by the Word of God. In bringing these questions unavoidably to the surface, is not the Spirit preparing the way for the life-saving ministry of a Church revived in the fullness of the Lord of Creation? And could our Father be preparing to use this new technology to equip His Church for world evangelization?

What would happen, asks Richard Lovelace, if the whole planet is driven to call upon the name of the Lord, and if the information that is broadcast is that His name is Jesus?

## National Preparation

The trends within our own nation also give us compelling reasons to unite in prayer for spiritual awakening. From divine perspective, these are surely dramatic preparations.

The American people face their own crisis of meaning. We know that we are no longer at the center of world history, as we once were. Who are we, we wonder?

We are losing confidence about our future, too. Do we face a future of continued unemployment, recurring cycles of inflation, increasing national debt, and shrinking options for personal fulfillment? By one survey, 50 percent of Americans fret about national and personal prospects.

We have also undergone a serious ethical collapse and an erosion of trust. Theodore White said, "The great issue in America is whether or not, as in the past, Americans can trust each other." A breakdown in natural leadership has helped to accelerate this erosion of trust. Many of us are losing faith in people we once called experts. Pollster Louis Harris notes that the "index of alienation" has climbed steadily from 29 percent in 1966 to 58 percent today. Could this be further preparation for a demonstration of trust and reconciliation displayed by a Church reunited around the glory of Christ (see John 17)?

In the face of all this upheaval and change, other positive preparations are in evidence. A spiritual hunt is underway. Our society is increasingly reaching out for connectedness with the world as we seek closer and deeper personal relationships and turn from the pursuit of things to pursuit of the sacred. Daniel Yankelovich in *New Rules* observes that we're moving toward an "ethic of commitment." Who has stirred up this pursuit?

*Pursuit of the Sacred.* Our society is far more religious than secularists would have us believe. According to George Gallup, American people as a whole continue to be the most openly religious and traditional of all western societies. Eighty-seven percent of Americans say that Christ has had a moral or ethical influence on their lives, and 81 percent consider Jesus divine. More than three-fourths of Americans say that Jesus is alive and in the heavenly realm and that "He lives in and cares for you."

College students, too, are caught up in the growing religious ferment. The proportion of college students who say that religion is important has grown from 39 percent to 59 percent over the past five years. Two-thirds of the unchurched pray, believe in Jesus Christ as the Son of God, and in life after death.

The soil is being prepared for something unusual. Gallup remarks: "Americans are a people of deep religious roots, roots that when watered with kindness and compassion will once more grow."

Recently, Connecticut Mutual Life Insurance Company published a report of its study of the impact of religious commitment on American attitudes. The authors concluded, "religious belief is rapidly becoming a more powerful factor in American life than whether someone is liberal or conservative, male or female, young or old. This may be only the beginning of a trend that could change the face of America." Because of the profound nature of their findings, the authors actually repeated the survey three times to see if a mistake had been made!

*Pursuit of the Neighbor.* I also see preparation for awakening as Americans look for deeper commitments in their relationships not only to God, but to one another. Often we feel like an aggregate of strangers, a society fragmented by colliding interests. We are in need not only of a sense of common purpose, but also of relationship to one another in achieving that purpose. Yankelovich has found that 40 percent of Americans are currently involved in a search for community. Sociologist Daniel Bell writes of one way we're finding it: "Probably in no other country in the world is there such a high degree of voluntary communal activity." Another social analyst says the demand for therapy is being replaced by a "demand for access to the world."

Is our growing national pursuit of meaningful, giving relationships another brick in the fireplace—another sign of dramatic preparations for spiritual awakening? What if Christ, in the midst of a spiritually awakened church, were able to capture this cultural trend and turn it into blessings for the nations? What if God were to move us as a nation out of either isolationist or crusade mentalities into a servant mentality? Is it not possible to believe that the impact of the gospel upon our country could foster an increasingly generous and giving America, where success is measured not just by profit but also by justice and love in the humble service of others. Obviously this would also have far-reaching implications for the credibility and spread of the gospel worldwide.

## The Vitality of World Christianity
*Pentecostals.* Some would claim that the explosion of the Pentecostal movement worldwide is proof that revival has

come. Certainly it is one demonstration of vitality in world Christianity, and may be, in the words of Peter Wagner, evidence that we're on "the crest of the wave" in global awakening and outreach. Pentecostal and charismatic churches are growing faster than any other Christian groups with an estimated 65 million. The world's largest churches are Pentecostal, and are found in the Third World: Central Church in Seoul (300,000), Jotabeche Church in Santiago (80,000), and Congregacao Cristo Sao Paulo (62,000). The charismatic movement has reached a vast array of socioeconomic classes throughout the world with the gospel, contextualized in a way that often "fits" Third World cultures most effectively.

If what we see now in many parts of the Church is just the crest of global awakening, then what a glorious floodtide lies ahead. If the current explosion of the Church is but the "sunrise of missions" (Donald McGavran), then what are we and the world ultimately being prepared *for*?

*Growing Numbers.* More people have become Christians since World War II than in all the rest of church history. The number of Christians worldwide is increasing at a rate of 78,000 a day, with over 1,600 new churches every week. Churches in East Asia and South Asia are growing by 360,000 and 447,000 converts per year, respectively. If the current trend continues, by the year 2000, 60 percent of the world's Christians will live in the Third World.

Of course, it is true that approximately 1 billion of the world's Christians need to be re-evangelized. But this still leaves over 450 million Christians worldwide who are "active" in that they are attending church at least once a week, and at least 250 million are evangelicals. Active evangelical Christians are certainly capable of sharing Christ with their nominal Christian friends in a new and powerful way, as God gives renewed vision of Christ's fullness through awakening. Many of the one billion nominals are just as ready to be released by revival into a genuine saving faith that mobilizes them for the task before us.

Even though there are 30 times as many people in the world to be won to Christ as there were in the first century—50 million then compared to 4.3 billion now—the *potential* work force today is 50,000 times as large as it was at the beginning, at least

250 million! One mission strategist calculates that at the beginning of the Christian era there was one witness for every 30,000 people worldwide, but now there is one to every 17, with one to every nine of those we regard as totally unreached, as almost all of the first century's population were!

*Open Doors.* Much of the world's population is accessible to Christian witnesses coming from the outside. Within parts of Southeast Asia, the Philippines, Taiwan and Japan, there are as many as 200 million people who can be openly reached with the gospel. Right now there are more than enough open doors to claim the attention of tens of thousands of new missionaries worldwide. Further, research indicates more individuals and segments of populations worldwide are receptive to Christ than at any other time in the last 2,000 years. Even among the 36 or so countries, with a population of nearly 2 billion, who don't allow foreign missionaries, God has opened the way for a new breed of missionaries to enter in the role of Christian doctors, engineers, teachers.

*Sophistication.* In addition, the Church has developed unprecedented sophistication and proliferation in such methods and channels as mass media, computers, linguistics, and missionary organizations. The job ahead of us is smaller than the job behind because of those potentially effective resources.

*Cooperation.* Finally, there's the genuine miracle of evangelical cooperation. The Covenant developed at the Lausanne Congress on World Evangelization in 1974 has become a dynamic compass for unified action in outreach. We now have an international body capable of responding together to Christ's global cause. Fruits of this unity include cooperative research, international conferences on missionary strategy with more than 30 since 1974, publications, the sharing of resources and technology, and a growing worldwide movement of prayer. As never before we are sharing our God-given gifts in a global evangelistic partnership. For example, through international conferences, modern technology and ease of travel, God is using revived parts of His Church to teach others how to evangelize.

Continued cross-pollinization from African and Asian Christians is greatly enhancing the evangelistic and social impact of the Western church in valuable ways! The number of missionaries being sent from Asian churches today is greater than the size of the whole European missionary force to Asia 150 years ago. In the Third World Church, over 400 missionary societies have already launched out 15,000 people. They challenge us in the West to catch up with them and to pray for revival for ourselves.

The implications of what's happening are staggering. What if among the over one billion Christians, God is preparing a community of conscience ready to be awakened and galvanized for biblical action on a variety of global issues?

What if awakening came to the worldwide Church so there was solidarity between Christians in the northern and southern hemispheres? What impact would that have for world evangelization among the two billion poorest of the earth? What if a thoroughly awakened Church were to ask itself: How can we work together to reach with the gospel the remaining three billion unreached of the world?

What if revival came to the 950,000 Christians already sprinkled within many unreached people-groups? Is it biblically conceivable that, prior to any new missionary penetration, these Christian minorities, freshly empowered by Christ, might accomplish far more in the advancement of the gospel than we had dreamed possible?

## The Vision within American Christianity

With 370,000 U.S. churches ministering to 144 million adults, there is currently one church for every 43 adults in our country. In most other countries, the ratio is closer to one *Christian* for every 43 adults. Are these God's beachheads, prepared to disseminate the impact of a coming wide-scale awakening?

Maybe the most significant evidence of revival at hand is the heart preparation within American evangelicalism. Dramatic preparations are evident in the growing belief that we *are* on the verge of spiritual awakening. This faith is a gift of God. Lewis Drummond has found that 85 percent of evangelicals believe this. And *Christianity Today* discovered almost 40 percent of Christian college students felt that the greatest need of the Church was for spiritual renewal. It appears that many are groping toward both local and worldwide awakening at a depth and breadth of new proportions. In 1983, a coalition on revival, with a highly acclaimed 40-person steering committee, formed to document an agenda for revival for the next decade.

Even the recently elected president of the National Council of Churches has begun his term calling for spiritual awakening in this traditionally liberal ecumenical agency. And the Sojourners Community in Washington, D.C., with all its emphasis on social justice, is gearing up for revival preaching campaigns in major cities nationwide.

One stirring of faith is the rapid formation of pools of renewal over the past 20 years that should encourage us all that a full outpouring may be at hand. Let's look at some:

*Mainline Renewal.* Movements for evangelical renewal began surfacing simultaneously in the larger denominations around 1967. They are growing.

*Theological Renewal.* Clergy persons under 30 today are more orthodox and evangelical than in recent memory. A good deal of this is directly related to the growing evangelical influence within our major seminaries.

*Charismatic Renewal.* Nearly one in five adults, 19 percent, considers himself or herself charismatic, though many of them have not spoken in tongues. Aggressive lay involvement has been strengthened as the charismatic thrust encourages the priesthood of all believers at a variety of levels through the exercise of spiritual gifts.

*Life-style renewal.* Millions of evangelicals are re-examining their attitudes toward economic life-styles. For some, renewal in this area has already begun.

*Social and Political Renewal.* To integrate spiritual and social concerns is a rising urgency. Evangelicals for Social Action, Voice of Calvary, Sojourners, and others are providing models and instruction for many of us.

*Moral Renewal.* Similarly, God is bringing forth moral renewal within the Church and society at large. In earlier awakenings, this development was called "the reformation of manners." An example is Jerry Falwell, who sees his work as a neo-evangelical reform movement, restoring active evangelical social presence against all forms of moral corruption.

*Peace Renewal.* And in the face of nuclear holocaust, to find another pool of renewal is not surprising. Many voices, especially in the historic peace churches, are calling for political action and are urging Christians to pray for a peace revival as the only hope of avoiding nuclear disaster.

*Catholic Renewal.* Nearly 5 million of the 40 million evangelicals in our country are Roman Catholics. Out of the Catholic Church has also come the Cursillo Movement—meaning "short course in Christianity"—a renewal movement focusing on personal piety, relationships, conversion and evangelism. On-going accountability groups further the renewing process. Cursillo is now offered by Episcopalians, Lutherans and others.

Is the coming awakening, for which God is preparing us, for the whole Church? If so, we should not be surprised at preparations in any part of that Body—Catholic, Orthodox or Protestant.

*Missions Renewal.* Tremendous renewal also dots the landscape of North American involvement in world evangelization, led by people and groups such as Ralph Winter, Leighton Ford, Orlando Costos, the Fuller School of World Missions, World Vision, and the Overseas Mission Study Center. The Church is focusing as never before on the task of reaching almost 3 billion totally unreached people—sometimes called the concern for the "hidden peoples" or the "frontiers"—and doing so with a strong sense of the possibility of extensive church growth by the end of the century.

Dramatic preparations for spiritual awakening throughout the worldwide Church are obvious. We sense how dramatically God seems to be setting the stage—building the fireplace—for a major new burst of heat and light. If God is preparing the Church and the world for revival, should we not expect it to be at hand? Of course, we should!

Bringing it closer to home: What if members of all kinds of renewal groups within American evangelicalism dug trenches toward one another in concerts of prayer so the waters of renewal might flow together? What currents—even floods—of revival might we see? Is a movement of concerted prayer the most strategic trench we could dig? It is my conviction that it is, and that this is why God is rapidly bringing united prayer to the

# 6

# PACESETTERS: LEADING
# THE WAY TO THE
# THRESHOLD

Pacesetter Frank Laubach, father of modern literacy, confessed that "prayer is the mightiest power on earth. Enough of us, if we prayed enough, could save the world—if we prayed enough!" In support of his dream, Laubach sought to mobilize a worldwide army of 10 million praying people.

Two centuries earlier, pacesetter John Wesley was equally clear on his commitment to mobilize concerted prayer: "Give me one hundred preachers who fear nothing but sin and desire nothing but God and I care not a straw whether they be clergy or laymen; such alone will shake the gates of hell and set up the Kingdom of heaven on earth. God does nothing but in answer to prayer." Toward this end, his fellow pacesetter in revival, George Whitefield, prayed "Lord, the Christian world is cast into a deep sleep; send forth I beseech thee some faithful and true pastors to awaken them out of it."

The renowned apostle of prayer, George Müeller, makes it clear in his autobiography that his primary reason for establishing orphan houses in nineteenth-century England went beyond salvaging abandoned young people. He wanted to "prove" the power of total, prayerful dependence on Christ, and thus set a pace for others to follow in his steps. Writes he, "The first and primary object of my ministry was that God might be magnified and this through answered prayer."

In the late 1850s, many ran his race with him. A young Scottish student attached himself to Müeller to study his life of faith. When he heard of the spread of concerted prayer in the United States in 1857-58, later called the third awakening, the young man, already convinced of the power of prayer by Müeller's example, went forth to call fellow Christians throughout England to join with him in revival prayer. That pacesetter's singular effort laid a groundwork for awakening that prevailed within and beyond the British empire for many years.

With such good reason to have hope for the worldwide revival in our time, we need to be praying that our Father will give His Church a multitude of such Christ-centered pacesetters—young and old alike—to spearhead concerts of prayer.

Previously, I outlined five basic theses upon which this entire book is built. The *fifth* thesis states that a movement of united prayer is normally initiated by pioneers of faith who first of all embrace God's global redemptive purpose and set the pace for serving it through concerted prayer, encouraging many others thereby to follow. Throughout biblical and church history, God has relied on a faithful few who sought Him with all their hearts and, as a result, generated spiritual surge in their generation all out of proportion to their numbers. I call these pioneers of faith "pacesetters" of a movement of prayer.

Could you be one of them?

Of course, most of us may feel incapable of mobilizing even 10 people, let alone our whole generation! However, a pacesetter's first responsibility is to stand and knock at the threshold of awakening with an unflagging desire to enter into the fullness of Christ Himself. Any of us can do that. And, as we knock, we can then begin to genuinely share our desires with others. We will very naturally be found, in the title of Jonathan Edwards's little volume, making "a humble attempt to promote explicit agreement and visible union of all God's people in extraordinary prayer."

## SECRET SERVICE AGENTS

I believe God is at this very moment preparing a whole band

of pacesetters to take us to the threshold. They may never be broadly organized under any particular name, such as the Evangelical Alliance in the 1800s or the Friends Missionary Prayer Band in India today, but they will nonetheless serve the Body of Christ in the most strategic way any of us could—by mobilizing concerted prayer in tune with prospects that so strongly encourage us to expect and seek spiritual awakening right now.

So, where are they? Think of them for a moment as God's "secret service agents."

Recently I was speaking at a large missions conference attended by President and Mrs. Gerald Ford. Scattered throughout the diverse audience were several secret service agents, who, though they looked just like everyone else sitting there, had a far different agenda on their minds. As hard as I tried, I could only locate one of them.

I thought that day about God's secret agents, these pacesetters of a prayer movement. I know they were in the audience, too. Certainly they also look just like most others; they are no better than other Christians, nor are they more spiritual. However, they are more likely to be desperate for a new work of God in their own lives, as well as in the Church. For a time we may be totally unaware of who they are as they faithfully launch on in determined prayer, bearing a unique agenda—spiritual awakening—on their hearts. But eventually we will be able to pick them out—they are hard to hide, and who knows, we may even join them!

Pacesetters are God's *gift* to the Body of Christ. They function in that role not by their own choice but by the sovereign call of God. Just as God gives the spiritual gifts of faith and prayer and praying people and a prayer movement, so does He give the gift of pacesetting. Hebrews 11 echoes this truth. If we have the faith to believe that, we have the faith to begin asking God to raise up pacesetters today.

In another day, when it seemed there was no one who cared enough about God's Kingdom to intercede (Isa. 59:16), the Lord promised to Isaiah: "I have posted watchmen on your walls, O Jerusalem; they will never be silent day or night. You who call on the Lord, give yourselves no rest, and give him no rest till he establishes Jerusalem and makes her the praise of the earth"

(Isa. 62:6-7). Posted or appointed by the living God to scale the wall where they can see the current landscape of God's purposes, these pacesetters study the needs of the world outside the wall and the needs of God's people inside the wall. Informed, they then give themselves relentlessly to prayer, taking no rest for themselves and giving no rest to the Lord until He establishes Jerusalem—awakens and revives His Church—and makes her His praise before all nations, fulfilling Christ's global cause through His Church.

Of course, many of us are fascinated by spiritual awakening. Some are even intensely concerned. Others are willing to do whatever they can to see it come to pass—whether preaching, praying, reordering priorities, or just cleaning up their lives. But then there are those called to a ministry of intercession who set the pace for a movement of united prayer in which God intends all of us eventually to participate. Their ministry becomes God's special effort to lead us all beyond interest, concern, and good deeds into the tough-minded strategy of concerted prayer.

As a result of growth in prayer, as much as anything, these day-to-day Christians catch the fire of truth, a theology of passion, a zeal for the coming Kingdom. Increasingly they understand the glorious hope they are praying toward. They grasp fuller implications of the person and work of Christ, recognizing that two issues are involved: (1) What Christ does for us and in us (fullness) and (2) all He wants to do through His Church to establish His Kingdom throughout the earth (fulfillment).

Pacesetters of this sort summon all of us ahead to the threshold, quite naturally. By virtue of the certainty before us all for spiritual awakening, they invite us to join them in repenting of worldly preoccupations of self-serving interests, and of unbelief. Their restless longings help many others to grow dissatisfied over the comparatively marginal impact our abundant resources are having against the kingdom of darkness around us and worldwide. We also learn from them how to rejoice in hope, abounding with a vision of the possibilities for Christ's Kingdom in our generation.

Thus in it all, they keep us sharp on the two vivid sweeps in spiritual awakening: (1) the Lordship of Christ among His people, demonstrated as He fills His praying Church with Himself;

(2) the Lordship of Christ among the nations, demonstrated through His praying Church as He fulfills His global cause.

God-given pacesetters are in the first fruits of a movement of prayer. Scouting out the land, looking for men and women of prayer, they harvest the growing number whom God has prepared for the ministry of intercession—recruiting, mobilizing, and organizing in prayer others who desire spiritual awakening.

So they become midwives to a revitalized witness of the gospel, spearheading the way for additional pioneers of faith who, most assuredly, will spring out of prayer and revival to serve Christ across geographical, cultural, linguistic and other human barriers that keep millions from the knowledge of salvation. And the tool these pacesetters use to accomplish this massive movement has historically been called "concerts of prayer."

Diagram 1 illustrates how these ideas mesh:

* Awakening: When God wakes us up to see Christ in new ways, so that together we trust, love, and obey Him in new ways, so that we move with Him in new ways to fulfill His global cause.

**Diagram 1**

Think of the potential! Suppose God has given enough pacesetters in the United States alone to get at least 10,000 Christians praying with them for spiritual awakening. If these 10,000 were to unite in concerts of prayer for two hours a month, that would mean 240,000 hours of united prayer for awakening each year. If those same 10,000 people also spent 10 minutes at the end of each day praying for the same issues, that would be an additional 600,000 hours a year.

If these 10,000 would be persistent to integrate the agenda of spiritual awakening into the prayer experiences they regularly share with others in the local churches and small groups to which they belong for a total of one additional hour of praying each month, that would add another 120,000 hours of prayer while encouraging many others to be on their knees to seek God's face. All of these efforts add up to almost one million additional hours of prayer for revival each year!

Of course, Scripture teaches that our Father refuses to respond to a mere piling up of our words for their own sake (Matt. 6:7-8). Still, what do you think would be the difference in the life of the Church one year from today, if it were saturated with one million hours of genuine intercession for awakening and world evangelization? And what if, in addition, that year of prayer set the pace for a large scale movement of united prayer whose momentum continues long past the first 12 months?

## THE COSTS

As exciting as it all sounds, however, pacesetters will pay a price. Part of the price will be brokenness over what we see in ourselves, in our church, our nation, and our world that dishonors the name of Christ, hinders His Kingdom's advance, and robs God of His glory. As someone has said, "Revival is not organized, it is agonized," and so is a movement of prayer for revival.

It also costs a daily discipline that never ceases. To live consistently, pacesetters must develop single-minded devotion to Christ and to His global cause; they must also cultivate a vigilance in life-style to reflect all they desire and hope for.

They sometimes pay the cost of being misunderstood. Breaking with the herd mentality in order to serve the Church at this level, they may make many of us uncomfortable at first. Some of us may initially despise them even.

In the book, *Praying Hyde* the reader walks with a nineteenth-century missionary in India whose clear assignment from God was to be a pacesetter in prayer. He was greatly mis-understood during his time there not only by his fellow mission-aries but also by many of his supporters back home. Because of his fervent prayer life, he was judged as someone bizarre, irre-sponsible, and even uncooperative. But his example has moved many of us to a prayer life we might not otherwise have known.

Jesus warned of this rejection in Matthew 10. It was one of the reactions His workers could expect when they went to har-vest the fruits of the coming revival. By pulling people together in prayerful anticipation of the Kingdom they may create dissen-tion; pacesetters will suffer rejection and even persecution. Revival seekers, by both their desperation and their hope, chal-lenge the status quo. The call to concerted prayer even when sounded in all humility and love will end one of two ways: in deci-sive devotion or in decisive division.

There is also the cost of spiritual warfare. If any group of people will be opposed by the Enemy, it will be those who give themselves to prayer. No wonder Paul told the Ephesian Chris-tians to clothe themselves with armor sufficient for a battle beyond the flesh and blood before they gave themselves to con-stant prayer for "all the saints" (fullness) and for "ambassadors in chains" (fulfillment) (Eph. 6:10-20). Even the high priest Joshua, in the days of Zechariah, could not assume his priestly ministry of intercession in the Holy of Holies until Satan had been soundly rebuked and Joshua had been delivered from his adversary's false accusations (Zech. 3).

Pacesetters must be prepared for the additional cost involved as they become answers to their own prayers. They themselves may be sent by God to carry the gospel to the unreached peoples for whose sake they prayed. And that will always be costly, for any of us.

## WILL YOU BE ONE?

Has God called you to be a pacesetter? Has He called you to get on the wall and set the pace for others who will climb the wall to join you, some of whom may eventually go over the wall to take the gospel to the ends of the earth? Are you willing to stand at that vantage point where you can look not only far beyond the wall to God's purposes for the whole earth but also at the crumbling ruins and marvelous potential inside the wall? And most of all, will you stand where you are able to look up and seek the face of the living God in whom lies all answers for both inside and outside the wall?

In an hour when the Church often feels as if it were up against the wall, is God calling you and me to break through that paralysis of faith? Make Isaiah's motto in 62:6-7 yours: "Take no rest, give no rest." Take no rest for yourself and give no rest to God until He has done, to the glory of His Son, everything He has promised to do? If God is calling you to be a pacesetter for a movement of prayer, you may be most concerned that if you step out in that role, you will find yourself standing alone. That was my greatest fear when I first sensed this was God's assignment for me. However, I have since discovered something wonderful through my travels here and abroad: many others are being posted on the walls. I am not alone, and neither are you.

The Moravians, who for a hundred years backed their revival and missionary thrusts with a nonstop, 24-hour prayer chain, called their eighteenth-century pacesetting "Herrnhut," the German word for "Lord's watch," referring specifically to the passage in Isaiah 62:6-7. There's a "Lord's watch" waiting for you, too, even if it's only two or three others at the start.

Lewis Drummond believes this. In his book, *The Awakening That Must Come*, he surveys many of the pools of renewal throughout the Church and sees in them the promise of an even greater work of God before us. One of the great benefits from these pools, Drummond remarks, is that they are producing those whose hearts are channeled toward a ministry of concerted prayer. The pacesetters are already there:

> The answer to this most basic essential question should be obvious. Has not the renewal, charismatic, deeper life, and other profound movings of the Holy Spirit given the contemporary church that very band of dedicated believers who could serve as God's praying remnant to precipitate a general great awakening? Surely this is true. What a potential the church has today in the renewed people of God, even if they be few in number.[1]

And yet our greatest assurance that we can become persuasive pacesetters lies in our intimate link with the Chief pacesetter of prayer: the Lord Jesus. He it is who has first become the author and completer of faith for all of us (Heb. 12:2); who has not only pioneered our way into God's presence but remains there like a high priest to represent us every time we come to the throne of grace (Heb. 3:1; 4:14-16). He has done so at great personal sacrifice, opening the lines of communication by His cross (Heb. 10:19-22). In essence, He is the wall on which all the watchmen stand. As He calls us to set the pace with Him in prayer (Heb. 13:10-15) He also guarantees our success (Heb. 13:20,21).

If you want to serve with Him as a pacesetter, then the next part of this book will be helpful to you. In it we look at principles of mobilizing, organizing, and equipping a movement of prayer for the world. The remaining chapters are written to make your work on the wall manageable and effective.

And yet, I've often found great motivation for bringing others to the threshold, as I've uncovered practical ways to get them joined in praying with me toward the vision.

What I've learned is what I now want to share.

# PART II

## STEPS TOWARD A
## MOVEMENT OF PRAYER
## FOR THE WORLD

# 7

# THREE STEPS TO GET US STARTED

Wherever you go, you will probably find three kinds of Christians: those unaware that history is happening; those who watch history happen; and those who make history happen.

Fortunately, God has called all of us to be more than observers of life. Our activities, when done in obedience to the Lordship of Christ, allow us to play a part in making history happen—in shaping the future of His Kingdom. Pacesetters understand this fact. And, they know this is preeminently so in our life of prayer together.

As Peter says (my paraphrase): "The fulfillment of all things is on top of you. Therefore think clearly about the way things really are, and then discipline yourself in the most strategic response you can give: prayer. Tie all of this together by loving each other with a love so deep that it looks beyond all of our petty differences and even our sins to see His kingdom" (1 Pet. 4:7,8). Or, as Paul put it to the leader of one of the most fruitful missionary churches of his day, "I urge, then, first of all [or, of highest priority], that requests, prayers, intercession and thanksgiving be made for everyone . . . . This is good, and pleases God our Savior, who wants all men to be saved and to come to a knowledge of the truth" (1 Tim. 2:1-4).

In a movement of prayer for spiritual awakening, we cease to be spectators as we take initiative toward the outcome of history! Our life together presses for the fulfillment of Christ's global cause in a way nothing else can.

Let us now explore three preliminary steps which every pacesetter should take to mobilize concerted prayer for spiritual awakening.

## REPENTANCE: MAKING ROOM FOR SPIRITUAL AWAKENING

Just a few years prior to the spiritual awakenings in the New England colonies in the early 1700s, Puritan leaders in Massachusetts declared, "God hath a controversy with his New England People." They called for united repentance and prayer for a new outpouring of the Spirit. In the same attitude, delegates at the 1981 American Festival of Evangelism were given small pins made of sackcloth and ashes to wear on their dresses or lapels as an outward sign of their willingness to unite in repentance. All of this reflects the great call to revival prayer in 2 Chronicles 7:14: "If my people . . . turn from their wicked ways, and seek my face . . . . "

Repentance is the first step toward a prayer movement. It is perhaps the very best sign of a new sense of God's presence. In facing our sins we make room for deeper fellowship with Christ. Repentance reorders our lives and prepares us to encounter all that spiritual awakening will bring. Jack Miller understands: "It is simply impossible for a man to meet the Lord of glory in the full revelation of his majesty and not be grieved by his particular sins and want to confess them."[1] In realistic self-appraisal we must, as E. Stanley Jones acknowledged, "lay at his feet a self of which we are ashamed."

And yet repentance does not stop here. By a revolution of our vision for Christ, we are transformed in how we think and act and feel in our priorities and our relationships so that we might fully trust, love, and obey Him, and therefore effectively move with Him to fulfill His global cause. Thus repentance is not a negative step, it is a corrective one. By repenting in the presence of Christ we discover even more about Him and how we can serve Him.

But repent we must. How can we proclaim righteousness

and truth in the gospel until we have humbled ourselves and repented of our own sins and deceptions? If we are grieving, quenching, resisting, or lying to the Spirit, we can never lay hold on the power of the Holy Spirit to be His witnesses.

The sins we confess often define what it is we are prepared to seek from God. As His light dispels some of our blindness, we want to seek even more light. The more God shows us of evil in ourselves the more we will want to intercede regarding evil wherever it is found. The more God purges us of sin, the more zealous we will be to see His whole house cleansed and become a "place of prayer for all nations" (Mark 11:15-18).

Let us explore some specific areas for confession that are critical if our repentance is to make room for spiritual awakening.

### Lack of Faith

In Romans 14, Paul says that whatever is not of faith is sin. It is of the flesh. It may express itself in a lack of full enthusiasm for the things of God, in an absence of joy and praise, or in a cold heart toward the Lord Himself. The Father sent His Son into the wilderness so that He might be tested in this area of faith. Was He willing to give priority to God's Word and not to bread alone? Was He willing to give priority to God's ways and not take a shortcut to retrieve the kingdoms of earth? And, no matter what the situation, was He willing to trust God to be everything to Him that He had promised? In the same way, those who make room for spiritual awakening must cast aside, in repentance, every attitude of unbelief. We must name whatever paralyzes our faith. We must repent and believe the gospel.

We need to repent for our lack of desire for the Kingdom. We have compromised God's glory; we've been ill prepared to jealously guard it. We have been casually content with our lack of spiritual power and satisfied with mediocrity. Through Isaiah, God says to us: "These people come near to me with their mouths and honor me with their lips, but their hearts are far from me" (Isa. 29:13). And again: "A spirit of prostitution is in their hearts; they do not acknowledge the Lord . . . . When they go with their flocks and herds to seek the Lord, they will not find him; he has withdrawn himself from them" (Hos. 5:4,6).

We need to repent not so much of perversion but of indifference; not so much of pride as of preoccupation; not of failure but of frivolity; the sin we must often name is the sin of settling for second best. Not only have we lacked serious study and earnest obedience to God's Word, but we have demonstrated the shallowness of our desires by the sin of prayerlessness.

## Fleshly Indulgences

According to Galatians 5, sins of the flesh cannot withstand an atmosphere of revival. Where have we indulged in lustful thoughts, or justified covetousness, or pursued material things? Where do we need to face envy and aggressive demands for our own desires and achievements to the neglect and hurt of others?

We need to become honest with our Father at every point at which we have shadowed God's glory, because we have failed to see ourselves before Christ as we really are. Our Father loves us too much to answer our prayers for spiritual awakening if, in reality, we are asking Him for help so that we can indulge in thoughts and actions of which He is unworthy (Jas. 4:3).

## Relationships with Others

Reconciliation to one another must keep pace with all other efforts to mobilize a movement of united prayer if we are to succeed in the formation of a concerted effort and find the awakening for which we pray.

Many of us need to begin by thinking about our relationships with people in our families. Where is there lovelessness? Where have I brought shame, unworthiness, and loss of self-esteem to others? Whom have I insulted or oppressed, and whose sense of self-esteem have I lowered, or whose confidence of God's work in their lives have I retarded? Whom have I manipulated or exploited, and whom have I refused to forgive?

## Spiritual Pride

We must face all the ways we use to appear more committed to Christ than we really are. Jesus' greatest wrath was aimed at the hypocrisy of spiritual leaders. God wants real people, not phonies.

Often the love of power has replaced the power of love. We can be pursuing the good in wrong ways, relying on past successes in organizations or methods—and even on ourselves—instead of the living God. As our society cries out for a response to its many needs, many of us evangelicals may be responding because we like to be at the center of attention, having others depend on us, more than because we really desire to see Christ glorified.

Some of us may also need to confess the spiritual pride we feel as specially molded instruments of God—pacesetters—for the promotion of prayer, revival, and the advancement of Christ's kingdom. Or, the pride in prayer that says "I'm thankful I'm not like others" (see Luke 18:11).

### National Sins

Those involved in a movement of prayer for the world must be willing to identify with the sins of our nation and begin to lead the way in national repentance. We need to repent of the sins of America, past and present, because we *are* Americans. Most of us need to undergo critical self-examination to determine how much of the status quo in our society we have really accepted, sometimes even with biblical rationalizations.

Look at the city or community in which you live. What sins are clearly evident to you? In what ways do you share responsibility for divorce, pornographic materials, street crimes, alcohol in the high schools, neglect of the poor? In what ways have these sins encroached on your personal life, your family's life, or your church's life?

If we recognize unholy commitments, whether in business or life-style, reflected in our economic choices as Americans, we must say so to the Lord. Wherever we see ourselves taking refuge under a nuclear umbrella, and for all practical purposes replacing God with the bomb as the ultimate security in our lives, we must repent. Whenever we sense that, along with other Americans, we are benefiting from the poverty and suffering of others—often in the Third World—we must acknowledge it and ask forgiveness. And then we must be ready to change.

Looking at repentance at this level in past revivals, Donald Dayton ponders:

I begin to wonder what forces might be
unleashed in our world if our understandings of sin
and evil were to become historically concrete—if we
should again be able to name racism, prejudice, war,
manipulation, and oppression for the sins that they
are. What would happen if our decisions for Christ
should become decisions against the forces of evil in
our world? This fuller understanding of biblical conversion was Finney's vision, and it is one we need to
recover.[2]

## Disobedience to the Great Commission

We must also take seriously areas of disobedience to the
Great Commission. In the words of Ron Sider, we must uncover
a "holy dissatisfaction with the church and society that callously
tolerates widespread injustice and quietly forgets 2,000,000,000
people who have never heard of Christ."

Often we can become so occupied with the missionary
endeavors in which we are involved, that we do not squarely
face how much is *not* being done. The average Christian group in
America does not give itself to a strategy for penetrating the
kingdom of darkness in their own community, let alone to the
ends of the earth. Many of us must confess that we have trouble
caring about people who have never heard of Christ and who are
cut off from Him by major human barriers. Some of us, who have
spent hours debating what God will do with unbelieving people
who die in ignorance of the gospel, need to face what God will do
with disciples who have knowingly refused to move out to claim
His promises in reaching the unreached. Once we do, our first
option will be to repent.

We must be willing, says John White, to face "how casually
we have paraded a dwarfed and shriveled Christianity before the
world" and how we have failed to keep both of the greatest com-
mandments that Jesus gave us. We have neither loved God with
all of our hearts, nor have we loved our neighbors for the sake of
Christ.

We need to realize that, for all our talk about world evangelization, we are doing little about it. Andrew Murray faced the
same problem. In his call for a movement of prayer for spiritual

awakening, *The Key to the Missionary Problem,* he recognized the importance of repentance.

And so it is critical that pacesetters lead the way in open repentance. It is we who must get this difficult and awkward ball rolling—genuinely not for special effects—if our other efforts at mobilizing prayer are to bear fruit.

## UNITY: PROVIDING WINESKINS FOR SPIRITUAL AWAKENING

Unity within the Body of Christ can provide the wineskins that capture and pour out the new wine of spiritual awakening.

Of course, in one sense, unity is the result of spiritual awakening. For example, the Evangelical Alliance, the first formal expression of broad-scale Protestant ecumenicalism, was founded in 1846 as a result of the vision developed in over a hundred years of awakenings. That experience was equally shared in Acts 2 where the entire Body of Christ on earth at that time was united as a result of the outpouring of the Holy Spirit.

I believe that unity among Christians is also a prerequisite to spiritual awakening. A movement of prayer brings together the best of both worlds: Christians uniting in love to pray.

The kingdom of God involves *community,* the beginning of the great work of reconciliation that will one day engulf the whole universe. We receive one another in the same way that Christ receives us. Just as spiritual awakening leads us into a dying world, so community teaches us how to first die for each other.

Our unity with one another either verifies or denies ourselves, our church, our neighbors, our nation, and our world—our unity with Christ (John 17). Since spiritual awakening revitalizes the whole Church, our pursuit of awakening must also demonstrate as best we can a life together that testifies to what we really believe about the Church. Are we willing to trust God for a great deal more unity and to disagree with each other about a great deal less? It is naive to think that our heavenly coach can fire up a winning team that is suited up in different uniforms and refuses to work as a team! That refuses even to huddle together just to *pray* for unity and victory.

Despite all of our diverse programs and ministries, I believe the Church in America shares much in common. While we often differ sociologically, ethnically, culturally, methodologically, and sometimes doctrinally, most Christians do not differ over the Lordship of Christ and the authority of Scripture. David Hubbard remarked to the Fourth Annual Convocation of Christian Leaders: "As Christians our fine tuning is different, but we have much more common ground than we realize." Yale church historian Kenneth Scott Latourette found that different kinds of Christianity shared a basic core of belief in Christ as Lord, the authority of Scripture, and the need to advance the gospel.

Since the Middle Ages, the major issues around which Christians have most often been divided have not been those of doctrine, but those of church order or ethics. Most antagonism has been due, frankly, to insufficient love. This is why Billheimer's *Love Covers* is so timely and prophetic and so widely read right now. Love covers these denominational, sacramental, and experiential differences. After all, the catalysts in the Great Awakening represented three different theologies: Pietistic Lutheranism, Puritan Calvinism, and Wesleyan Armenianism. Somehow they moved together and flowed together and worked together.

With all the cultural and structural diversity of the Christian movement in the past 2,000 years, these unifying factors explain both its resilience and its expansion, even in the place of formidable barriers. And it is their basic care that forms the focus of a prayer movement for the world.

Most of us, in fact, are united in a growing desire for a deeper devotion to the Lord. Christ is at the center of our faith. Moving toward Him in prayer we will naturally move us toward one another. In the *Pursuit of God,* Tozer describes how a hundred pianos, all tuned to the same fork are automatically tuned toward each other. Is that not what a concert of prayer is all about?

Or take some of the moral concerns that most American Christians hold in common today: (1) the sanctity of human life, (2) the restoration of the family, (3) the stewardship of creation, (4) the moral revitalization of our political processes, (5) justice for the poor, (6) freedom from nuclear holocaust, and (7) reaching the unreached. The time has come to also agree on the necessity and power of prayer if we are to see any change.

Furthermore, across the denominational mosaic there seems to be a growing agreement that we must break out of ecclesiastical ghettos and get on with loving the world together.

Some may argue that irreparable divisions exist between Pentecostals and non-Pentecostals, or between conciliars and evangelicals, or Protestants and Catholics, but it may not be as insurmountable as it first appeared.

John R. W. Stott, perhaps the leading theologian in worldwide evangelicalism, studied declarations from both the World Council of Churches and the Vatican, and compared them to the Lausanne Covenant. Stott then drew up 10 common affirmations between these major camps of Christendom, affirmations that could become the initial agenda for concerted prayer:

1. The Church is sent into the world.
2. The Church's mission in the world includes evangelism and social action.
3. The content of evangelism is derived from the Bible.
4. The gospel centers on Christ crucified and risen.
5. Salvation is offered to sinners in the gospel through Jesus Christ.
6. Conversion is demanded by the gospel.
7. True conversion invariably leads to costly discipleship.
8. The whole Church needs to be mobilized and trained for evangelism.
9. The Church can evangelize only when it is renewed.
10. The power of the Holy Spirit is indispensable to evangelism.[3]

John Stott provided quotations from the Lausanne Covenant, together with Roman Catholic and Conciliar documents, to illustrate these common affirmations. At the same time, he made it clear—and continues to do so—that alongside this apparent convergence serious theological divergences remain, which must be faced with integrity and must not be swept under the rug.

Richard Hutcheson, author of *Mainline Churches and the Evangelicals*, says that mainline churches must recognize the vitality of the evangelical movement and meet it positively and affirmatively. "The most effective single method of coping with diversity is to pray . . . . The church is God's, its future is in God's hands."

Clearly, despite other differences, most Christians share many similarities in our sense of mission to the world. Just as there is one body through many members, we have one mission through many ministries. Bonhoffer reminds us, in *Cost of Discipleship,* that Christ's calling us into His mission to the world should "transcend all our previous divisions and establish a new and steadfast fellowship in Jesus." God has given us a commission vast enough, as well as difficult enough, to demand an unselfish involvement that pulls together divided Christian forces into biblical unity for the sake of the gospel.

True, some people talk about the emerging task—encouraging existing churches worldwide, while others talk about the unfinished task—the reaching of the totally unreached. But this should create no division, for the former encourages prayer for the fullness of Christ in His Church and the latter for the fulfillment of His global cause. And that is the balanced agenda for a concert of prayer.

Since 1974, the worldwide Lausanne Movement, joining evangelical forces of all denominations around the Lausanne Covenant, has been a miracle of God toward that end. It is in the spirit that concerts of prayer must expand.

Finally in most Christian groups, members ask each other: "Who is hungry or thirsty to know more of Christ and His glory?" I believe this is the starting place for unity in prayer for spiritual awakening. You might call it "the brotherhood of the dissatisfied." Isaiah called it restlessness (Isa. 62:7).

Each of the pools of renewal previously studied were marked by a strong intention to seek the Lordship of Christ in specific areas. And most leaders within any given pool recognize that a movement of prayer is the one place where we can all agree to unite in our restless pursuit of Christ, regardless of our individual contributions to His Kingdom.

This is the genius of concerted prayer. It gives us an umbrella under which all kinds of committed Christians can unite, pressing forward in intercession about the 90 percent on which we do agree regarding spiritual awakening, and putting the other 10 percent before Christ to arbitrate as awakening comes.

Unity within a movement of prayer also prepares new wineskins for God's mission to the world. It is tough for non-Christians to oppose a gospel that is being promulgated by a diverse coalition of godly people who, through united faith and prayer, have also become united in heart and mind with the Lord and His global cause! Such a bond will encourage us to press on beyond prayer into the work God calls us to. It will create a Church united in the battle that can be won no other way. It will provide the Lord with a strong and sturdy barn into which He may gather the wheat.

To this second step of unity all pacesetters of concerted prayer must be unswervingly committed.

## DAILY DISCIPLINES: GETTING IN SHAPE FOR SPIRITUAL AWAKENING

If we really believe that God will answer our prayers for revival, then we need to prepare ourselves for the answers before they come. A concert of prayer can be as much an escape from the cause of Christ as attending a Michael Jackson concert! We can busy ourselves in a cozy group that prays for the world with no real intention of getting further involved. A daily discipline that reflects what we are praying can be the antidote for this. Jonathan Edwards was right in step with this when he wrote in *An Humble Attempt* about the necessity of diligence and discipline for those who prayed for revival:

> And if ministers and people should, by particular agreement and joint resolution, set themselves, in a solemn and extraordinary manner, from time to time, to pray for the revival of religion in the world, it would naturally tend more to *awaken in them a concern about things of this nature,* and more of a desire after such a mercy. It would engage them to more attention to such an affair, make them more inquisitive about it and ready to use endeavors to promote what they, with so many others, spend so much time in praying for. It would *make them more ready* to rejoice, and praise God, when they see or hear of any thing of that nature or tendency . . . .
> For persons to be thus engaged in extraordinary

prayer for the revival and flourishing state of religion
in the world, will naturally lead each one to reflect on
himself, and consider how religion flourishes in his
own heart, and how far his example contributes to
that for which he is praying.[4]

## What Comprises a "Daily Discipline"?

Being a part of a regular concert of prayer, of course, is in
itself a primary discipline that can get us in shape for a life of sacrifice. Concerted prayer becomes a microcosm involving many
of the ministry dynamics needed to reach the whole world.
When we seek the coming of God's Kingdom, we are living out
the Kingdom by how we pray. In prayer we learn how to participate in other actions into which God will lead us.

Prayer, discipleship, and ministry work together. Prayer
without discipleship and ministry can turn into a powerless
pietism. But discipleship and ministry without prayer can
become formal and dead. As we grow as disciples in ministry,
we force ourselves to face the reality of our impotence apart
from God's continued renewal in our lives. Even when we fail, it
benefits us by driving us back to more determined prayer.

In concerts of prayer we're already thinking and planning in
full expectation of awakening. In addition, we should *act as if* our
vision for "fullness and fulfillment" is already abundantly realized. For revival to have staying power in us, we must reorder
our own lives and the life and ministry of our churches, so that
two or three decades after God answers, the renewed intervention of His Kingdom still continues in force. Comparing Isaiah
58, which connects awakening with disciplined efforts at compassion and justice, with Isaiah 60, which connects awakening
with the sovereign power of God, puts such a "daily discipline"
in proper perspective.

## How Do We Get Started?

*First,* we must faithfully respond to all that Christ means to
us now. We must be sure we are faithful to what we see of Christ
now in order to be faithful to the much more we will know of Him
as He answers our prayers. If the Christian life is committing all
I see of myself to all I see of Christ for all I see of His global

cause then when seeking His face I must give Christ my active obedience today.

*Second,* we must get involved in daily study of Scripture. People united in concerted prayer will be people of the Word. We need to do all we can to keep clear what it is we are praying toward. That is the key mental discipline in a movement of prayer. We must let Scripture speak to us especially about the meaning of the cross. The cross is at the heart of what we seek. It reveals the depth of our sinful condition; the love and justice of God; the ways of God and His Kingdom; the value God places on human life, including the billions who have no knowledge of His Son; and what is required of us as we seek to fulfill Christ's global cause.

*Third,* we need to develop a daily discipline that integrates a vision for the world into daily discipleship within the environment of united prayer. In my earlier book, *In the Gap,* I discuss initial daily disciplines needed to equip you to live like a world Christian. Among other things, I suggest a simple daily plan involving only 15 minutes a day that consists of the following disciplines (see diagram 2 below):

## A World Christian Discipline
*Fifteen Minutes a Day*

| | |
|---|---|
| 0-5 | Bible Study—What Scripture teaches on Christ's global cause |
| 6-9 | Study other books on world evangelization |
| 10-12 | Intercessory prayer |
| 13-14 | Share with another Christian what you are learning |
| 15 | Listen—ask God to speak to you as He chooses. |

**Diagram 2**

- 5 minutes—Study what Scripture teaches on Christ's global cause. Almost 50 percent of the verses in the Bible touch on this subject.
- 4 minutes—Study other sources on world evangelization. You might read a book on evangelization, marking where you stop and picking it up there the following day.
- 3 minutes—Pray for the world, based on what you have discovered in the previous nine minutes. You literally reach out

to a world of people who cannot pray for themselves.

- 2 minutes—Share with one other Christian what God has given to you in these nine minutes of "vision-building" and three minutes of prayer. This way you deposit a vision which God can use in the life of another Christian to direct him into more strategic involvement in His global cause, especially in the prospect of revival.
- 1 minute—Be still before the Lord, asking Him to speak to you any way He may choose regarding fullness and fulfillment, based on the preceding 14 minutes.

If the 10,000 pacesetters I projected earlier would discipline themselves like this for the coming revival every day for a year, it would result in another one million hours a year coupled with their one million hours of praying for revival. What impact do you think this effort would have on Christ's global cause as they continue to pray together?

There are three overriding steps a pacesetter must follow to mobilize a movement of prayer for the world: (1) repentance, (2) unity and (3) daily discipline. We are making room for spiritual awakening, joining our lives together into vessels that effectively carry His new wine of revival and getting in shape for a ministry to the world that will accelerate as God answers.

# MOBILIZING A MOVEMENT OF PRAYER
## You Can Do It!

So you want to be a pacesetter in a movement of concerted prayer for the world. Great! Past the first three steps, how do you proceed next?

### PROBLEMS WITH PRAYER

Let us begin by being honest with each other. Prayer is sometimes dull, difficult, and spasmodic for everyone, including us pacesetters! Why is this? To understand the problems is to proceed with greater effectiveness in helping others on to concerted prayer.

1. We may have prayed, and prayed boldly, and not seen our prayer answered. We came away feeling that we either didn't deserve to have our prayer answered, that we failed to pray hard enough, or that maybe God simply didn't care.

2. Some of us have limited perspective of what prayer does. We suffer from historical ignorance—we never studied the topic in Scripture or in a class or in church history. Our deficiency leads us to a lack of hope. What are God's ways? What has God promised? Who does He intend to be in your life, in the life of the Church, and before the nation?

3. We each have a hidden aversion to a God who is holy and

sovereign. As fallen human beings, we in the natural, seek to hide from God's presence, just as Adam did in the beginning. How often do we busy up our lives, for example, with "Christian" activities so we can excuse ourselves from getting down to business in serious prayer?

4. We may be afraid of His answers. When God answers our prayers, His decisions and actions cannot be controlled by us. Considering the impact and changes that spiritual awakening brings, do we really want it? If we are afraid of risks—of being thrust forward into new life disciplines and ministries that could change the whole course of our involvement in the world—of course we will hesitate to pray.

5. These practical problems may initially block our mobilizing efforts. But, take heart, all of them can be overcome. For remember prayer is a gift of God. A movement of concerted prayer must come from Him also. It is He, not we, who must persuade people to take up the work of prayer for awakening. Our mobilizing efforts are not so much like rolling heavy boulders up an incline until finally, if we reach the top, they take off rapidly down the other side. Rather we are opening the doors to a large menagerie to set free newly hatched eaglets to fly forth in faith.

If you know that this is something God has called you to do, then there are no problems; there is only a threshold toward which to move. Following are some principles that have been important for me as I grow to understand my role as pacesetter.

## PRINCIPLES FOR MOBILIZATION

*First,* keep your efforts at mobilization biblical. Remember, the frontline in world evangelization is the Word of God and prayer. Scripture is the common meeting ground in our agenda for prayer for every Christian, no matter what pool of renewal or denomination they come from. Scripture provides us a conceptual framework by which we may interpret events in the Church and the world, as well as our own personal needs and desires. With a strong scriptural foundation beneath us we can form prayers together on which we all agree.

*Second,* set the pace in prayer yourself, even if initially no one else joins you. Remember Zechariah 8:20-21? Those who call others to prayer conclude their invitation with the words, "I myself am going." In other words, even if no one else joins me, prayer is so strategic and the needs are so great that I must press on.

*Third,* as you seek to mobilize others, be humble. Standing at the threshold knocking does not make me any more spiritual than those who have yet to join me. My role may be catalytic, even prophetic, but I am still a disciple-in-the-making, just as others are.

*Fourth,* integrate the agenda of spiritual awakening into every other prayer situation. Do this, for instance, when you are called on to pray during your weekly small-group Bible study. The more you integrate, the more you alert others to your concerted prayer vision, and to the good reasons to get involved.

*Fifth,* begin with the few. Don't be dismayed if that is all there is for awhile. Looking back on how God raised up little prayer bands as "droplets of revival," China missionary Maria Monson in an event we reported earlier writes:

> The Lord knew that there was a greater possibility of the few having prayer fellowship in oneness of spirit, than the many. Let him then lead step by step into fellowship with the little group of others who are on the same wavelength. It is the oneness of spirit that is important, not the numbers who gather to pray.[1]

God is already raising up people of prayer long before you begin to mobilize them. Where will you find these few? Let me suggest two prime candidates: (1) those who are seeking after Christ, who want a deeper reality in their walk with Him; (2) those who have a sense of mandate to redirect their lives for maximum ministry to the world.

*Sixth,* seek the seekers. How can you do this effectively? You could begin by widely circulating an invitation for others to join those of you who have begun, and see who turns up.

One practical approach which I have used for several years is a survey. A survey can be used formally during a church service or large group meeting or informally in individual conversation. If you do a formal survey, participants should take only three or four minutes to answer these questions:

1. Do you believe our church or fellowship is in need of God to wake us up to see Christ's fullness—for us, in us, through us—in new ways? Yes or no.

2. If so, do you believe that this new work of God in our lives would be best pursued in a sustained, united movement of prayer? Yes or no.

3. If God were to awaken us this way, in answer to a united movement of prayer, do you believe it would have a strategic impact, not only locally, but on the fulfillment of Christ's global cause in our generation? Yes or no.

This is not an ideal questionnaire, since it demands only yes or no answers. But if you make it an informal survey, over coffee let's say, you can go further and discuss with people why they have responded as they have.

I've found that 80 to 90 percent of those surveyed will respond positively to all three questions. At the next meeting you can report the percentage of positive response to each question. You can even conclude: "So it appears that the most logical step for us to take is to be a part of one another in united prayer for spiritual awakening. We have great news! Why don't we all act on our convictions and try to be there."

The point is God will have His concerts of prayer, and we must not set the number of those involved. It may be two; or it may encompass your whole church or campus. I know of concerts throughout our nation, all of which are clearly God-given, that cover the whole spectrum from 5 to 500 to one thousand. Regardless of the number you start with, never stop praying for more seekers. Jesus, in Matthew 9:37-38, calls us to pray for laborers for the harvest; only in answer to prayer will the laborers be thrust out. It would seem equally true that we need also to pray for the people who pray, since that is where the thrust begins.

*Seventh,* be enthusiastic. People need to know that you really believe in what you're doing. But don't force the issue too far, because there is a time when people are ready to seek, and a time when they are not.

*Eighth,* listen for barriers to prayer. Are people afraid of what it will cost them? Have they had bad experiences? Is their vision fuzzy about what they are praying toward? Are they struggling to integrate the issues of spiritual awakening into their problems of daily life? Is it possible that there is sin in their lives that prevents them from drawing near to God? Are there broken relationships with other Christians that have soured them on Kingdom concerns?

*Ninth,* as you begin to understand these barriers, it is important to help people see that their involvement can meet their felt needs. Most of us approach any new challenges on the basis of "what's in it for me?" Help people to see that concerted prayer is compatible to who they are, relevant to what they need, and desirable in achieving God's life objectives for them.

Our mobilizing efforts must help leaders of our churches and campus movements to recognize that concerts of prayer can meet their felt needs, too. In other words, leaders should see a concert of prayer as an important step in helping them bring their whole fellowship into Christian maturity, toward which they are striving. The better they see that, the more quickly these leaders will endorse their people's involvement. Help them see that:

• The concert of prayer is establishing a *foundation* for spiritual awakening and world evangelization.

• The concert of prayer provides a unique environment where all kinds of Christians can grow together and affirm their role in worldwide evangelization, whether as senders or goers.

• The concert of prayer helps promote visible unity in the Body of Christ that will assist the advancement of the gospel right where they live.

• The concert of prayer encourages and equips people to be more devoted to and skilled in prayer, and thus to serve more effectively the Christian fellowships from which they come.

• Concerts of prayer can help participants avoid competition between the individual Christian churches and fellowships from which the participants come. It can also enhance their enthusiasm for and faithfulness to their own church or fellowship.

*Tenth,* fire imaginations with the biblical and historical patterns of spiritual awakening, and with evidence that God is preparing for another such work today. Give them a new vision of the Church, a new vision of God's work among the nations, a new vision of hope about the future and the advancement of God's Kingdom.

*Eleventh,* show people that concerts of prayer are manageable. Maybe your concert will be two hours one evening a month, 20 minutes once a week after each worship service, or 15 minutes after each campus fellowship meeting. Show people that the concert won't demand an unreasonable amount of time. Even 15 minutes, if clearly on target, can be a concert of prayer.

*Twelfth,* once you get them there, get them into the action. Have different individuals lead various components of the meeting, do research on information to be prayed about, recruit others, or send out a little newsletter to all regular participants (more on this later).

*Thirteenth,* use this book to help you mobilize and train others. You might do so by having them read through it at a chapter a week. Or, you may want to form a small group to study the book together prior to incorporating newcomers into the ongoing concert of prayer. To help you, a seven-session, small group study guide is found in the back of this book. Also, the "Recovery Series" of the World Christian Video provides 8 to 11 weeks of exciting training possibilities (see back of book).

*Fourteenth,* tap into the growing network of other united prayer efforts. The National Prayer Committee can help you do this.[2] We need to hear what God is doing in the variety of corporate prayer expressions, and we need to communicate with each other about what we are learning from God about revival prayer, about concerted prayer, about mobilizing prayer, and about answers to our prayers. Those who have studied previous awakenings note that one critical human contribution to expanding prayer movements was clear, accurate, sufficient communication between those who prayed.

*Fifteenth,* expect a battle. When it comes don't let it throw you. Satan's greatest concern, next to preventing the gospel from reaching those who haven't heard, is to sabotage prayer movements that call for God to revive His Church and advance His Kingdom. He will try to discourage you, whether it be by interruptions as you pray together, by dwindling numbers, or by those who misunderstand and even question your efforts at prayer with, say, charges of spiritual elitism. The battle is sure to become toughest as your prayer group increasingly experiences the hand-to-hand cosmic warfare described in Daniel 9 and 10, Ephesians 6, and Revelation 12. Concerts of prayer are serious business.

## USE OF A COVENANT

Jonathan Goforth, the great missionary to China of the last century, found that one secret of revival on the mission field involved a "covenant in prayer, on the part of missionaries, that persisted until the revival came."

When he wrote his volume on prayer concerts, Edwards noted the practical side of maintaining a "spirit of covenant":

> But yet, as a proper guard against negligence and unsteadiness, and a prudent preservative from yielding to a disposition—to which persons might be liable, through the prevalence of indolence and listlessness—to excuse themselves on trivial occasions, it was proposed, that those who united in this affair should resolve with themselves, that if, by urgent business, or otherwise, they were hindered from joining with others on the very day agreed on, yet they would not wholly neglect bearing their part in the duty proposed, but would take the first convenient day following for that purpose.[3]

In a covenant, a group of people affirm that God has called them together for a specific purpose. A covenant states the intention of, and gives identity to, those who are prepared to be faithful to that calling. It also states the prayer movement's focus and its expectations. It forges us together in a sense of common mission.

You may want to include in it statements regarding: (1) the shape of the concert itself; (2) the intention of its members to participate regularly; (3) their intention to carry the issues with them back to their own daily prayer life; (4) the willingness of concert participants to integrate the agenda for spiritual awakening into all other times of prayer with Christians; (5) your intention to seek those whom God may be preparing to be a part of your prayer concert.

In Madison, we have a concert of prayer covenant. Maybe it will give you some guidelines (see diagram 3).

## POSSIBLE PITFALLS

The path to every worthwhile endeavor is filled with pitfalls; mobilizing a prayer movement is no exception. I can name at least three pitfalls you should beware of.

*First,* avoid a naive optimism that expects immediate response on the part of everyone you invite to join. Keep your eyes fixed on Christ rather than on immediate circumstances or human enthusiasm.

*Second,* never forget that you are a servant who is helping fellow Christians become all they are meant to be. In your fervor to make things happen, be sure you do not come across to your friends as prideful, self-righteous, a know-it-all, or disrespectful of what God has already done for them.

*Third,* we who mobilize prayer in a "Christian" country like America must always remember that our priority in prayer is for a new demonstration of the Lordship of Christ in His Church. It is not for the theocratization of our society at large. It is for spiritual awakening rather than cultural renaissance though that may come. It is for the fulfillment of the Great Commission rather than the rallying of forces around patriotic ideals. The pressure will be there for us Americans to allow our prayer movement to slide away from the Kingdom's agenda and toward a civil/religious exercise for endorsing fuzzy forms of moral renewal. Of course, Kingdom prayers on behalf of our nation are always welcome—and can result in moral renewal.

## A CONSULTATION ON CONCERTS OF PRAYER

If you are mobilizing prayer in a community-wide or campus-wide effort, you may need to hold a one-time consultation with church or campus leaders. you will want to determine together what steps to take to get praying people united. Such a consultation can help to insure that what we do is truly a cooperative effort.

In the back of this book is a suggested outline for such a one-

# Concerts of Prayer for Global Awakening
## A COVENANT

*This is what the Lord Almighty says: Many peoples and the inhabitants of many cities will yet come, and the inhabitants of one city will go to another and say, "Let us go at once to entreat the Lord and seek the Lord Almighty. I myself am going" . . . In those days ten from all languages and nations will take firm hold of one Jew by the edge of his robe and say, "Let us go with you, because we have heard that God is with you!"—Zechariah 8:20-23*

BY THE GRACE OF GOD and for His glory, we enter into a covenant of intercession for spiritual awakening. In doing so, we give high priority and increasing urgency to regular gatherings in concerts of prayer that seek the fullness of Christ in His Church for the fulfillment of His purposes among the nations.

AS WE GATHER in Jesus' name, we will come prepared, in mind and heart, to intercede (by praise, repentance, request) for spiritual awakening locally and world-wide, in the Church and among the nations. Accordingly, we will also join together to look for the following identifiable trends, both within our Christian fellowship(s), in our city and throughout the nations, in answer to our prayers:

1) The revived and unmistakable sense of God's presence and glory, in holiness and love and power, centered in the Lord Jesus Christ.

2) Resulting in the recovery, by repentance and faith, of full commitment, unity, holiness and love within the Church.

3) Leading to the revitalization of the Church's on-going ministries, primarily in evangelism, discipleship, compassion and justice.

4) Culminating in a mighty expansion of these ministries among the billions currently beyond the reach of the Gospel, filling the earth with the knowledge of the glory of God.

RECOGNIZING that spiritual awakening is born in and sustained by a movement of prayer, we will also ask God to raise up others to join us in concerts of prayer, and wherever appropriate invite them to enter with us into this covenant.

day meeting of leaders and a set of proposals for discussion.

The one-day outline and the proposals described there have been used by the National Prayer Committee in national and regional gatherings. They have effectively galvanized leaders to commit themselves and their people to concerted prayer. The result of the meetings has produced something like this:

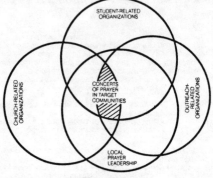

**Diagram 4**

## FORMING A STEERING COMMITTEE

It's easier to steer a bike once its moving. But unless some steering goes on after you have started, an accident is inevitable.

History shows that in most revivals there have been aberrations as one group or another has veered away into a variety of sub-biblical tangents. This could happen to your movement of prayer for revival. So, once it is underway, part of your responsibility in mobilizing it is to steer it on course. Do not try this alone. Form a steering committee.

That steering committee may initially consist of the original three or four who joined you when your concert of prayer began. Or, it may consist of leaders on your campus or in your community who as a result of a consultation expressed a strong commitment to the concert of prayer idea.

What are the responsibilities of the steering committee?

*First,* be faithful in attending. Every other responsibility will be impossible to carry out unless the committee is regularly involved. You are setting an example as well.

*Second,* the steering committee should meet between concerts of prayer—unless the concerts are held frequently—to evaluate what's happening and to take corrective action when necessary. Ask questions like: Where is the prayer concert now? Where would God like it to be? How do we get from here to there? You may discuss the way the latest concert meeting was organized or the tone of the meeting. Was there a strong sense of direction, orderliness, and faith? How did people pray? What does this tell you about the extent and depth in their understanding of issues on spiritual awakening? Was your understanding weak or off target? How can you insure that next time your praying will be more in line with the specific reason for the concert?

Some steering committees have found it very helpful to use the grid in diagram 5 for analyzing each prayer meeting to determine if a good balance was maintained. In chapter 9 we will discuss in more detail how to use this helpful tool.

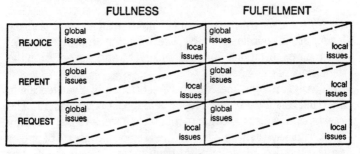

Diagram 5

At times your steering committee may want to involve other members of your concert in a brief time of evaluation. Encourage others to participate as much as possible in vision, planning, and evaluating the prayer movement. Other issues to be considered in evaluation times are outlined in detail later.

*Third,* the committee should pray for concert participants. God acts as a result of your prayers, and His work while you meet in prayer is as basic as what He does after you meet. As we enter new dimensions of spiritual aggression, we must keep the concert before the Lord, asking Him to lead it by His direction, organization, and agenda, and to protect it against all the attacks of the evil one. The steering committee also should pray that the other pray-ers will not become discouraged and that God will keep them faithful to what He has called them to do.

It may seem strange to have a prayer meeting to pray for a prayer meeting; after all, who will then pray for the prayer meeting that prays for the prayer meeting, ad infinitum? Of course, the ultimate one praying for all pray-ers is the one who ever lives to make intercession for us (Heb. 7:25). Still, I know your steering committee will not regret the time it spends praying for the concerts of prayer.

*Fourth,* the steering committee should facilitate communication between meetings. Communicating with participants is especially important if your concert meets no more often than once a month. A letter in which the committee makes suggestions for sharpening the prayer movement or highlights guidelines for the next concert of prayer is helpful. The letter can also keep participants updated on issues that need to be addressed in prayer and to report to them on fast-breaking answers.

*Fifth* and finally, the steering committee should give primary leadership in coordinating the concerts of prayer. By their model and their exhortations, the leaders set the atmosphere from the very start of the meeting.

Two years ago, the National Association of Evangelicals in Portland called for united prayer among Christian leaders. The response was strong. Leaders met once a week to fast and pray for spiritual awakening. They formed regional concerts of prayer on the last Friday evening of each month. Once the prayer movement was underway, two committees were set in place. One was a 40-person executive committee, comprised of leaders from various denominational and interdenominational groups within the city, who acted more as an advisory council.

Eight members of that group branched off to comprise a second committee—the steering committee. They have been responsible not only for keeping the prayer movement alive and growing, but for nurturing the concerts. They have held all-day seminars for participants, and recently they brought in a teaching team from the National Prayer Committee to train participants and to help carry the prayer work to a new level of intensity.

If they can do it, in God's time, so can you!

# 9

# ORGANIZING A CONCERT OF PRAYER
## Of Course You Can!

There you are in your venue—a large living room, a lounge on campus, or a church sanctuary. Before you, 25 eager people sit ready to be joined in revival prayer. You and three or four others have been praying for this moment for months. The clock strikes 7:00 P.M. as one more person slips through the back door. It is time to begin your first concert of prayer.

Now what? Despite your best recruitment efforts, unless you know how to organize and lead the meeting it will probably end up like a lot of other prayer meetings—a lot of talk about prayer but little prayer! Or worse yet, just plain boring.

Don't despair! You can lead an exciting concert of prayer!

## VARIETY IS THE SPICE . . .

This chapter presents ideas that you and your steering committee can implement. You will find more suggestions than you can handle all at once. There are many creative ways a concert of prayer can establish a format that includes the freedom and active discipline that will allow the Holy Spirit to pray through the whole group. The following is a basic structure that reflects important principles, with enough variety to give color and music to the format. After all, you are leading a concert of prayer!

*First,* determine where you will meet. I suggest you secure a location that is central to your community or campus. You may want to move the concert from church to church. If you seek to interface lay people with students, try a concert of prayer on the campus in your community, thus allowing the students to host the prayer meeting.

*Second,* maintain a regular and convenient schedule. All of us suffer from over-scheduling, hyperactivity, and too many demands. It is important that your concert meet on the same day and hour every time, to avoid confusion.

Should you meet once a week, once a month, once a quarter? Morning, noon, or night? Thirty minutes, one hour, three hours? As the prayer movement progresses, changes in each of these may be necessary. Extraordinary prayer is not determined so much by how long or how often you pray, but by the fact that you do pray, that you pray for those things most on God's heart, and that you do so together.

*Third,* encourage variations of posture during the meeting. Tell people they're free to pray sitting, kneeling, standing, walking, or even flat on their faces.

Encourage variations on how the group shows its agreement with particular prayers. For example, suggest that during one period in the concert someone finish a prayer with a phrase like "in Jesus' name." Immediately the entire group might join in on the closing "amen" to the prayer, expressing audible agreement with the pray-er on what was said.

*Fourth,* encourage variation in the length of prayers. Assure people that prayers of one sentence are fine; so are prayers of one or two minutes as long as the prayer comes from the heart and is in keeping with the Word of God.

*Fifth,* vary how group prayer is directed. At times a leader may call out, "Let's just have a time of rejoicing" or "Will someone lead us in prayers of repentance regarding the sins of the Church." Or you may be very practical: "For the next few minutes as we pray fullness prayers, let's name specific churches where we would like to see God work"; or, "As we pray for a little while on fulfillment issues, feel free to state both the name of your own neighbors and people groups far away among whom you would like to see the gospel at work."

In the early stages of developing concerts, it is important that leadership be more directive so that people understand what to pray about as well as how to maintain balance in the topics. When people gather they are often tired, are preoccupied with other pressures, or have not thought about spiritual awakening in the last 24 hours. Strong leadership at the beginning of the meeting can help override a lot of these difficulties. Take time to reintroduce the two major themes in spiritual awakening—fullness and fulfillment—and to highlight some of the issues under each theme on which the concert should focus.

I recommend that part of the time the concept prays all together as a group, even if it eventually grows to 300 or 400 people! You can have times during the concert when the group breaks into smaller huddles, too. If you divide the concert in half—one half for fullness and one half for fulfillment—take 10 minutes or so to stop praying as a large group and start praying in huddles in between halves and at the end of the concert.

## A SUGGESTED FORMAT

Variety in format is important. Diagram 7 shows a format that has been helpful to a number of concerts with which I have been in touch. It is a format we have been using regularly in Madison with occasional variation over the past four years.

### Suggested Format for a Two-hour Concert of Prayer

- Assign a leader to guide each concert.
- Enter quietly. Prepare for a ministry of intercession (3 min.).
- Sing a hymn (3 min.).
- Present an overview of concerts for newcomers and to keep the purpose and prayer agenda clear (5 min.).
- Teach on biblical roots of prayer, revival, and missions, using passage assigned for private meditation during the previous concert (5 min.).
- Recount historical roots from history or the Church today on what God has done with and through those who prayed for fullness and fulfillment (5 min.).
- Sing a hymn (3 min.).

- The ministry of intercession:
  —Concentrate on fullness agenda (40 min.).
  —Concentrate on fulfillment agenda (40 min.).
- Sing the Doxology (1 min.).
- Reflect individually and privately on how God led us to pray; jot down things to pray about until the next concert (3 min.).
- Assign a Scripture passage to reflect on until the next concert that will build understanding on prayer, awakening, and missions (3 min.).
- In between concerts, encourage members to continue to reflect and pray on the issues on which the concerts focus.

### Diagram 7

No matter what format you follow, it is helpful for your concert to maintain the following elements somewhere during the meeting:

- Praise God in song and prayer.
- Invite Christ to be the "conductor" of the meeting.
- Confess and pray for cleansing.
- Tell "Why we are here."
- Teach a brief Bible lesson regarding fullness and fulfillment.
- Report on what God has done in the past or is doing today in response to movements of prayer.
- Ask for testimonies from those whose lives are being transformed by their involvement in the concerts.
- Review specific guidelines the steering committee feels would help keep the concert on target.
- Review some specific issues that help make up the agenda of fullness and fulfillment.
- Spend an extended time of prayer for fullness and fulfillment.
- End with a word of promise from Scripture on how God answers prayer.
- Record the prayers that have been offered so you can watch for the answers.
- Suggest a passage for each participant to meditate on in preparation for the next concert.

Now, let me highlight a few of these elements. Place a sign at the entrance to the meeting room reminding people to enter quietly. Encourage people to get to the concert a few minutes early to collect their thoughts and get ready to pray.

You can invite Christ to be Lord of the concert simply through a brief prayer at the beginning, asking Jesus to conduct your symphony of intercession. It helps the whole group to sense that Jesus is present with them, so they can be accepting of each other, be honest in their prayers, and be bold in what they ask.

Exhortation from Scripture, review of other prayer movements, and personal testimonies can encourage the whole group to press on in their prayers. Every concert needs to sense that it is moving somewhere, building on previous concerts, and preparing its participants for the answers God will give. We must build into people a sense of hope and a knowledge of what we are praying toward. Of course, reports from those who are experiencing personal revival can be helpful here. You may also invite a missionary, or a Christian international student, or others who have recently traveled to other parts of the country or world to share what they are seeing God do in answer to prayer.

I recommend placing a map where it is visible to everyone. During prayer, someone may wish to look up and scan the world map to recall an issue they need to address.

You may ask certain participants, a few days before the meeting, to research various topics recommended by the steering committee to give more depth to prayers at the concert. By how they pray, the researchers can help the whole concert join them with greater understanding.

It is critical that participants be reminded that the agenda is two-fold: fullness and fulfillment. Without clear and direct leadership at this point, the prayer meeting will tend to move toward prayer for fullness rather than fulfillment and toward prayer for oneself rather than the Church at large. That is why I recommend that the actual time given to intercession be divided into two distinct portions: half for prayer for fullness and half for fulfillment.

At the start of the first half, mention what fullness refers to. Give a sampling of issues normally addressed in fullness praying.

Then have a leader begin that segment by opening with a fullness prayer. When it is time to enter the second segment, a hymn or chorus might be sung to end the first. Then the leader can briefly define fulfillment praying, give illustrations of issues involved and lead out with the first fulfillment prayer.

I recommend that every participant be given a reproduction of the grid presented in the previous chapter (diagram 5) before actually entering into the fullness/fulfillment prayer time.

Give participants five minutes of quiet to fill in one issue which comes to mind for each of the 12 triangles of the grid. By keeping the grid in front of them when they begin to pray, they will know clearly what they ought to be praying about when it becomes appropriate in the flow of the "symphony."

I highly recommend that five minutes or so be given at the end for reflection and personal review of the prayer meeting. During that time participants might write in their notebooks what God has said to them during the two hours of prayer—key issues on which the group seemed to be in strong agreement, or issues that had special meaning for any particular participant. In fact, for a minute or two the group might discuss one or two concerns the Spirit led the concert to emphasize during that particular meeting.

These could also be written down in their "concert diaries." A Korean pastor calls his "the Book of the Kingdom" to pray over in personal prayer times and to review in preparation for the next concert. Thomas Goodwin, a seventeenth-century Puritan divine and aide to Oliver Cromwell, reminds us in *The Return of Prayers* that there is a return on our prayers. We must not give in to the sin of praying for something while failing to watch how God answers. Then we can praise Him for what He does and take courage to ask for even more.

## MORE GUIDELINES

Some of the following will be more relevant in the early days of your concert, some later on. At times it might be good to publish pertinent guidelines and send them to participants between prayer meetings.

• Remind participants to enter the room quietly.

• Encourage them to think of themselves not only as a family in

prayer, but as a team involved in a ministry of prayer.
- Define the concert of prayer as both a school of prayer and a ministry of prayer: a time to learn as well as a time to give.
- Remind them that concerts of prayer are a distinctive type of prayer meeting. A concert of prayer is a ministry of intercession, a ministry to the Church and to the world with a specific target: spiritual awakening—fullness and fulfillment issues.
- Encourage people not to feel self-conscious. Remind them that any prayer they make—made according to the Word of God, from a heart of faith, and in Jesus' name—is acceptable to Him.
- Encourage sensitivity to varieties of praying. You may have Pentecostals and non-Pentecostals, educated and less educated, rich and poor, young and old, etc. Ask participants to accept one another's prayer styles.
- Suggest that people listen carefully to one another's prayers, seeking not only to express agreement when appropriate but also to look for ways to build on one another's prayers. Sometimes a whole series of prayers may build one on the other around a specific topic until that area is covered by the group.
- Remind participants about the length of their prayers. They are praying in a group, so they should think of others and not just of themselves in what they choose to pray about and how they construct their prayers.
- Don't hesitate to praise God at points along the way. Try to do so within the context of the reason for concerts: the grand sweeps of concern for fullness and fulfillment.
- There are three paces of intercession: solidarity, advocacy, and pursuit. Acknowledge these paces and encourage people to develop their prayers along all three lines.
- Give guidelines on times of silence. Silence can be very significant. At times, God may call us to be quiet enough before Him that we might hear all He is asking us to do. There are many things a concert of prayer can pray about but there may be only a few things it should pray about on any specific occasion. During times of silence, you not only have opportunity to review what has already been prayed, but you can ask God to lead you even more clearly about what you must pray before the concert is over.

- Encourage asking God questions and then pausing to listen. Many of the psalms appear to be this type of praying. It may be appropriate for someone to lead out in prayer with a series of questions, each followed by a few moments of silence.
- Singing may be appropriate at times in order to strengthen the faith and vision of the group for the ministry of intercession and to get our eyes more firmly back on Christ and His purposes. Again, it is important that all singing fit the specific agenda and purpose of concerts.
- Confession is an important part of intercession. Sometimes the confessions may be for individual lives, sometimes for local churches or the Church worldwide; at other times they may need to confess the sins of our nation and of our world. They may need to confess lovelessness, unbelief, disobedience or cry out to God in repentance for their ineffective impact with the gospel. In all confession, participants must be sure that the burden is not primarily for themselves—their sins, their helplessness, their needs—but is for the whole Church, beginning with the church where they live. In all confession, the concert must continue to move away from the problems and look away to the person of Christ, in whom there is forgiveness.
- Publish a statement of faith broad enough to allow any genuine Christian to participate, but clear enough to ensure that praying does not end up on a doctrinal tangent. I recommend the *Lausanne Covenant on World Evangelization*, a widely used statement. (A copy may be obtained by writing to C.W.E., Whitefield House, 186 Kennington Park Rd., London SE11 4BT, England.)
- Encourage people to think about their prayers before they begin, using the grid if necessary.
- Encourage people to pray frequently about those things God has led them to pray for since the last concert.
- As you pray, encourage participants to use Scripture in forming the requests they make. Encourage people to open their Bibles during the time of prayer and to actually turn to passages and pray them back to the Lord in their own words.
- Reassure people that there is nothing wrong with moving from general issues to more specific ones. Most of the prayers of

Scripture are prayers formed in generalities though for specific situations or people.

- Remind people that even when they pray for "local concerns"—either for themselves or their church or their city—they need to be encouraged to examine the global implications of God's answers to those prayers, and to say so to Him.

- Remind them to avoid the "privatization" of their requests. It is possible to pray about fullness and me or fulfillment and me and never get down to praying for fullness and fulfillment as it relates to the Lord and His global cause.

- Remind them that they are holding one another accountable in their daily prayer lives, as well as in their daily disciplines, to be living out what they pray together in concert.

- Encourage faithfulness in attending the concerts of prayer. Remember, it may be months or years before all prayers are answered. Periodically, review your covenant if you form one.

- Remind people to keep a balance between the real and ideal as they evaluate the meetings. The real is never what we want it to be, but most of our ideals are usually unattainable. Without this balance, participants might give up and withdraw from the concerts or try to place the blame on others or go off and start their own groups. Welcome feedback to the steering committee if participants have ways to strengthen the concerts.

- Encourage members of the concert to be responsible for research on specific prayer issues, such as needs of our society, missions concerns, or specific people groups to be reached. This way, they will be better equipped to give intelligent leadership in prayer during the next concert.

- Remind them to come prepared with hearts primed to pray. On some occasions participants may find it helpful to fast a meal. Leave this to the discretion of each participant.

- Suggest that participants bring friends to the concerts. Encourage them to orient their friends to both the purpose and format of the concerts before they arrive.

You can put your guidelines in writing or just mention some of them at the beginning of a concert event.

One last suggestion: You could distribute a list of issues to be addressed in concerts under fullness and fulfillment, similar to the one that is outlined in the next chapter. You could either give participants an extended list all at once or distribute briefer lists at the end of each concert. With that list you may also include a sample copy of the concert of prayer grid for their own reference.

Such are some of the nuts-and-bolts concerns with which every pacesetter must be concerned. In the next chapter, we want to give tough-minded thinking to expanding our agenda in prayer.

# 10

# AGENDA FOR CONCERTED PRAYER
## Shape of Prayers to Come

For a moment, stand with me by the throne of God, where John stood in Revelation 4 and listen in on the prayers of the saints at the First Solid Church in Anywhere, U.S.A. What do you hear? What themes are struck when a little group in that church meets to pray once a month? Do their prayers fit the setting you see around here at the throne, encircled with myriads of hymning angels and lamps of furious fire? Do you hear what John heard in Revelation 5 and 8 as he focused on the prayers of God's people ascending like smoke from an altar of incense?

Do you hear prayers about global redemption (Rev. 5) and global justice (Rev. 8:1-4)? Are the people at First Solid getting to the heart of spiritual awakening? Are they praying strategic prayers that call for the Church to know Christ in a new way and for the advancing of His Kingdom? Do you hear them moving forward with rejoicing, repenting and bold request?

There is a chance you don't—not if they are struggling with how to pray the way *I* do sometimes. But there is no reason to be discouraged, either with them or ourselves. If we keep in view the two clear themes in the Word of God, which both touch spiritual awakening (fullness, fulfillment), and if we work at growing our prayer agenda around each one, it won't be long before our prayers will truly mingle with the aromatic incense of intercession that has been ascending to the Father from the beginning.

## GET IT GROWING

If, as I have said, the front line in world evangelization is the Word of God and prayer, then the best place to begin growing your prayer agenda is to unearth all that the Scriptures teach on the themes of fullness and fulfillment. You'll find enough issues to keep a concert of prayer breathing and moving forever!

To help you, I suggest that you take two inexpensive Bibles. In one, underline with a pink highlighting pen all the references that have to do with the subject of fullness—you might begin with Isaiah or Ephesians. In the other Bible, underline with a yellow pen all the references that have to do with fulfillment. That might be a good start for your concert of prayer. You can take some of the verses and use them as prayer targets in each concert.

However you do it, it is important that your prayers reflect the biblical dimensions on God's Kingdom. As you study Scripture and then as you meet in concerts of prayer, constantly think about God's intentions for the Church and for the world by asking the following questions to enlarge your prayer concerns:

• What is the scope and content of God's purpose for history, the Church and the nations?
• In specific ways, what would it look like for God's Kingdom, described for us in Scripture, to invade the Church? The world? Your own life?
• How extensive might the impact of His Kingdom grow to be upon His people and His world?
• Why is the fullness of Christ and His Church so essential for the fulfillment of His purposes in the earth?
• How has His purpose unfolded so far?
• Where have there been problems?
• What has been responsible for victories?
• Where are we in God's purposes now? What is left to do? How will it get done?
• Biblically speaking, how can each of us fit in most strategically?

These questions aren't designed to discourage us from praying for personal concerns and issues each of us have. But if we are involved in prayer for spiritual awakening, we must somehow relate even the most personal prayers to the larger scope of God's purposes. How else does one give breadth and depth to prayers that are a part of his or her daily walk? The above question can help.

Let's keep working at growing our agenda. Try this mind-expanding approach on for size: "If God were to answer your requests—whatever they may be—to the fullest extent you can imagine possible—based on who you know Him to be and what He has said in His Word—what might be the impact of those answers on spiritual awakening—fullness in the Church, fulfillment of the global cause?" Better read that question again!

For instance, let's say you are a college student whose father has recently become unemployed; it appears there may not be enough money for you to stay at school for another quarter. You might have to leave school and go to work. How should you pray about this? Of course, you might pray that God would comfort your father and somehow supply the funds, and that's okay. But using the question I just gave you, you might be led to also pray that God would use this experience in ways that change the world.

How? To teach you and your father new dimensions of trusting Him which later you can share with other Christians to build them up in fullness of faith. Or, you might pray that God will allow you to experience the helplessness and vulnerability that comes with "poverty," as temporary as it may be, long enough to help you to understand something of what life is like for most of the world's unreached peoples and to care for them more deeply.

Let's take another area: praying for missionaries and missionary work. For many, this is a very dull and unexciting obligation. So where do you begin to change this? Go back to our question. If you take the missionary and his or her ministry and break down all items for prayer into two columns of fullness and fulfillment, it will start to make new sense. For example, praying for a missionary's relationship to God is a prayer for fullness. But praying for a missionary's ability to communicate the gospel is a prayer for fulfillment. Both areas are critical, if our prayers are going to be true to the scope of God's kingdom and the impact of spiritual awakening.

To pray, for example, for the conversion of Islamic religious leaders in a Muslim country where your missionary is working is a prayer for fulfillment. To pray that a body of believers be gathered into an evangelizing fellowship within a village of that country is also prayer for fulfillment. But to pray that your missionary there will have loving relationships with other missionaries on his or her team is a prayer for fullness. Most missionaries struggle with this at one time or another. They often long for true spiritual awakening for themselves that not only restores them to a new vision of Christ but, in turn, to a deeper love for each other and the people they have come to serve. To what extent could you imagine God answering prayers here?

Of course, there are many other sources for growing your prayer agenda. Information gleaned from both secular and Christian publications can help.[2] Books like Patrick Johnstone's *Operation World* (STL Books, #2 Industrial Park Rd., Waynesboro, GA 30830), prayer guides such as *Global Prayer Digest* (1605 East Elizabeth Street, Pasadena, California 91104), or magazines like *World Christian* (Box 40010, Pasadena, California 91104), and *Sojourners* (P.O. Box 29272, Washington, D.C. 20017) can give you up-to-date background information. Evangelical Missions Information Service is worth every penny for its weekly publications (Box 794, Wheaton, Illinois 60189).

The book you hold right now has insights on prayer issues for the Church and the world on almost every single page. I suggest that every committed member of your concert of prayer obtain a copy to refer to when they seek to prime their pump in personal preparation for your next gathering. You might review chapter five, then go through the issues listed on the next few pages for a start, placing a star (*) in the margin at every statement or fact that ought to be addressed in prayer. Bring the book with you to upcoming concerts and refer to it during the meeting, picking one or two issues that you will voice in prayer. In addition, you might fuel prayer by reading suggestions from the back of the book.

And don't forget the prayer grid we gave you earlier. Write in awakening issues that currently concern you. How would you fill in each of the 12 triangles if you had to right now? Growing your agenda is simply a matter of the Father helping you add additional items to each triangle as you read, listen, travel, and interact with others, and as you press on in prayer yourself.

By keeping clear the balance in prayer for spiritual awakening, the grid will be your faithful guide toward the shape of prayers to come. For example, it reminds you that many of your concerns in spiritual awakening have both local and global dimensions. Both must be addressed. You must fight the tendency to concentrate on either dimension to the exclusion of the other. In the same sense, it leads you to keep a balance between rejoicing in what God is already doing (or promises to do), expressing repentance for the things in us and in the Church-at-large that hinder or ignore what God wants to do, and, of course, requesting God's actions for specific concerns under fullness and fulfillment. It will also help you resist the tendency to pray for fullness issues to the neglect of fulfillment ones; to pray only for those things that are closest and most directly related to your own felt needs while neglecting or ignoring the bulk of issues that lie beyond your own experience of "fullness," that touch fulfillment worldwide.

## ISSUES FOR PRAYER

The rest of this chapter contains a list of issues under fullness and fulfillment which our concert of prayer in Madison has addressed at one time or another. They will get you started toward filling out the 12 triangles on your grid. You can add other issues as God teaches you what He wants you and your concert of prayer to cover. At the end of each list is space for you to add areas that you want to pray for which I have missed.

In fact, it is important to always keep asking the Father what He wants you to pray about, no matter how long your own list grows. The direction He wants your next concert of prayer to move might be totally different from your past list of ideas. That is as it should be. After all, He is both composer and conductor.

### Issues to Address in Prayer for Fullness
• That God would give a global awakening to His Church, helping us to know Christ well enough so we trust, love and obey

Him, so we move with Him in new ways for the fulfillment of His global cause in our generation.

- That the Church would be united in faith, acknowledging Christ as its head in every respect, unveiling His glory before a watching world.
- That the Church would awaken to the universal authority of Christ, which is the basis of her commitment to the advancing of His Kingdom.
- That God would fill us with hope, giving us a clear vision of what the Church is moving toward so that out of that hope would spring faith and love.
- That the Spirit would bring to ultimate fruitfulness and impact the current renewing work He is already accomplishing in parts of the Body of Christ.
- That the Church would see the need to seek global awakening and renewal for a new mission thrust.
- For God to make us aware of others who have a similar burden for spiritual awakening, so that we might unite our hearts together in prayer.
- For God to raise up many prayer bands of "world Christians" on our campuses, in our churches and mission agencies, and throughout His Church worldwide.
- That God would show us our needs and our weaknesses so thoroughly that we become desperate in our seeking and utterly dependent on Him.
- For God to open us to deeper ministries of the Holy Spirit, so He could be poured out on us as fully as God intends.
- That the Spirit would share with His Church the truths of Christ and reveal Him to us.
- For new awareness of God's holiness and the Church's need to be holy as He is, if we are to have a significant impact for His glory.
- For God to convict us of every area of sin so that we might be led into the holiness of Jesus.
- That God would help those who are praying with us in our concerts of prayer to live a daily life that reflects all we have prayed for together.
- For a fresh sense of God's love for the world, and rekindling of our love for Him.

## ADVOCACY: STANDING UP FOR OTHERS

During and after the Vietnam War, many Americans wore bracelets called "MIA (Missing in Action) bracelets." Each person wore his or her bracelet until the missing serviceman was found. We were advocates for those in enemy hands who could not advocate for themselves.

That is a good model for the second pace of intercessory prayer: advocacy. Having first aligned ourselves with God and His Word, we next align ourselves with those who cannot pray for themselves.

Andrew Murray said, "My drawing nigh to God is of one piece with my intercourse with men and earth." Out of intimacy with Christ comes responsibility for others, in prayer. Out of love for God, advocacy becomes an act of love for our neighbors. Like the second statue at Pembroke College, advocacy is love pleading on its knees. We begin to see that God intends prayer to be a way for us to release His loving power into the lives of others.

A biblical model of this approach is God's assignment to the high priest in Exodus 28:29-30. Every time he came into the holy of holies to intercede on behalf of Israel, he bore stones on his vestments on which were inscribed the names of each of the tribes of Israel, not unlike an MIA bracelet, as a remembrance before the Lord. When we gather for a concert of prayer, we too need to come wearing on our hearts, as it were, names of those in the Church and in the world on whose behalf we are advocating. This is part of our holy priesthood (1 Pet. 2).

And the beautiful thing about loving others in prayer is that there are really no limits as to how far our love can go. What if you could travel anywhere in the world, to anyone in deep need, and stretch forth a loving hand to help them? Prayer allows you to have just such a limitless mission. As far as God can go—either geographically, culturally, physically, or spiritually—prayer can go. Our advocating requests actually touch people where they are because God is already there to touch them according to what we ask. Isn't that exciting?

If we are going to take the power of advocacy seriously then we need to deepen our understanding of those for whom we pray and for others who need our prayers. We need to develop

- That God would give us a new heart of love. That God would move us to seek it until we are willing to take the whole world into our hearts.
- That God would bring reconciliation to His Church, so that all Christians can become transparent before God and each other; that we would unite for the sake of Christ in repentance and forgiveness.
- Wherever there are major rifts and divisions within the Body of Christ, that God would heal those divisions so that the gospel would have greater credibility as the world observes "how we love one another."
- For members of our local church; for our immaturities and selfish demands that divert our pastor's vision for spiritual awakening and deplete his energies in advancing Christ's Kingdom.
- For the grace to accept every enablement God sends for us for choosing the best, and doing what maximizes Christ's glory.
- That God would forgive us for the times we fail to choose what is just and to do what glorifies Christ.
- That God would convict us of our pride and divisiveness, open our ears and eyes to hear and see one another the way God does, and to help us minister to one another in the power of Christ.
- That God would help us repent of everything that prevents us from following Christ without limits, even to the ends of the earth: sin, unbelief, preoccupation, and self-serving.
- That God would overrule all internal barriers within the Church that would hinder the advancement of the gospel—paralysis of faith, preoccupations, parochialism, and indifference.
- That Christians would be set free to reorganize their lifestyles so that they can better respond to people's deepest needs in effective ways, especially in places where the gospel has not yet come.
- That God would break the hold of money in the life of the Church, and that we would be delivered from its power, allurement, and folly.
- That God would give believers, beginning in our own concert

of prayer, transparency with one another, humility, brokenness, and reconciliation wherever it is needed.

- That God would renew our world vision and our faith to move forward to face the challenge of reaching the nations, beginning where we live.
- That God would educate His people about His heart for the world and how He sees the world, so that our acts of obedience would correspond to the facts.
- For the Spirit of God to so empower us as a missionary spirit, that He will make us a missionary Church.
- That God would give His people wholehearted zeal for His worldwide purposes.
- That God would deliver us from drifting, aimlessness, and fruitlessness, and set us on a straight and level path in urgency for His Kingdom.
- That the Church worldwide might be unified to fulfill the Great Commission in our generation, especially among the 2.5 billion people who can only be reached by major new effort in cross-cultural evangelism.
- That God would give us such gratitude for all He has done already for us personally and collectively, that we would delight to bring what we have found to those who have never heard.
- For a spirit of "surrender" within the Church and a willingness to do whatever God calls us to do, at whatever price.
- That the Spirit would summon Christians to accountability before Christ in the sharing of our unique blessings in Him with the billions locked away in extreme spiritual and physical poverty. That we would repent of hoarding the gospel, so that we might release its full impact of love and justice worldwide.
- That God would fill His people with hearts of compassion for the earth's unreached, until we come to the place where, like Christ, we are ready to die for them.
- That we would awaken to the world-sized part God has given to each one of us and to His global Church, with our world-sized potential in His plan for the nations.
- That God would help us actively desire to overflow in ministry to the world around and beyond us.
- For God to help us see every "human limitation" or "handi-

Verlene Kirkland

Peg Wagner

Constantin

Elana

Rodica

Ruth Johnson

Fred Savage

0502                        13116107

                        18      4390434
                        BRA
                        75      7706102           REG   13.50
                        PANTYHOSE
                        75      7706102           REG    1.79
                        PANTYHOSE
                        07      5531501A           REG    1.79
                        WOMN SPORTWR
                        57                        REG   45.00
                                                  C       -00
                        38      4942104A
                        LINGERIE               REG      36.00
                                              SUBTOTAL    .08
                                              TAX         .00

                    W6011007202504196411387/0

11/21/88        3 DC      TTL      67.08

# SEARS
## MAPLEWOOD, MINNESOTA

RETAIN FOR COMPARISON WITH MONTHLY
STATEMENT OR FOR RETURN OR EXCHANGE

0502          131122/107          36038

| 18 | 43904384 | | |
|---|---|---|---|
| BRA | | REG | 13.50 |
| 75 | 77061032 | | |
| PANTYHOSE | | REG | 1.79 |
| 75 | 77061032 | | |
| PANTYHOSE | | REG | 1.79 |
| 07 | 55315016 | | |
| WOMN SPORTWR | | REG | 15.00 |
| 57 | | CR | 1.00- |
| 38 | 49421066 | | |
| LINGERIE | | REG | 36.00 |
| | | STL | 67.08 |
| | | TAX | .00 |

W6011007202504196118B/0

11/21/86      3 DC      TTL      67.08


THERE'S MORE FOR YOUR LIFE AT SEARS

I AGREE TO PAY THIS CHARGE ACCORDING TO
MY DISCOVER CARDMEMBER AGREEMENT AND I
AUTHORIZE  THE ISSUER TO PAY SEARS.

cap" as a gift which, once liberated, builds up the Church and advances the Kingdom.

- That God would give mature leadership for the solid discipling of national churches, especially in those countries and among those people where we have recently seen such spiritual vitality and evangelistic ferment—such as Nigeria, Kenya, South Korea, Philippines, India, Brazil, Columbia, Norway, Poland, China, and many others.
- That Christian groups and churches would be awakened with a vision of how God has sovereignly teamed them up, giving them unique experiences and gifts so that together they might fulfill strategic missions that touch the ends of the earth.
- That those being won to Christ around the world right now could immediately sense their calling not only to join themselves to Christ but also to enter wholeheartedly into His global cause.
- That God would raise up pioneers of faith to lead the Church to embrace the new things God wants to do through us in this generation, beginning in prayer.
- That God would raise up godly visionary leaders to take His people on into our mission of redemption and healing among all nations and peoples.
- That God would give many churches and teams around the world new dreams and visions for specific missions to the world.
- That God would help His Church identify the starting place for such dreams: that we would discover the resources and gifts in the Body of Christ and how to use these unique blessings God has given us to share with families of the earth.
- That God would bring commitment to Christ and His global cause among the hundreds of thousands of Christian students worldwide, and prepare them to assume leadership and sacrifice to carry out that commitment.
- That the Church would be filled with victorious optimism in keeping with God's love and purposes for the whole earth, and step forth boldly in the light of that victory, for fulfillment of God's promises through us for this generation.
- 
-

- 
- 

## Issues in Praying for Fulfillment

- For God to be glorified throughout the earth, among all people everywhere. Tell Him you want this to happen and tell Him what it will mean to you personally when it does.

- For the climax of history that depends, to a large degree, on the compassionate, Spirit-empowered witness of Christ's worldwide Church.

- That God would receive new praise in the earth, not only for what He is presently doing in the Church, but especially for all He does through the Church to reach, salvage, and fulfill unreached peoples around the world.

- That Christ's global cause of love and justice will prevail. It is a life or death issue! People without Christ everywhere lack an inheritance in God's Kingdom and have no way to receive His salvation.

- For churches of maturing disciples to be planted within every people group within this generation.

- For bold new thrusts in world evangelization through the intentional, sacrificial penetration of major human barriers worldwide.

- For awakening and spiritual hunger among the 2.5 billion people, such as Muslims, Chinese, Hindus, Buddhists, who have yet to hear of Christ. That they may have a new sense of reality of God and an awakened desire to seek Him.

- For those millions who have heard of Christ and have some understanding of the gospel, including nominal Christians, but have yet to come to full "birth" in a commitment to the Lordship of Christ in their lives. That they may be reborn into faithful and obedient servants of Christ in this generation. If just this one prayer were answered, it would have an unprecedented impact for world evangelization.

- For Satan to be bound and fully routed. That Christ's victory on the cross would break Satan's hold on nations and cultures.

- That God would defeat the diverse strategies of Satan and his kingdom as they manifest themselves through many day-to-day "powers" that often literally enslave multitudes—nationalism, militarism, traditionalism, technocracy, racism, scientism, secularism, expansionism, materialism—and keep them blind to the grace of God.

- For world leaders and governments, and for the outcome of world events. All of these can directly affect the free flowing of the gospel within a nation or within a people-group (1 Tim. 2:1-4).

- That the gospel would have such an impact that the lordship of Christ might be brought to bear on the decisions of earthly rulers. And that in turn, their judgments would bring justice, mercy, and dignity as well as true peace to the nations.

- That God would raise up God-fearing, righteous leaders to be placed in positions of authority and influence in such areas as government, education, judicial, media, medicine, business, and commerce, as well as in homes and churches.

- For major global issues that impinge upon a world mission thrust and are part of the moral darkness that must be penetrated by the gospel and the planting of responsible communities of disciples among the billions who have yet to hear. Such issues include global hunger, nuclear proliferation, and political and economic oppression.

- For those in prison, the fairness of the judicial system, effective law enforcement, and compassion to victims and families.

- For justice throughout our land, throughout the world, so that people who are made in the image of God would find fair treatment and know the righteousness of God.

- That God would have mercy at every point where we sense that His judgments may be imminent. That His power to curse or bless would become apparent to those who are standing under His judgment.

- That God would overthrow governments that rob their people of basic human rights, oppressing them and exploiting them cruelly, and keeping them from the gospel.

- That God would convict the leaders of the world who hold our planet under the threat of massive destruction; that He would provide wisdom for a way out of this horror.

- For mission agencies, the vessels through which God often thrusts forth laborers into the harvest. Pray that they will be purified and reshaped to channel the new wine of revival to the ends of the earth.

- For God's people everywhere to see those nearby whose ways of living differ from them enough to cut them off from the regular witness of the gospel—to see them and reach them. We need special sensitivity to the poor, oppressed, friendless.
- That individual churches around the world will adopt some of the earth's unreached people groups, taking them as their special focus for prayer and action.
- For specific people groups (there are more than 17,000) beyond the reach of the gospel. Ask God to give your church and His people in many places the wisdom to know how to reach them. Ask God to show: What opportunities now exist? What barriers stand in the way? What will it take for Christians to cross those barriers? How might Christians best do this now? As He answers, turn those answers into points for further intercession for the specific group and your group's role in serving them.
- That God would give to the Church the gift of "apostles" (1 Cor. 12:28). We need hundreds of thousands of cross-cultural messengers to be sent out by churches around the world. Ask God to give the Church wisdom to know who these people are, to set them apart for the work to which He has called them, and to send them forth by a movement of prayer and sacrifice.
- That God would deploy a new force of self-supporting (tentmaking) witnesses to relocate among those people of the earth closed to professional missionary outreach. That lay people would get a vision for this for themselves.
- For all current efforts to research and formulate mission strategy, to effectively deploy a new generation of missionaries.
- For technical areas of mission outreach such as Bible translation, Bible correspondence courses, Christian radio and TV, theological education by extension (TEE), saturation evangelism, student work worldwide, medical mission relief and aid ministries, and short-term missions.
- Since a major aspect of Jesus' ministry to the unreached involved the casting out of demons, the healing of the lame and the deaf and the blind, the raising of the dead, and many other miracles, ask God to give His Church worldwide whatever signs and wonders are needed to confirm the Word

before an unbelieving world.

- Pray for those who are either accessible to a Christian witness from the outside, or who are responsive to whatever witness is already there but which needs more workers.

- That God would help us be keenly aware of the opportunities He is giving us now to testify of Christ to the unreached world.

- For those people and places where the doors are open for hundreds of additional laborers to enter. That the doors would remain open and that workers would soon be found to walk through them.

- For the Christian Church within every country. That God would raise up out of revival a new mission thrust from every nation and people-group where communities of disciples already exist.

- That God would raise up men and women with specific gifts and proven experience in training and evangelism who will be able to work in conjunction with local churches in host countries, or with other missionaries.

- For suffering Christians who often experience temptations, oppressions, and persecutions because they aggressively operate with the gospel in the whirlpool created by two diametrically opposed spiritual powers. Pray especially for those facing increased dangers from revolutions and terrorism.

- For specific missionary movements in the third world. Today, there are 15,000 third world missionaries sent out by more than 300 third world agencies.

- For specific evangelical North American missionary societies. For their organizational and personnel needs, and for particular outreaches and mission projects.

- For America as a major sending base of missionary personnel. Of the eighty thousand Protestant missionaries worldwide, almost sixty thousand come from North America. Pray that God would revive the Church in our nation so that the base of Christians here, containing 80 percent of the evangelical resources of the world and 70 percent of its trained Christians, might continue to release these God-given blessings for ministry to the earth's unreached. Pray that the revival will enrich the quality of the missionaries who go.

- For the unreached "nations" in America. The unique United States ethno-cultural panorama includes 120 ethnic groups speaking over 100 different languages. At least 3 million in the United States have no knowledge of Christ and no one near them who is like them to tell them of Christ. Tens of millions more, many locked away among the urban poor of our cities, are out of touch with compassionate, witnessing Christians, or see little credibility in the gospel.
- For the 300,000 international students on our campuses, many from the major "closed" countries. For the millions of international visitors in the United States every year.
- For God to raise up a new movement of "senders" worldwide—people who know God has called them to send a new force of cross-cultural witnesses and who embrace that assignment with the same vision and sacrifices as those who go.
- 
- 
- 
- 

So you see, growing your prayer agenda for a concert isn't all that hard. In fact, it is quite exciting! Combining all the issues gleaned from Scripture, expanding your current prayer list so that personal requests reflect dimensions of fullness and fulfillment, and gradually adding newer issues to your prayer strategy, as the above empty spaces suggest, will remain right on target for revival. You'll certainly not get bored!

To take a practical first step right now, return to the "grid" in chapter 8, and, using the 12 triangles it gives you, fill in each with one prayer issue from the suggestions in this chapter.

# HEY, LEADER
# STRIKE UP THE BAND
## Marching Out in a Concert of Prayer

If fellowship with the Father and Son is like walking in the light (1 John 1:5-7), then a concert of prayer is like a group of Christians, in fellowship with God and each other, who have formed a marching band in the light—a parade set loose in the courts of heaven, marching to the ends of the earth. Is this similar to what Paul had in mind when he wrote of armies of pray-ers in Ephesians 6?

What are the paces our Leader wants to put us through? What beat do we march to? In this final chapter, you'll get answers that will take your concerts of prayer off toward the sunrise of spiritual awakening like one grand victory procession.

### THE THREE PACES OF INTERCESSION

Recently I strolled in the gardens of Pembroke College, one of 35 colleges that make up Oxford University in England. As a young man, George Whitefield studied at Pembroke. There he was converted and joined in the fellowship of concerted prayer called the "holy club," that included the Wesleys.

Near the oldest building of the college stands three statues, depicting key aspects of prayer. The first figure is seated with its head in its hands, thinking of things eternal. The second is on his knees, hands clasped, arms outstretched toward heaven.

The third figure stands erect, with shield and sword, ready to do battle. As I looked at these three figures, I recalled the force of prayer in the ministry of George Whitefield himself and thought of the three paces of intercession the Lord brings us through when He calls us to strike up a concert of prayer. They are solidarity, advocacy, and pursuit.

Like the seated statue, part of intercession is coming into agreement with God, pondering on what He wants and then desiring it with Him—in other words, solidarity. At other times intercession, like the kneeling figure, calls us to bleed with the Father, particularly on behalf of those situations and peoples where others will not or cannot pray. So, we become advocates for them. But then on some issues God calls us to march into a real battle, to press His purposes forward with unflagging zeal and at any cost until we see accomplished what He has burdened us to pray for. Pursuing prayer takes over at this point.

These intensifying paces are endorsed in our Lord's teaching. Sometimes He told us to ask—simply agreeing with God; sometimes to seek, which includes doing so on behalf of others; and sometimes to knock, clearly the most aggressive of the three and the most demanding.

One concert of prayer in which I have participated for years includes only two people—my wife Robyne and myself. It is the most important time of united prayer in my schedule, and it comes every day. In this mini-concert we have experienced all three paces. We have prayed through Scripture, at one time working through the whole book of Psalms, to realign our hearts' desires with the ways of God. We have actually picked the same passages, written out individual prayers reflecting to God our responses to what He said to us in His Word, and then read our prayers to each other at the close of the day. After that, we got on our knees to blend our insights together in a time of solidarity praying.

We have also spent time as advocates in at least two ways: (1) for each of the nations of the world, using such tools as *Operation World: Handbook for World Intercession;* (2) over every personal letter that comes to our house from friends and ministries around the world.

The last couple of years, however, our Father has also led us into persistent, pursuing prayer on issues where the stakes seem so great to us that we feel we would be irresponsible if we did not keep aggressively knocking. For one thing, He has asked us to diligently seek Him for a very close walk with the Lord Jesus, giving us 1 Corinthians 6:17 as a picture of what He wants. We are praying for revival in our home. He has also charged us to persist in prayer for specific crises (abortion), people (churches in Madison), and people-groups (castes in India) until He answers, as in the Luke 19 parable of the widow pestering the judge.

In our monthly Madison concerts of prayer we have gone through the same three paces. Of course, the direction of our "parade"—spiritual awakening—has never changed. And we try to play the score the way we know the Composer has written it: the treble clef is fullness and the bass clef fulfillment. We never seek to march without playing both clefs, measure by measure or issue by issue.

But there are times when God changes the tempo on us. For example, though we agree with the Lord that we want to see Him raise up a praying Church in this generation (solidarity), and though we pray for specific situations where it seems that prayer movements are beginning to emerge (advocacy), we feel compelled to regularly concentrate on asking God to bring forth a mighty prayer movement within Madison to advance His Kingdom worldwide (pursuit).

Let us look at these three paces a little more closely.

## SOLIDARITY: AGREEING WITH GOD

In solidarity, we align ourselves, in prayer, with what God has shown us in His Word and agree with Him saying, "Father, we want what you want." As Martin Luther defined it: "Prayer is not overcoming God's reluctance; it is laying hold of his highest willingness." A friend of mine calls it "jumping on God's bandwagon." Praying in solidarity recognizes that the only thing beyond the reach of our prayers is anything outside the will of God.

Here is where praying "in Jesus' name" finds its true meaning. This is not a phrase to be tacked on at the end to indicate that our prayer is finished. Jesus meant for us to pray with the authority that comes from linking our standing before the Father with Christ's standing, our character with His character, and our reputation with His. We are saying "Father, your Son's life-perspectives, His life-directions, and His life-mission are ours; they shape everything we're asking you to do." For in the final analysis, prayer is a Person—we are allied with the risen Christ. When we ask in His name, we can never want too much from the Father (John 14:16).

In solidarity praying, then, we identify first of all not with the world's battery of needs and longings, but with Jesus' desire to please the Father. God's kingdom must control our agenda in prayer, not what culture defines for us as possible or impossible, but what God said will actually *be*.

To seek first God's Kingdom is to desire the spread of the reign of Jesus Christ. Such desire in prayer will include, according to John Stott:

> Ourselves, until every single department of our life—home, marriage, and family, personal morality, professional life and business ethics, bank balance, tax returns, life-style, citizenship—is joyfully and freely submitted to Christ. It will continue in our immediate environment, with the acceptance of evangelistic responsibility towards our relatives, colleagues, neighbors and friends. And it will also reach out in global concern for the missionary witness of the church . . .
>
> God is King, has inaugurated his saving reign through Christ, and has a right to rule in the lives of his creatures. Our ambition, then, is to seek first his Kingdom, to cherish the passionate desire that his name should receive from men the honor which is due to it.[1]

Solidarity praying calls us to pray with a desire that every dimension of the new heaven and the new earth may be brought to pass. As we pray for specific Kingdom concerns for our world—such as justice, peace, reconciliation, and wholeness—we should do so with words that anticipate a full breakthrough of

God's Kingdom. We should want all of what God wants, and be willing to say so—now!

Our prayers should express global-sized desires, especially as we see more of the plans of our global God. No matter what concerns we may bring to God in prayer, we need to be sure that we focus our praying on the whole Church and the whole world. Regarding desires for the whole Body of Christ, Edwards writes:

> Such being the state of things in this future promised glorious day of the church's prosperity, surely it is worth praying for. Nor is there any one thing whatsoever, if we viewed things aright, for which a regard to the glory of God, a concern for the Kingdom and honor of our Redeemer, a love to his people, pity to perishing sinners, love to our fellow creatures in general, compassion to mankind under their various and sore calamities and miseries, a desire of their temporal and spiritual prosperity, love to our country, our neighbors, and friends, yea, and to our own souls—would dispose us to be so much in prayer, as for the dawning of this happy day, and the accomplishment of this glorious event.[2]

Although people resist praying in generalities, due in part to our technological bent, we may be taught to pray in more specific analytical details. Most of us do need to learn how to pray meaningfully in generalities. We need to agree with God far more on the multiple sweeps of His plan no matter what the specifics may be. Again, those six weeks of prayer I spent with five men in my church in Kent in 1970 were more a time of reminding our Father and ourselves of the teachings in the book of Ephesians than it was praying in detail for every problem of our church. There is a direct correlation between our solidarity praying and the many blessings that have come from that church since.

If you study the great prayers of the Scripture, you will see that, in almost every case, the individual was aligning himself or herself and the people and situations, with the will of God. It is as if each one surveyed past ways and promises of God, took a sounding on what God was doing in the present, gained perspective on where He was headed in the future, and then asked, "How can we be joined with our Father in the past, present, and future of His will? And how can we show this by the way we pray?"

In the same way, we too must be careful not to push our own agenda on God. We must spend time, first of all, listening, waiting, learning from Him, conforming our agenda to His, and then with boldness and joy, coming to agreement. How do we listen and learn?

1. *Study the Scriptures.* In the Bible God reveals His will, and in our prayers He fulfills it. In Scripture we see God's character, His works, and His purposes; then we ask for His actions on the basis of what we see. As stated in *An Humble Attempt*: "For, undoubtedly, that which God abundantly makes the subject of his promises, God's people should abundantly make the subject of their prayers. It also affords them the strongest assurances that their prayers shall be successful."[3]

2. *Be aware of the ministry of the Spirit in your life.* He gave us God's Word and has come to us to represent God's Son in our lives. The Scriptures call us to "pray in the Spirit." The Holy Spirit *is* a praying spirit, and He longs to pray through us (Rom. 8:27; 1 Cor. 2:9-13; Gal. 4:6; Eph. 2:18; 6:17-18).

3. *Learn what God is doing today.* Match the hard facts against the reports of all He has done before. This will help you become better prepared to interpret what God desires to do, and you will become bolder in asking Him for it.

4. *Talk to others about what you want to say to the Father,* so that you can sharpen and balance one another. I am struck by how often in group prayer meetings we launch into one prayer after another, with only the briefest time to discuss our requests. How valuable to use a significant portion of time to determine what we can all agree on regarding a specific issue based on our knowledge of Scripture and of the situation. Then, after discussion and agreement, we can turn together to concerted prayer on the issue with full confidence.

This was the pattern in Acts 4 when the early Church stood up to persecution by united prayer. Luke tells us they were able to pray with one voice. How did a Church that size pray with such unity? A study of the prayer itself (4:24-30) shows that they took time to discuss both the Word and the situation before they spoke to God.

Here is a key point at which praise and thanksgiving assume prominence. In solidarity praying, praise becomes a critical expression of where we stand vis-à-vis the will of God. You will recall that one of the three approaches to fullness and fulfillment praying on the grid is "rejoice"—both praise and thanksgiving.

True intercession is itself an act of worship and praise. We are telling our Father how much His glory, desires, and purposes mean to us. We are saying that we are so committed to His Son that we want all He has to give of Himself to His church and to His world. Saint Anthony said: "We pray as much as we desire, we desire as much as we love." In solidarity praying we are cleaving to the Father in love (Ps. 91:14).

In praising God, we move beyond disappointment and into hope and joy. Since our natural inclination is to load the first thoughts of our prayers with "give me, help me, and do this for me," praise becomes a bold step of appropriating what we already have because of who God is and what He has promised. In praise, much of our unbelief and doubt will vanish away like mist before the rising sun. We need to live, said John R. Mott, "on the upmost limits of our faith, not on our doubts." Praise takes us there.

What are the upmost limits for you? Do you expect God to answer your prayers? Do you expect Him to do so with world-wide implications? Do you expect Him to take seriously your agreements with Him for spiritual awakening? Are you prepared to show Him such faith, even before you ask, with joy and praise to Him? Andrew Murray said, "And to the faith that knows it gets what it asks, prayer is not a work or a burden but a joy and a triumph; it becomes a necessity and a second nature."

Learning to pray in solidarity with the Father was Jesus' desire for us. When the disciples came to Him, asking Him to teach them how to pray, they weren't asking for an all-day seminar on prayer. "Teach us how to pray" meant: "Jesus, Master, we have watched you praying for the past two years, and we see how fully in line your prayers are with your Father. Teach us how to pray in a way that is fully in line with who you are and how you pray." Jesus gave them a solidarity prayer, often called the "Lord's Prayer." Not one that said, "Thy will be changed," but rather, "Thy will be done." "God is bound to answer every prayer that conforms to this pattern. Can our prayers be brought within the scope of this prayer? Then it is certain of answer, for the pattern is divinely given."[4]

The Lord's Prayer breaks down into two major parts. The first three requests deal with fulfillment concerns; the second three deal with fullness. Each of the leading verbs in the Greek are in the imperative, almost as if Jesus is giving us permission to command God. How can He do that? Because He knows that to pray along these lines is to be in total harmony with what God is already prepared to do.

Here is my own paraphrase of the Lord's Prayer which may help to draw together all we have learned so far in this section on solidarity:

*Fulfillment*

Our gracious Father, to whom all the resources and the eternal praises of heaven belong: reveal your glory so that all peoples may praise you!

Expand your Kingdom to the ends of the earth— let it break through with the gospel wherever it has never come before!

Fulfill your grand purpose of redemption for all the nations, and as you do this, we also ask . . .

*Fullness*

Provide us and your people around the world with the essentials we need to live and work with Christ in fulfilling His cause in our generation.

Preserve the circle of love that binds your people to yourself and to one another, here and around the world, so that we can more effectively move out in the critical challenge of loving those yet to be reached for Christ in every nation.

Empower us and your Church around the world to win over all opposition and all trials, so that your salvation may break through every barrier, especially those erected by the evil one himself.

intelligently targeted compassion. This is what Jesus had in mind in Matthew 9 when, out of His own compassion, He called His disciples to look clearly at the people in need, then to pray on behalf of those who could not or would not pray for themselves.

I saw this uniquely demonstrated by a Swedish mission society. In any new situation, their initial missionary strategy was to have their missionaries spend the first month on location—in an urban enclave, let's say—in prayer and fasting, advocating for those who had not yet heard of Christ. Throughout the month their schedule consisted of four major activities: (1) a periodic light meal and (2) sleep, (3) a few hours a day walking the streets looking on the faces of the people they had come to serve and greeting them, and then (4) returning to their room to spend hours together advocating for those they had seen. Not until 30 days later would they take up more direct work of service and evangelism.

Many of us, however, have never caught this strategy. A friend of mine recently had an experience that shows how often we lose sight of the importance of such advocacy. At a meeting of 3,000 pastors he noted, by the raising of their hands, that most had a number of members from their congregations who had secular employment in parts of the Muslim world. But when he asked how many pastors had groups in their churches regularly advocating on behalf of these witnesses for Christ and for their Muslim friends, as we might expect them to do for professional overseas missionaries, virtually none raised their hands. Their churches need to develop intelligently targeted compassion that matched their fruitfulness in sending out witnesses.

A model of intelligently targeted compassion is given to us by Daniel's prayer in Daniel 9. In it he goes over his situation with the Lord, almost like arguing his case in a divine courtroom on behalf of his people Israel, and on behalf of the nations who mock their disgrace. For us too, there may be no higher honor we bestow on God than to clearly and logically unfold our case for His Kingdom as it touches critical needs of the Church and the nations today. I have found *Operation World* and the *World Christian Encyclopedia* very helpful tools as I follow Daniel's model in my advocating. They almost function like a lawyer's brief for me.

Advocating prayers bear directly on the two-fold agenda for concerts. Take the fullness dimension of spiritual awakening for example. Scripture encourages us, not only to identify God's people and their needs but to advocate changes as God works in His Church. As we pray for fullness we need to be praying "for all of us," even if we are praying repentance prayers that may not seem to directly apply to actions we have taken. When God gives us insights into the needs of other Christians, He does not give them so that we might criticize them but so we might advocate on their behalf and ours.

We also need to advocate regarding the fulfillment of God's purposes among unbelievers. Have you ever supported someone who was helpless, who was depending on you to guide them, feed them, or run their errands? In the same way, we come to the aid of those who are spiritually helpless. Our prayers stand in the gap between unbelievers and the God who loves them as we intercede that they might see and understand clearly who Jesus is. Proverbs 31:8-9 says, "Speak up for those who cannot speak for themselves, for the rights of all who are destitute. Speak up and judge fairly; defend the rights of the poor and the needy." Prayer for those under God's judgment who cannot speak up for themselves is their greatest hope.

When Stanley Mooneyham wrote *What Do You Say to a Hungry World?* I thought advocacy in concerts of prayer: what do we say on behalf of a hungry world? If we are truly worried about those stripped of food, justice, and—most of all—the hope of eternal life, the most unreasonable thing we could ever do is to neglect to carefully discuss them with our Father and to take up their cause before His throne of grace.

## PURSUIT: PRESSING ON FOR A CHANGE

Not long ago David Wells stunned some of us with an article in *Christianity Today* titled, "Prayer: Rebellion Against the Status Quo." Did you ever think of prayer that way? As Jesus observed, the Kingdom of God forcefully advances as forceful men lay hold of it (see Matt. 11:12). Does this ever happen through prayer? If so, could we call such prayer rebellion? The answer is yes.

Out of the paces of solidarity and advocacy may come, on

some issues, a more intense tempo that feels and looks like one of rebellion. In these cases, God has assigned us the specific responsibility of pursuing Him relentlessly until His will is carried out in full. In so doing, we are saying to Him, "Father the time has come for you to act. There must be delay no longer. You have convinced us that you are ready. Accordingly, we will press on in prayer until you bring the change."

Maybe this is what some mean when they talk about having a burden in prayer. There are some issues under fullness and fulfillment that may burden an individual, or even a whole concert of prayer, and we are not able to shake them. Then it must be borne. Maybe this is what others mean by "the prayer of faith": God gives us the faith to believe that He is ready to move, so much so that we cannot stop asking Him to do it until it happens.

In any case, pursuing prayer is prayer on a mission. It is diligent, fervent, constant, persevering, determined, and convinced! This praying comes closest to the Greek words used for prayer in the New Testament that translate "to petition," "to beg," "to express with a cry." As Luther said of his house dog: "If only I could pray the way my dog looks at the morsel on my plate, all his thoughts concentrated on it."

Whenever George Müeller and his wife faced a persistent and frequent lack of resources to service the children in their orphanages, they moved into pursuing prayer:

> Would it have been right to charge God with unfaithfulness? Would it have been right to distrust Him? Would it have been right to say, it is useless to pray? By no means. This, on the contrary I did: I thanked God for all the help He had given me in connection with the whole of the enlargement; I thanked Him for enabling me to overcome so many and such great difficulties . . . instead of distrusting God, I looked upon this delay of the full answer to prayer, only as a trial of faith, and therefore resolved, that, instead of praying once a day . . . we should now meet daily three times, to bring this before God.[5]

Let me give you an illustration of this experience from my

own life. In 1980, my wife, Robyne, and I adopted an infant from South India. We had already agreed with God in solidarity that we wanted Him to bring forth His Kingdom among those who are beyond the reach of the gospel. Such praying drew us to care about the orphan children of India—we met some during our travels there. So, we began to advocate for this needy group.

In time, our Father brought to our attention little Adam and asked us to adopt him. The tempo picked up. Now we prayed daily for a little life whom we had been totally unaware of four weeks before. As the adoption procedures grew unexpectedly complicated, it became clear that Adam's journey out of Kerala, India and into Madison, Wisconsin was mined with frustrations and bureaucratic dead ends. Our praying quickly resembled pursuant prayer. We prayed: "Father, we know that you want this boy in our family. We believe the time has come for you to act. So we will pursue you for Adam's release until he has joined us in our home." Not only emotionally straining, it also became a crisis of confidence. In the fight of faith we "rebelled" against the Enemy, clothed with authority in the full armor of Christ. God won the victory, and we have a delightful Indian son in our home to prove it. A daughter from near Bombay also joined us later—again, after determined, pursuant prayer.

I have seen the same intensifying of pace and tempo on a particular issue in a concert of prayer movement. In fact, my most moving concert of pursuant prayer came as I listened to brothers and sisters from India. We had gathered for a week to plan strategies for the evangelization of their nation. On the last night we met, these leaders set aside all planning and work and suggested we lie prostrate on our faces in prayer. For the next three hours, I heard prayers such as I had never heard before. They prayed, "Father, what we've talked about all these days is really nothing new—we've discussed such strategies for hundreds of years. What we need is a movement of prayer for spiritual awakening in the life of the Indian Church, if the millions of our nation are to learn of Christ. We believe this is what you would like to do and, as a result, to bring all of India under the sound of the gospel before the close of this generation. We are no longer satisfied with things as they are. Father, pour out all you intend to do, for the time has come for you to act. And if the taking of any of our lives physically contributes to that end, we here tonight gladly give you our lives for Jesus' sake."

Have you ever heard anyone pray like that? That's pursuing prayer.

Prayer that pursues is, by other terms, prayer that "longs." In Romans 8, we are told that in the same way that creation groans to be set free, God's children groan for their resurrection bodies. Even so, the Spirit when He prays for God's purposes in creation and the Church to be fulfilled, does so with groanings that cannot be uttered. Sometimes, the same Holy Spirit leads us to pray for things we are convinced, for God's glory, we ourselves cannot live without. Our longing may be for His work among others in the Body of Christ or for a particular ministry to the world.

It is this kind of longing that John Knox revealed when he prayed, "Give me Scotland or I die!" Francis Zavier expressed it when he stood on the shores of China and cried, "O rock, rock, when wilt thou open to my Lord?" It is seen in the constant prayer of General William Booth, founder of the Salvation Army. Under persecution, facing the great needs of nineteenth-century England, but convinced from the God of the book of Acts that God was ready to move, he repeated over and over: "Do it again, Lord, do it again!"

### Prayer as Suffering

Pursuing prayer becomes a ministry of suffering. I begin to learn how to hurt and cry about the things that break God's heart. This may be the most significant experience any of us will have of fellowship in Christ's travails. The anguish we feel may go beyond words. Here is where fasting as well begins to make real sense. We may literally lose our appetites, or may want to use mealtime to pray.

It is necessary for all of us to ponder what it could cost us to get serious with the Father in concerted prayer. What we pray for we must also be ready to die for. In some ways, the praying may be the first phase in the laying down of our lives in some specific way for Christ's sake and the gospel's.

## Prayer as Renewal

There will be pursuant prayer toward the fullness dimension of spiritual awakening. On some issues we will cry out to God day and night, that He might deliver His elect (Luke 18:6-8). We will pray for God to lead a broken and helpless Church out of defeat and into victory for His Son.

## Prayer as Intercession

We will also pursue God on behalf of the nations. In pursuant prayer we reach the sharpest edge of front lines work in world evangelization. A friend of mine who took a tour of missionary work stations throughout the Muslim world returned with a startling revelation: wherever he found the gospel making inroads in Muslim communities, he found missionaries who were giving themselves to hours of intercessory prayer each day—pursuant prayer.

What might happen in your concert of prayer as God moves you toward pursuant prayer for the nations? He might lead you to "adopt" particular people groups that have yet to be reached for the gospel. This, in fact, was part of the strategy in prayer mobilization explored recently at the International Prayer Assembly in Korea. As your prayer concert learns solidarity and advocacy, you might find yourselves led by God's Spirit to believe, for example, that He was ready now to penetrate a Muslim refugee enclave in London with the gospel of Christ. What if your concert began to pursue the advancement of Christ's Kingdom in this situation with the same intensity it would pursue missionary work among the refugees if you were suddenly sent out as a team to work with them? Such has actually happened. What if God raised up hundreds of movements of prayer within our nation alone to focus in that way on specific unreached peoples? The potential is thrilling.

J.O. Fraser, missionary among the Lisu people in Burma, wrote back to his British prayer group and challenged them to move from advocating prayer to pursuant prayer. He said:

> I am not asking you just to give "help" in prayer
> as a sort of sideline, but I am trying to roll the main

responsibility of this prayer warfare on you. I want
you to take the burden of these people upon your
shoulders. I want you to wrestle with God for them.
I do not want so much to be a regimental commander
in this matter as an intelligence officer. I shall feel
more and more that a big responsibility rests upon
me to keep you well informed.[6]

Like a band on parade, your concert of prayer marches forth
in an aggressive ministry of intercession. The Leader, who has
struck up the band, may put you through different paces and different tempos at different times:

- Solidarity:  Agreeing with God. "Father, we want what you
  want."
- Advocacy:  Standing up for others. "Father, they need what
  you have."
- Pursuit:  Pressing on for a change. "Father, the time has
  come for you to act."

Your responsibility and mine is to be sure that we keep in
step, side by side, as our instruments blend together in one
great fanfare of victory.

Eventually, like a triumphal procession, the concert will bring
forth the sweet fragrance of Christ in spiritual awakening (2 Cor.
2). And it will become apparent that ultimately you paraded for
the sake of the world—you marched to the ends of the earth.

Did I just hear someone blow a whistle?

# Postscript

# TRY THE NEXT SEVEN YEARS, FOR A START!

Since we have referred to Edwards and his *An Humble Attempt* so often, let's end our book with another word of perspective and encouragement from this New England Puritan visionary.

To complete his call for prayer, Edwards presented his generation with a final challenge: Meet in monthly concerts of prayer on a sustained basis for seven years, he instructed. Then, pause to evaluate what God has done, to determine if you should keep on.

Seven years? In our "instant" society that may seem preposterous. After all, it is hard enough to convince most of us to be consistent on anything for seven weeks!

But Edwards was onto something that every concert of prayer must face. The Father may not choose to make spiritual awakening visible the very first time we pray for it. And for some time, despite our prayers, many peoples of earth remain cloistered in darkness.

We are not to be shaken by this, however. God has called us to be faithful in prayer, first of all. Christ's Kingdom will come. But we must rally to Him fully enough (Col. 1:18-20) that even though His global cause seems to advance painfully slow, we still do nothing less, in love for Him and each other, than to keep on praying—for fullness and fulfillment. That is what love demands. Edwards understood.

And yet we remain faithful in hope. Ultimately—even if it be after seven years—our united appeal to the Father will intensify and accelerate the Kingdom's coming. The morning will dawn for our generation. With healing power, Christ will reveal Himself grandly in the midst of His Church before the eyes of the nations as the hope of glory (Col. 1:27). To that end we must struggle in prayer with all the energy God gives us (Col. 1:28–2:3; 4:12).

Anyone out there besides Edwards want to join me in a concert of prayer? . . . for the next (gulp) seven years?

Where can you begin? Meeting 15 minutes a week with your closest friends is a good step. For those of us who are married, the starting place can be—should be—our spouses and families. If unity with our spouses is a guarantee that our prayers are effective (1 Pet. 3:7), then surely sharing a concert of prayer with them—even if only five minutes a day—is a proper path towards such unity.

The point is that we *must* begin. And the time has come. Gathering at the threshold remains our highest priority (1 Tim. 2:1-8).

# PACESETTERS
## Small Group Study Guide

Welcome, potential pacesetter! The term "pacesetter" comes from chapter 6. You may want to read it now to find out who you might become by the end of these studies of *Concerts of Prayer.*

The seven sessions are designed for those who think God might want them to help mobilize concerted prayer and need to talk it through with others. Ideally your group should consist of 5-8 potential pacesetters. The more you have the less time each has to participate in the discussions.

Each session lasts 90 minutes in order to achieve maximum discussion. The time suggestions below reflect the practicalness of this approach. Of course, the sessions can be explored in a variety of settings, such as during a weekly meeting, over seven Saturday morning gatherings, or in total throughout a single weekend retreat.

The discussion facilitator should be familiar with the book and this Study Guide before Session I begins. All group members, however, should have read the "Introduction" to the book before the first meeting.

Each 90-minute session contains the following segments:

I. *Prayer Passage* (15 min.). Read the assigned verses

and then discuss these 5 questions each time:

   a.  What prompted the prayer movement described here?

   b.  What can you learn about important characteristics of a prayer movement? Be specific.

   c.  What focus and impact did this prayer movement have on God's people?

   d.  What focus and impact did this prayer movement have on the nations?

   e.  What are two or three principles that you could apply from this passage to a united prayer movement today? Discuss either in terms of one in which you're involved, or one which you would like to encourage into being.

II.  *Prayer Time* (15 min.). In each session, begin your opening prayer time by quietly reviewing the list of possible prayer targets at the end of chapter 10. Each group member should select one issue for himself/herself under "Fullness" and under "Fulfillment." Then, spend the remainder of the 15 minutes praying over your selections. Pray as well in response to the passage and for the session itself.

III.  *Study* (50 min.). Questions are listed below for each session, with time suggestions for each period of discussion.

IV.  *Mini-Concert of Prayer* (10 min.). By using insights, challenges and visions generated in your study, fuel your united prayer for spiritual awakening and world evangelization.

V.  *Assignment.* Be sure to be faithful to the Lord and your group by thoughtfully reading the assigned chapters for the next session. If you do these sessions on a single weekend retreat, however, the whole book should be completed beforehand.

# SESSION I

*Prayer Passage:* Acts 1:1-14; 2:1-21 (15 min.)
*Prayer Time:* Fullness and Fulfillment (50 min.)
*Study of Introduction* (to be read beforehand) (50 min.)

1. What is your most positive experience with corporate prayer? Why was it so positive? (5 min.)
2. What is your most discouraging experience with corporate prayer? What could have made it more meaningful? (5 min.)
3. What do you hope to gain from these sessions for your personal prayer life? (3 min.)
4. In what ways do you hope to use your discoveries from these sessions to actively assist efforts at united prayer? (3 min.)
5. This book is about "concerts of prayer." The term stimulates musical imagery. Draw as many parallels from the world of music to united prayer as you can. For example: Jesus "conducts" us as we pray together. (3 min.)
6. How do these parallels suggest the possibility of new and exciting dimensions to prayer for you? (3 min.)
7. Take an overview of the "Contents" at the front of the book. Which chapter seems to fascinate you the most right now? Why? Which one looks most promising for you? (5 min.)
8. Read the covenant suggested on page 167. Can you imagine yourself being part of a prayer movement that captures the spirit of this covenant? If so, how might it differ from other prayer experiences you have had in the past? (9 min.)
9. Let's experiment with your current prayer life. What are the two most significant prayer requests you've focused on personally over the past month? Share one of them with the group. Then, determine how you would respond to this question: If God were to answer this one area to the fullest extent I could imagine possible—based on what He has said in His word and who I know Him to be—what might be the impact of that answer for Christ's global cause? (This helps to illustrate something of the unique focus of a concert of prayer.) Discuss your responses. Then ask: What if you

started to pray this way about everything, every day? What
if you were united with others who prayed the same way?
What differences might this make? (14 min.)

*Mini-Concert of Prayer* (10 min.)
*Assignment for Session II:* Read chapters 1 and 2.

# SESSION II

*Prayer Passage:* Psalm 102:1-22 (15 min.)
*Prayer Time:* Fullness and Fulfillment (15 min.)
*Study of Chapter 1 and 2* (50 min.)

1. In what ways do you sometimes feel like an "ordinary person"? How does David's opening parable give you new perspective on yourself? Do you have any hope that God might be willing to surprise you this way? Describe it (5 min.)
2. What evidences do you see around you of tremors that suggest we may be on the verge of a new shaking in the Church—of spiritual awakening? Be specific. (3 min.)
3. Read Richard Lovelace's statement on page 33. Do you agree? Why or why not? (3 min.)
4. Discuss your reactions to the five "theses" outlined on page 41. Where do you agree or disagree? If all of us could agree, what practical differences would that make for us or for the Church at large? (10 min.)
5. Suggest some differences and unique benefits which can be found in concerted (corporate) prayer over private prayer. Then discuss: Do you sense that today concerted prayer needs to be restored to its priority in the Church? Why or why not? (8 min.)
6. What do you understand to be the distinctives of a concert of prayer over other kinds of prayer experiences? Why would it be important to keep these distinctives in clear view? (10 min.)
7. In light of what God is doing to mobilize concerted prayer worldwide, what would be an important next step for you to take? For your study group to take? (11 min.)

*Mini-Concert of Prayer* (10 min.)
*Assignment for Session III:* Read chapters 3 and 4.

# SESSION III

*Prayer Passage:* Hosea 5:13–6:3; 14:1-9 (15 min.)
*Prayer Time:* Fullness and Fulfillment (15 min.)
*Study of Chapters 3 and 4* (50 min.)

1. Name a time in your own life when you felt yourself to be in the same discouraging position as the remnant group to whom God sent Zechariah. How did you handle it? How was your approach like or unlike the one envisioned in Zechariah 8? (5 min.)
2. Consider the four hallmarks of a united prayer movement—attitude, agenda, impact, ignition. Discuss: Do these seem comprehensive enough to you? Why or why not? Describe how you might expect them to unfold in your own situation (such as your church, campus fellowship, city or organization). Be specific. Then answer: Would God be willing to make this vision a reality in your situation? Why or why not? (10 min.)
3. How would you define "spiritual awakening"? Write out a two-three sentence definition using your own words. Then, share your definitions with one another. Discuss: How are your definitions similar? How do they differ? How do the differences help to round out each individual definition? (10 min.)
4. Now read the definitions provided in chapter 4 by J. Edwin Orr, Richard Lovelace and David Bryant. Discuss: How are they similar? How do they differ? How do the differences help to round out each individual definition? Finally: What do these three definitions add to the ideas your group compiled under question 3 above? What do your ideas add to *them*? (15 min.)
5. In light of all your discussions in this session, how convinced are *you* of the need for spiritual awakening in the Church today? If, in answer to a united prayer movement in which you participated, God were to grant spiritual awakening—what changes might that bring to your life? What changes

might it bring to your Christian group or fellowship?

*Mini-Concert of Prayer* (10 min.)
*Assignment for Session IV:* Read chapter 5.

# SESSION IV

*Prayer Passage:* 2 Chronicles 15 (15 min.)
*Prayer Time:* Fullness and Fulfillment (15 min.)
*Study of Chapter 5* (50 min.)

1. Define the word "hope." Describe the last time you had a personal experience of hope. (5 min.)
2. David outlines four good reasons why we should hope for and pray toward spiritual awakening: the divine pattern, the dark prospects, the disturbing paralysis and the dramatic preparations. Take each one separately. Spend 10 minutes discussing each one using the following questions:
   a. How would you summarize this reason in two or three sentences? Does it give us hope?
   b. What about it is still not clear to you? Where do you have questions on it?
   c. What additional evidences of it do you see, beyond what David describes?
   d. How might all of this change the way we pray individually and corporately?

3. What evidences do you see of these four reasons—pattern, prospects, paralysis, preparations *right around you*? What reasons do *you* have to hope for and pray toward spiritual awakening? (5 min.)

*Mini-Concert of Prayer* (10 min.)
*Assignment for Session V:* Read chapters 6 and 7.

# SESSION V

*Prayer Passage:* Joel 1:5-14; 2:11-25 (15 min.)
*Prayer Time:* Fullness and Fulfillment (15 min.)
*Study of Chapters 6 and 7* (50 min.)

1. Working together, draw up a list of as many synonyms (either words or phrases) as you can of the word "pacesetter." Then discuss: Is this a role you want to assume in an emerging God-given movement of united prayer? (5 min.)
2. Next discuss how ready you feel you are to assume a pacesetter's "statement of intent" similar in spirit to the one below:

   "By the grace of God, for Christ's glory and in the Spirit's strength, it is my wholehearted intention to encourage and assist concerted prayer for spiritual awakening and world evangelization in the Christian fellowship to which God sends me."

   Discuss: What appears possible for *you* in such a statement? What looks too overwhelming or challenging for you right now? How would you rewrite it to better express the role you believe God has given you at the moment? (10 min.)
3. How would you define the word "repentance"? What are areas where you need to repent as a step toward concerted prayer? What are areas where your Christian fellowship may need to do so? Be specific. (8 min.)
4. Do you believe the kind of unity in prayer about which David writes is really possible in your situation (fellowship, church, city, organization)? Why or why not? What is possible right now? Be specific. (8 min.)
5. How are you currently preparing yourself to be as fully involved in spiritual awakening and world evangelization as God will allow you? Does this preparation involve a daily discipline that reflects what you are praying for? Describe this for the group. What do you think of David's suggestions for a daily discipline? (8 min.)
6. In what ways do you see the steps of repentance, unity and

discipline to be important in anyone's attempts to help mobilize concerted prayer? What can you do to encourage such steps in your efforts at mobilizing prayer? (11 min.)

*Mini-Concert of Prayer* (10 min.)
*Assignment for Session VI:* Read chapters 8 and 9.

# SESSION VI

*Prayer Passage:* Acts 4:1-4, 23-31 (15 min.)
*Prayer Time:* Fullness and Fulfillment (15 min.)
*Study of Chapters 8 and 9* (50 min.)

1. In the past, what things have most discouraged you away from aggressive, consistent, personal prayer? Be specific. Do you know others who have experienced the same things? Describe why facing these issues yourself can help you mobilize others into concerted prayer. (8 min.)
2. David presents 15 principles for mobilizing concerted prayer. Discuss any eight of them very briefly, using these three questions: Does this principle look like it would work in your situation? Why or why not? If it does, what would be one important next step you could take to implement it? (15 min.)
3. Do you see any possibilities of forming a steering committee to help guide a united prayer movement in your area? If so, discuss briefly how it might happen. (5 min.)
4. Do you see any possibilities of sponsoring a consultation on concerted prayer in your area? If so, discuss briefly how it might happen. (5 min.)
5. Have you ever led a united prayer meeting before? If so, which ideas discussed in chapter 9 did you follow? Which ideas do you *wish* you had known? Discuss one or two ideas apiece, and do so briefly. (10 min.)
6. What do you think of the Concert of Prayer format suggested on page 173: How would you like to alter it to more effectively fit your situation or your group? (5 min.)
7. As this session closes, do you feel better equipped to become a pacesetter? (2 min.)

*Mini-Concert of Prayer* (10 min.)
*Assignment for Session VII:* Read chapters 10 and 11 and "Postscript."

# SESSION VII

*Prayer Passage:* Luke 11:1-13 (15 min.)
*Prayer Time:* Fullness and Fulfillment (15 min.)
*Study of Chapters 10 and 11 and "Postscript"* (50 min.)

1. What are additional issues your study group could add to the preliminary listing David provides in chapter 10 under the heading "Fullness"? And also, under "Fulfillment"? As a group, try to come up with 3-4 additional issues under each heading. (8 min.)
2. How have you personally experienced the three paces in intercession outlined by David in chapter 11? Be specific. Have you experienced them more in praying for fullness issues or fulfillment issues? Why is this? In what ways do you sense any need for growth in this area? (10 min.)
3. What difference could it make during a time of concerted prayer if each of us were able to recognize these three paces and how they work together? How might our ministry of corporate intercession become more effective? (5 min.)
4. As we end these seven study sessions, what do you sense to be the most strategic next step you could take individually? What might be steps two and three? (10 min.)
5. Do you sense that God has any assignment for your study group to carry out together in response to all you've explored in these sessions? If so, what? If so, when? If so, how? If so, why? (17 min.)

*Mini-Concert of Prayer* (10 min.)
*Post-Study Assignment:* Look over the Appendices and Bibliography. Then do the next thing God shows you to do!

# AGENDA
# FOR
# CONSULTATION ON
# CONCERTS OF PRAYER

(Place)

(Date)

(Time)

This is what the Lord Almighty says: "Many peoples and the inhabitants of many cities will yet come, and the inhabitants of one city will go to another and say, 'Let us go at once to entreat the Lord and seek the Lord Almighty. I myself am going.' In those days ten from all languages and nations will take firm hold of one Jew by the edge of his robe and say, 'Let us go with you, because we have heard that God is with you.'"

—Zechariah 8:20-23

## Introduction

Welcome . . . . . . . . . . . . . . . . . . . . . . . . . . . . . . . . . .5 minutes
Scripture Reading . . . . . . . . . . . . . . . . . . . . . . . .5 minutes
United Hymn and Prayer Time . . . . . . . . . . . . .15 minutes

Overview of the Consultation: Purpose and Agenda . . 5 minutes
Introductions of Consultation Participants . . . . . . . . .15 minutes
Case Studies of Current Prayer Movements . . . . . . .45 minutes

## Discussion of the Three Proposals

Presentation of *Proposal #1*—"A Call for Concerts of Prayer" . . . . . . . . . . . . . . . . . . . . . . . . . . . . . . . . . . . . . . .10 min.
Discussion of Proposal #1—What are the needs and opportunities for Concerts of Prayer? . . . . . . . . . . . . . . . . . .35 min.

Presentation of *Proposal #2*—"A Strategy for Mobilizing Concerts of Prayer" . . . . . . . . . . . . . . . . . . . . . . . . . . . .10 min.

Discussion of Proposal #2—What is the best approach for mobilizing Concerts of Prayer? . . . . . . . . . . . . . . . . . . . .50 min.

Break for Lunch . . . . . . . . . . . . . . . . . . . . . . . . . . . . . . . .50 min.

Presentation of *Proposal #3*—"A Cooperative Plan of Action for Concerts of Prayer" . . . . . . . . . . . . . . . . . . . . . . . .15 min.
Discussion of Proposal #3—How can we cooperate in practical terms to co-sponsor and assist local Concerts of Prayer? . . . . . . . . . . . . . . . . . . . . . . . . . . . . . . . . . . . . .75 min.

Break . . . . . . . . . . . . . . . . . . . . . . . . . . . . . . . . . . . . . . . . .15 min.

## Forming a Cooperative Plan of Action

Summary of discussions on Proposals 1,2,3 . . . . . . . . . .10 min.
Discussion: Where do we have consensus for a plan of action? . . . . . . . . . . . . . . . . . . . . . . . . . . . . . . . . . . . . . .60 min.
    * On a time frame for coordinating Concerts?
    * On an approach toward co-sponsorship of local

    Concerts?
 * On an approach toward cooperative assistance of
   local Concerts?

 * On ways to measure the quality and impact of local
   Concerts?

 * On a *facilitating* body (such as a steering committee)?
 * On immediate steps following this Consultation?

Statement of Action: Confirmation of a joint committee to a
    cooperative plan of action.....................30 min.


## Conclusion

Mini-Concert of Prayer ...........................30 min.
Depart to fulfill our commitments

# WORKING PROPOSALS FOR CONSULTATION

Based on our common vision for and commitment to united prayer for spiritual awakening and world evangelization, the following three proposals are set forth:

**PROPOSAL ONE—A Call for Concerts of Prayer**
In view of the great needs facing the Church internally, for revival and awakening;

And, in view of the great needs facing the Church externally, for the evangelization of the world and the worldwide advancement of Christ's Kingdom;

And, in view of the unprecedented opportunities calling the Church to seek Christ's fullness in our life together, for the fulfillment of His global mission;

And, recognizing that the prelude to and sustaining foundation for a new work of God in the Church is united prayer for spiritual awakening and world evangelization;

And, borrowing from history a term used to describe similar movements of united prayer during previous spiritual awakenings (Concerts of Prayer);

*it is proposed* that we here this day commit ourselves as Christian leaders to one another and the Church, to call for and to help mobilize local concerts of prayer for spiritual awakening and world evangelization.

**PROPOSAL TWO—A Strategy for Mobilizing Concerts of Prayer**
Based on our commitment to call for and assist Concerts of Prayer within the Church in our nation;

And, drawing from the praying constituents of national organizations and ministries within the three major spheres of churches, students and mission;

And, looking to local prayer leadership and prayer movements to

help steer and galvanize these praying people into grass-
roots efforts at Concerts of Prayer;

*it is proposed* that we here this day, as Christian leaders, cooperate in encouraging and serving our praying people by endorsing
and co-sponsoring local concerts of prayer. Linking with local
prayer leaders, we will assist our praying people into concerts of
prayer within our own community.

## PROPOSAL THREE—A Cooperative Plan of Action for Concerts of Prayer

Rising from consensus on the call for Concerts of Prayer (Proposal 1) and the strategy for mobilizing Concerts of Prayer (Proposal 2), *it is proposed* that we here as Christian leaders take
immediate steps toward co-sponsorship of local Concerts of
Prayer over the next two years. To be more precise, *it is proposed:*

1. That between (date) and (date), (total number) jointly-
sponsored concerts of prayer for spiritual awakening and world
evangelization be initiated and assisted where local prayer leadership is already evident.

2. That the movement of prayer be developed in at least four
phases:

* Concert of Prayer *endorsement*: local leaders and organiza-
    tions in the major spheres of churches, students and mis-
    sions make direct contact with their praying constituents,
    explaining the concert of prayer strategy and encouraging
    them to become part of a concert of prayer in their com-
    munity.

* Concert of Prayer *event*: Leaders and organizations in the
    major spheres of churches, students and mission coordi-
    nate with local prayer leaders and prayer committees to
    draw together their praying constituents into one initial
    concert of prayer within their own community.

* Concert of Prayer *movement*: As a result of the endorsements
    and rising from the event, on-going, community-wide con-
    certs of prayer emerge under the leadership of a local,
    trans-denominational steering committee, in cooperation
    with the mobilizing efforts of leaders and organizations
    from the three major spheres.

* Concert of Prayer *nurture*: In counsel with leaders and endorsing organizations in the three major spheres, the local steering committee work to sharpen, encourage, strengthen and expand the community-wide concert of prayer.

3. That, where appropriate, every effort be made to expand the base of supportive, co-sponsoring individuals and organizations.

4. That commitment and accountability for the concerts be kept primarily under the guidance of the local steering committee.

5. That evaluation of the concert of prayer movement be made by sponsoring groups, determining the impact on their own internal objectives with respect to spiritual awakening and world outreach. This should be done at specific checkpoints culminating in a major evaluation by (date), possibly through another community-wide consultation.

6. That helpful contact should be made with the National Prayer Committee (address below) which may suggest resources, facilitate some training, and provide information on the prayer movement nationwide.

---

For further help on such a consultation, write to:

> National Prayer Committee
> Concert of Prayer Project
> 233 Langdon Street
> Madison, WI 53703

A sample copy of a camera-ready "Invitation to a Concert of Prayer" is also available from the above address.

# A CALL TO PRAYER
# FOR SPIRITUAL AWAKENING AND
# WORLD EVANGELIZATION
# FROM THE 1984 INTERNATIONAL
# PRAYER ASSEMBLY, SEOUL, KOREA

God, in His Providence, has brought us together in Seoul, Korea, from 69 nations. We have sought His face and His guidance. He has impressed on us an urgent desire to call for an international prayer movement for spiritual awakening and world evangelization.

## Theological Basis

World evangelization is a sovereign work of the triune God through the ministry of Christ's church. The forces of darkness which block the spread of truth and the growth of the church cannot be displaced by human plans and efforts. Only the omnipotent Holy Spirit, applying the fruits of the finished work of Christ through a church constantly awakened through prayer, can deliver the lost from the power of Satan (Acts 26:17-18), as "the Lord adds daily those who are being saved" (Acts 4:47).

The awakening of the church is thus essential to the completion of world evangelization. The renewed church in Acts 2:42-47 was strengthened by apostolic teaching, by the Lord's Supper and by sharing fellowship. But these means of grace can only be empowered for us today through fervent and persistent prayer to the Father in the name of the crucified and risen Christ. Even after Pentecost, the apostles repeatedly returned to prayer for the church to be filled afresh with the Spirit and empowered to proclaim the Gospel with boldness, despite satanic resistance (Acts 4:23-31).

Prayer is God's appointed means through which the Spirit's power is released in evangelism. By prayer, the Spirit both empowers our witness and opens the blinded minds of unbelievers to seek and desire the Lord Jesus Christ as Savior. Our strong encouragement in believing prayer is our Lord's promise that He will answer us if we ask according to His will and in His name.

Before the Lord's return to judge all satanic rebellion and to consummate His Kingdom in power and glory, the Gospel must and will be preached, and disciples made, among every people on earth (Matt. 24:14; 28:19,20; Mark 13:10). Explicit agreement and visible union of God's people in extraordinary prayer for the awakening of the church and world evangelization is essential for the extension of the Kingdom of Christ through the preaching of the Gospel.

## Call to Prayer

We rejoice that in the last few years, in many parts of the world, the Holy Spirit has instilled a growing dependence on God, leading to increased unity in prayer within the Body of Christ, transcending denominational, national, ethnic and cultural divisions.

We confess that too often prayer is offered only for personal physical and financial needs, rather than for spiritual and material needs in the church, neighborhood and world.

We confess that frequently there is a lack of meaningful prayer by the congregation in services of the local church, as well as a general lack of personal and family prayer.

We confess that there is not enough emphasis on, training for, and dependence upon prayer from the pulpits, and in institutions training Christian workers.

We confess that too often dependence upon the Holy Spirit's role in prayer has been minimized, and mobilization of prayer has been without reliance upon Him.

We are constrained to call the Body of Christ worldwide to mobilize intercession for spiritual awakening in the church and world evangelization. We call specifically for:

1. The formation of interdenominational prayer committees, whenever possible through existing structures, on city, national, regional, continental and international levels.
2. The convening of national, regional, continental and international prayer assemblies as soon as this can adequately be implemented, and thereafter at regular intervals.

3. The establishing of information networks through personal visitation, literature, computer linkages, audio-visual media, and other means for the communication of prayer needs, emergencies, methods, reports of prayer movements worldwide, and prayer ministry resources.

4. The promotion of nurture and teaching on prayer life through seminars, workshops, literature and audio-visuals.

5. The encouragement of churches, theological seminaries, Christian institutions, para-church organizations, Christian leaders and pastors to give the highest priority and strongest emphasis to prayer, both in personal life and ministry.

6. Cooperation and participation of the church worldwide in the observance of specifically designated days of prayer.

We therefore call all believers to a specific and personal commitment to become prayer warriors for spiritual awakening and world evangelization.

---

For further information on the Lausanne Committee's Intercession Advisory Group or the International Prayer Assembly follow-up, contact the:

National Prayer Committee
Concert of Prayer Project
233 Langdon Street
Madison, WI 53703

# NOTES

## Introduction

1. J. Edwin Orr, *The Eager Feet: Evangelical Awakenings 1790-1830*, (Chicago: Moody Press, 1975), p. 95. Used by permission.

## Chapter 1

1. Lewis B. Smedes, "Preaching to Ordinary People" *Leadership*, (Fall, 1983), p. 115.
2. Ibid., p. 116 (italics added).
3. John Naisbitt, *Megatrends: Ten New Directions Transforming Our Lives*, (New York: Warner Books, Inc., 1982), p. 252. Used by permission.
4. Kenneth Scott Latourette, *A History of Christianity*, (New York: Harper and Row Publishers, Inc., 1953), no pg. number.
5. Samuel Shoemaker, *With the Holy Spirit and with Fire*, (Waco, TX: Word, Inc., 1973), p. 10.
6. James Newby, "Bruce Larson: Church Dreamer and Architect" *Eternity*, (October, 1983), p. 22.
7. Richard Lovelace, *Dynamics of Spiritual Life*, (Downers Grove, IL: Inter-Varsity Press, 1979), p. 425 (italics added). Used by permission.

## Chapter 2

1. O. Hallesby, *Prayer*, (Minneapolis: Augsburg Publishing House, 1975), p. 159.
2. Andrew Murray and Leona Choy, *Key to the Missionary Problem*, (Ft. Washington, PA: Christian Literature Crusade, Inc., 1980), no pg. number.
3. Lausanne Committee for World Evangelization, *Evangelism and Social*

*Responsibility,* Occasional Paper #21, 1981, p. 49.
4. George Peters, *Evangelical Missions Tomorrow,* (Pasadena, CA: William Carey Library Publications, 1977), p. 150-151 (italics added).
5. William Bright, "Interview" *Worldwide Challenge,* January, 1983, p. 8. Used by permission. Copyright Campus Crusade for Christ, Inc.


**Chapter 3**
1. Jonathan Edwards, *An Humble Attempt to Promote Explicit Agreement and Visible Union of God's People in Extraordinary Prayer for the Revival of Religion and the Advancement of Christ's Kingdom on Earth* in *The Words of President Edwards,* (New York: Princeton University Press, 1844).


**Chapter 4**
1. Ian Murray, *The Puritan Hope,* (Carlisle, PA: The Banner of Truth, 1971), p. 237-238. Used by permission.
2. Orr, *The Eager Feet,* p. 248 (italics added). Used by permission.
3. Lovelace, *Dynamics of Spiritual Life,* p. 21-22 (italics added). Used by permission.
4. Jonathan Edwards, *News Sheet #150,* Revival Prayer Fellowship.
5. Duncan Campbell, *News Sheet #149,* Revival Prayer Fellowship.
6. R.J. Lucas, *Fullness and Freedom,* (Downers Grove, IL: Inter-Varsity Press, 1983), p. 107. Used by permission.
7. Mark A. Noll and Nathan O. Hatch, *Eerdmans Handbook to Christianity in America,* (Grand Rapids: Wm. B. Eerdmans Publishing Co., 1983), p. 101.


**Chapter 5**
1. Lovelace, *Dynamics of Spiritual Life,* p. 367. Used by permission.
2. J. Edwin Orr, *The Fervent Prayer: The Worldwide Impact of the Great Awakenings of 1858,* (Chicago: Moody Press, 1974), p. 193. Used by permission.
3. Elton Trueblood, *The Incendiary Fellowship,* (New York: Harper and Row Publishers, Inc., 1978), p. 100.
4. Lausanne Committee for World Evangelization, *Occasional Paper #2: The Gospel and Culture,* p. 14.
5. Richard Halverson, "On the Threshold of Something Wonderful" *Eternity,* (March, 1984), p. 24-26.
6. Kenneth Kantzer, "Reflections: Five Years of Change" *Christianity Today,* (November 26, 1982), p. 13.
7. John White, *Flirting with the World: A Challenge to Loyalty,* (Wheaton, IL: Harold Shaw Publications, 1982), p. 142.
8. A.W. Tozer, *The Pursuit of God,* (Camp Hill, PA: Christian Publications, Inc., n.d.), p. 8. Used by permission.


**Chapter 6**
1. Lewis Drummond, *The Awakening That Must Come,* (Nashville: Broadman Press, 1978), p. 122. All rights reserved. Used by permission.

**Chapter 7**
1. John C. Miller, *Repentance and the Twentieth Century Man,* (Ft. Washington, PA: Christian Literature Crusade, Inc., 1980), p. 52.
2. Donald W. Dayton, "Engaging the World" *Sojourners,* (March, 1984), p. 19.
3. John R.W. Stott, "World Evangelization: Signs of Convergence and Divergence in Christian Understanding," *Third Way* (December 1, 1977). Used by permission.
4. Edwards, *An Humble Attempt,* no pg. number.

**Chapter 8**
1. Marie Monson, *The Awakening,* (Robesonia, PA: OMF Books, n.d.), p. 129. Used by permission.
2. For more help with this and all facets of prayer mobilization, contact the National Prayer Committee, Concert of Prayer Project, 233 Langdon St., Madison, Wisconsin, 53703. They have a wealth of personnel and resources on which to draw.
3. Edwards, *An Humble Attempt,* no pg. number.

**Chapter 9**
Another format that could be just as effective, though quite different from that given in this chapter, goes like this: Divide the two hours into equal segments of thirty minutes each. At the beginning of each half-hour segment someone presents a ten-minute exhortation on a general issue the steering committee feels must be addressed in that particular concert. After the ten-minute exhortation, the group proceeds to pray during the remaining twenty minutes. Then the next exhortation is given, and another twenty minutes of prayer follows, and so on throughout the two-hour period. Be sure to keep the exhortations biblically based and clear on the current situation. If your steering committee feels comfortable in giving leadership in this way, I strongly urge you to try it.

**Chapter 11**
1. John R.W. Stott, *Christian Counter-Culture,* (Downers Grove, IL: InterVarsity Press, 1978), p. 170. Used by permission.
2. Edwards, *An Humble Attempt,* no pg. number.
3. Ibid.
4. J. Oswald Sanders, *Prayer Power Unlimited* (Chicago: Moody Press, 1977), p. 107. Used by permission.
5. George Müeller, *Answers to Prayer,* (Chicago: Moody Press, n.d.), p. 49 (italics added). Used by permission.
6. J.O. Fraser and Mary E. Allbutt, eds., *Prayer of Faith,* (Robesonia, PA: OMF Books, n.d.), no pg. number. Used by permission.

# SELECTED BIBLIOGRAPHY

*Note:* Most books suggested here were consulted in the preparation of this book. They represent a broad range of evangelical and secular perspectives. Each offers you some of the very best research and analyses available on the specific topics under which they are listed.

They are arranged under the four main reasons to pray for and expect spiritual awakening and under a fifth topic: prayer. Works that fall under more than one topic have been placed where their primary attention is focused.

You are encouraged to continue exploring the issues raised in this book by dipping into some of these titles. This will help to sharpen the vision of your own concert of prayer.

## Paralysis

Christopher, Salley, and Behm, Ronald. *What Color Is Your God? Black Consciousness and the Christian Faith.* Downers Grove, IL: Inter-Varsity Press, 1981.

Guiness, Os. *The Gravedigger File.* Downers Grove, IL: Inter-Varsity Press, 1983.

Hatch, Nathan O., Noll, Mark A., Woodbridge, John D. *The Gospel in America.* Grand Rapids: Zondervan Publishing House, 1982.

Hubbard, David A. *Right Living in a World Gone Wrong.* Downers

Grove, IL: Inter-Varsity Press, 1981.

Johnston, Jon. *Will Evangelism Survive Its Own Popularity?* Grand Rapids: Zondervan Publishing House, 1980.

Krass, Alfred C. *Evangelizing Neopagan North America.* Scottdale, PA: Herald Press, 1982.

Linder, Robert D., and Pierard, Richard V. *Twilight of the Saints: Biblical Christianity and Civil Religion in America.* Downers Grove, IL: Inter-Varsity Press, 1977.

Perkins, John. *With Justice for All.* Ventura, CA: Regal Books, 1982.

Schaeffer, Francis. *Church at the End of the Twentieth Century.* Downers Grove, IL: Inter-Varsity Press, 1970.

————. *The Great Evangelical Disaster.* Westchester, IL: Crossway Books, 1984.

Schaeffer, Franky. *A Time for Anger.* Westchester, IL: Crossway Books, 1982.

Snyder, Howard A. *The Community of the King.* Downers Grove, IL: Inter-Varsity Press, 1977.

————. *The Problem of Wineskins: Church Renewal in the Technological Age.* Downers Grove, IL: Inter-Varsity Press, 1975.

Wallis, Jim. *Agenda for Biblical People.* New York: Harper and Row Publications, Inc., 1976.

————. *The Call to Conversion: Recovering the Gospel for These Times.* New York: Harper and Row Publications, Inc., 1983.

————. *Revive Us Again: A Sojourner's Story.* Nashville: Abingdon Press, 1983.

White, John. *Flirting with the World: A Challenge to Loyalty.* Wheaton, IL: Harold Shaw Publications, 1982.

————. *The Golden Cow: Materialism in the Twentieth-Century Church.* Downers Grove, IL: Inter-Varsity Press, 1979.

Yankelovich, Daniel. *New Rules.* New York: Bantam Books, Inc., 1982.

## Pattern

Berkhof, Hendrik. *Christ and the Powers.* Scottdale, PA: Herald Press, 1962.

Billheimer, Paul. *Love Covers.* Fort Washington, PA: Christian Literature Crusade, Inc., 1981.

Baluw, Johannes. *The Missionary Nature of the Church.* New York: McGraw-Hill Book Co., 1962.

Curnock, Nehemiah. *The Journal of John Wesley* (abridged). New York: Capricorn Books, 1963.

Dallimore, Arnold A. George Whitefield: *The Life and Times of the Great Evangelist of the Eighteenth Century Revival,* vol. 1 and vol. 2. Westchester, IL: Good News Publications, 1980.

Drummond, Lewis A. *The Awakening That Must Come.* Nashville: Broadman Press, 1978.

Edman, V. Raymond, ed. *Crisis Experiences.* Minneapolis: Bethany House Publications, n.d.

Edwards, Jonathan. *An Humble Attempt to Promote Explicit Agreement and Visible Union of God's People in Extraordinary Prayer for the Revival of Religion and the Advancement of Christ's Kingdom on Earth,* in *The Words of President Edwards,* 4 volumes. New York: 1844. Billy Graham Center Archives.

Finney, Charles. *Reflections on Revival.* Minneapolis: Bethany House Publications, 1979.

Gardner, John W. *Self-Renewal.* Rev. ed. New York: W.W. Norton & Co., Inc., 1981.

Glasser, Arthur F. and McGavran, Donald A. *Contemporary Theologies of Mission.* Grand Rapids: Baker Book House, 1983.

Goerner, H. Cornell. *All Nations in God's Purpose.* Nashville: Broadman Press, 1979.

Green, Michael. *I Believe in Satan's Downfall.* Grand Rapids: Wm. B. Eerdmans Publishing Co., 1981.

Griffiths, Michael C. *Who Really Sends the Missionary?* Chicago: Moody Press, 1972.

Hasler, Richard. *Journey with David Brainerd.* Downers Grove, IL: Inter-Varsity Press, 1981.

Hatch, Nathan O., Noll, Mark A., and Woodbridge, John D. *The Gospel in America—Themes in the Story of America's Evangelicals.* Grand Rapids: Zondervan Publishing House, 1979.

Hefley, James and Hefley, Marti. *By Their Blood: Christian Martyrs of the Twentieth Century.* Milford, MI: Mott Media, 1979.

Hershberger, Guy F., ed. *The Recovery of the Anabaptist Vision.* Scottdale, PA: Herald Press, 1957.

Hopkins, Howard. *John R. Mott: 1865-1955.* Grand Rapids: Wm. B. Eerdmans Publishing Co., 1980.

Jones, E. Stanley. *The Unshakeable Kingdom and the Unchanging Person.* Nashville: Abingdon Press, 1972.

Latourette, Kenneth S. *A History of Christianity.* New York: Harper and Row Publications, Inc., 1975.

Lovelace, Richard F. *Dynamics of Spiritual Life.* Downers Grove, IL: Inter-Varsity Press, 1979.

Lowman, Pete. *The Day of His Power.* Downers Grove, IL: Inter-Varsity Press, 1983.

Lucas, R.J., edited by Motyer, J.A. and Stott, J.R. *Fullness and Freedom.* Bible Speaks Today Series. Downers Grove, IL: Inter-Varsity Press, 1980.

Lyrene, Edward C., Jr. *Jonathan Edwards and the Concert of Prayer.* Unpublished graduate paper of Louisville Seminary: 1983.

McGavran, Donald. *Understanding Church Growth.* Rev. ed. Grand Rapids: Wm. B. Eerdmans Publishing Co., 1980.

McLoughlin, William G. *Revivals, Awakenings, and Reform: An Essay on Religion and Social Change in America, 1607 to 1977.* Chicago: University of Chicago Press, 1980.

Mallone, George H. *Furnace of Renewal: A Vision for the Church.* Downers Grove, IL: Inter-Varsity Press, 1981.

McQuilkin, Robertson. *The Great Omission.* Grand Rapids: Baker Book House, 1984.

Mellis, Charles J. *Committed Communities: Fresh Streams for World Missions.* Pasadena, CA: William Carey Library Publications, 1976.

Miller, C. John. *Repentance and the Twentieth Century Man.* Ft. Washington, PA: Christian Literature Crusade, Inc., 1980.

Monson, Marie. *The Awakening.* London: Lutterworth Press, 1959.

Murray, Iain H. *The Puritan Hope.* Carlisle, PA: The Banner of Truth, 1957.

Neill, Stephen. *A History of Christian Missions.* New York: Penguin Books, 1964.

Noll, Mark A., Hatch, Nathan O., eds. *Eerdmans' Handbook to Christianity in America.* Grand Rapids: Wm. B. Eerdmans Publishing Co., 1983.

Orr, J. Edwin. *Campus Aflame: Dynamic of Student Religious Revolution.* Ventura, CA: Regal Books, 1971.

_____ . *The Eager Feet: Evangelical Awakenings 1790-1830.* Chicago: Moody Press, 1975.

_____ . The Fervent Prayer: *The Worldwide Impact of the Great Awakenings of 1858.* Chicago: Moody Press, 1974.

_____ . *The Flaming Tongue: The Impact of 20th Century Revivals.* Chicago: Moody Press, 1973.

Roberts, Richard. *Revival.* Wheaton, IL: Tyndale House Publications, 1982.

Ryle, J.C. *Christian Leaders of the Eighteenth Century: Includes Whitefield, Wesley, Grimshaw, Romaine, Rowlands, Berridge, Venn, Walker, Harvey, Toplady and Fletcher.* Carlisle, PA: The Banner of

Schaeffer, Francis. *True Spirituality.* Wheaton, IL: Tyndale, 1971.

Shoemaker, Samuel M. *With the Holy Spirit and with Fire.* Waco, TX: Word, Inc., 1973.

Smith, Timothy. *Revivalism and Social Reform: American Protestantism on the Eve of the Civil War.* Baltimore: Johns Hopkins University Press, 1980.

Snyder, Howard. *The Radical Wesley.* Downers Grove, IL: Inter-Varsity Press, 1980.

Stott, John R. *Christian Mission in the Modern World.* Downers Grove, IL: Inter-Varsity Press, 1976.

Tozer, Aiden W. *The Pursuit of God.* Harrisburg, PA: Christian Publications, Inc., n.d.

Trueblood, Elton. *The Validity of the Christian Mission.* New York: Harper and Row Publications, Inc., 1972.

Tucker, Ruth A. *From Jerusalem to Irian Jaya.* Grand Rapids: Zondervan Publishing House, 1983.

Waren, Max. *I Believe in the Great Commission.* Grand Rapids: Wm. B. Eerdmans Publishing Co., 1976.

Whitefield, George. *George Whitefield's Journals.* Carlisle, PA: The Banner of Truth, 1978.

## Prayer

Baughen, Michael. *Breaking the Prayer Barrier: Getting Through to God.* Wheaton, IL: Harold Shaw Publications, 1981.

Bennett, Arthur, ed. *The Valley of Vision: A Collection of Puritan Prayers and Devotions.* Carlisle, PA: The Banner of Truth, 1975.

Bisagno, John. *The Power of Positive Praying.* Grand Rapids: Zondervan Publishing House, 1965.

Blaiklock, E.M. *The Positive Power of Prayer.* Ventura, CA: Regal, 1974.

Bounds, E.M. *The Essentials of Prayer.* Grand Rapids: Baker Book House, Direction Books, 1979.

————. *The Necessity of Prayer.* Grand Rapids: Baker Book House, Direction Books, 1976.

————. *The Possibilities of Prayer.* Grand Rapids: Baker Book House, Direction Books, 1979.

————. *Power Through Prayer.* Springdale, PA: Whitaker House, 1983.

————. *Prayer and Praying Men.* Grand Rapids: Baker Book

House, Direction Books, 1977.

———. *Purpose in Prayer.* Grand Rapids: Baker Book House, Direction Books, 1978.

———. *The Reality of Prayer.* Grand Rapids: Baker Book House, Direction Books, 1978.

———. *The Weapon of Prayer.* Grand Rapids: Baker Book House, Direction Books, 1975.

Chadwick, Samuel. *The Path of Prayer.* Fort Washington, PA: Christian Literature Crusade, Inc., 1963.

Christenson, Evelyn and Blake, Viola. *What Happens When Women Pray.* Wheaton, IL: Victor Books, 1975.

Dunnam, Maxie D. *The Workbook of Intercessory Prayer.* Nashville: The Upper Room, 1979.

Eastman, Dick. *The Hour that Changes the World.* Grand Rapids: Baker Book House, Direction Books, 1980.

———. *No Easy Road. Inspirational Thoughts on Prayer.* Rev. ed. Grand Rapids: Baker Book House, Direction Books, 1971.

Ellul, Jacques. *Prayer and the Modern Man.* New York: Seabury Press, Inc., 1973.

Everett, M. and Davis, Linda. *Prayer for Those Who Influence Your Family.* San Bernardino, CA: Campus Crusade for Christ International, 1980.

Finney, Charles G. *Prevailing Prayer.* Grand Rapids: Kregel Publications, 1975.

Getz, Gene. *Praying for One Another.* Wheaton, IL: Victor Books, 1982.

Goforth, Rosalind. *How I Know God Answers Prayer.* Chicago: Moody Press, n.d.

Goodwin, Thomas. *The Return of Prayers.* Grand Rapids: Baker Book House, Summit Books, 1979.

Gordon. S.D. *What It Will Take to Change the World.* Grand Rapids: Baker Book House, Direction Books, n.d.

Grubb, Norman P. *Rees Howells: Intercessor.* Ft. Washington, PA: Christian Literature Crusade, Inc., 1967.

Hallesby, O. *Prayer.* Minneapolis: Augsburg Publishing House, 1975.

Harvey, Edwin and Harvey, Lillian. *Kneeling We Triumph.* Chicago: Moody Press, 1974.

Hayford, Jack. *Prayer Is Invading the Impossible.* South Plainfield, NJ: Bridge Publishing Co., 1977.

Hubbard, David A. *The Practice of Prayer.* Downers Grove, IL: Inter-Varsity Press, 1983.

————— . *The Problem with Prayer Is.* Wheaton, IL: Tyndale House Publications, 1972.

Johnston, Russ and Rank, Maureen. *Dynamic Praying for Exciting Results.* Wheaton, IL: Tyndale House Publications, 1982.

Johnstone, Patrick J. *Operation World: A Handbook for World Intercession.* Midland Park, NJ: Send the Light Publishers, 1978.

Laubach, Frank C. *Prayer, the Mightiest Force in the World.* Old Tappan, NJ: Fleming H. Revell Co., 1959.

Lewis, C.S. *Letters to Malcolm: Chiefly on Prayer.* San Diego: Harcourt, Brace, Jovanovich, 1973.

Lindsell, Harold. *When You Pray.* Grand Rapids: Baker Book House, 1975.

McGaw, Francis A. *Praying Hyde.* Minneapolis: Bethany House Publications, 1970.

Manschreck, Clyde. *Prayers of the Reformers.* Epworth Press, 1958.

Morgan, G. Campbell. *The Practice of Prayer.* Grand Rapids: Baker Book House, Morgan Library, n.d.

Müeller, George. *Answers to Prayer.* Chicago: Moody Press, n.d.

Murray, Andrew, and Choy, Leona. *Key to the Missionary Problem.* Ft. Washington, PA: Christian Literature Crusade, Inc., 1980.

Murray, Andrew. *The Ministry of Intercession: A Plea for More Prayer.* Old Tappan, NJ: Fleming H. Revell Co., 1952.

————— . *The Prayer Life.* Chicago: Moody Press, Andrew Murray Series, n.d.

————— . *With Christ in the School of Prayer.* Old Tappan, NJ: Fleming H. Revell, Co., n.d.

National Prayer Committee. *Concerts of Prayer.* Cassette Tape Training Pocket. San Bernardino, CA: NPC, 1983.

Nouwen, Henri J. *With Open Hands.* Notre Dame, IN: Ave Maria Press, 1972.

Prime, Derek. *Created to Praise.* Downers Grove, IL: Inter-Varsity Press, 1981.

Rinker, Rosalind. *Prayer: Conversing with God.* Grand Rapids: Zondervan Publishing House, n.d.

————— . *Praying Together.* Rev. ed. Grand Rapids: Zondervan Publishing House, 1980.

Sanders, J. Oswald. *Prayer Power Unlimited.* Chicago: Moody Press, 1977.

Shoemaker, Helen S. *The Secret of Effective Prayer.* Waco, TX: Word, Inc., 1976.

Shedd, Charlie W. *How to Develop a Praying Church.* Nashville: Abingdon Press, 1964.

Taylor, Jack R. *Prayer: Life's Limitless Reach.* Nashville: Broadman Press, 1977.

Thielicke, Helmut. *Our Heavenly Father.* Grand Rapids: Baker Book House, Minister's Paperback Library Series, 1974.

Thomas, J. Moulton. *Prayer Power.* Waco, TX: Word, Inc., 1976.

Torrey, R.A. *How to Pray.* Chicago: Moody Press, n.d.

————. *The Power of Prayer.* Grand Rapids: Zondervan Publishing House, 1971.

Tozer, A.W. *The Knowledge of the Holy.* New York: Harper & Row Publications, Inc., 1978.

White, John. *Daring to Draw Near: People in Prayer.* Downers Grove, IL: Inter-Varsity Press, 1977.

*Great Commission Prayer Crusade Prayer Handbook,* vols. 1,2. San Bernardino, CA: Campus Crusade for Christ, 1975.

Laubach, Frank. *Open Window, Swinging Doors: Personal Diary of Dr. Frank Laubach.* Ventura, CA: Regal Books, 1955.

*1983 Prayer Group Directory.* South Bend, MD: Charismatic Renewal Service, 1983.

*Prayer: It's Deeper Dimensions.* Grand Rapids: Zondervan Publishing House, 1963.

*Prayers of the Middle Ages: Light from a Thousand Years.* Nashville: The Upper Room, 1954.

## Preparations

Barrett, David, ed. *World Christian Encyclopedia: A Comparative Survey of Churches and Religions in the Modern World, A.D. 1900 to 2000.* New York: Oxford University Press, Inc., 1982.

Bryant, David. *In the Gap: What It Means to Be a World Christian.* Ventura, CA: Regal Books, 1984.

Conn, Harvie. *Evangelism: Doing Justice and Preaching Grace.* Grand Rapids: Zondervan Publishing House, 1982.

Costas, Orlando E. *The Church and Its Mission: A Shattering Critique from the Third World.* Wheaton, IL: Tyndale House Publishers, 1974.

Dayton, Edward R. and Wilson, Samuel, eds. *The Future of World Evangelization.* Monrovia, CA: MARC, 1984.

Douglas, J.D., ed. *Let the Earth Hear His Voice: Lausanne Compendium.* Minneapolis: World Wide Publications, 1975.

Foster, Richard J. *Celebration of Discipline: Paths to Spiritual Growth.* New York: Harper & Row Publications, Inc., 1978.

————. *Freedom of Simplicity.* New York: Harper & Row Publications, Inc., 1981.

Frenchak, David and Keyes, Sharrel, eds. *Metro-Ministry.* Elgin, IL: David C. Cook Publishing Co., 1979.

Hayes, Dan. *Fireseeds of Spiritual Awakening.* San Bernardino, CA: Here's Life Publishers, 1983.

Hummel, Charles E. *Fire in the Fireplace: Contemporary Charismatic Renewal.* Downers Grove, IL: Inter-Varsity Press, 1977.

*Lausanne Occasional Papers: Thailand Reports #5-19.* Wheaton, IL: 1981.

Nelson, Marlin L. *The How and Why of Third World Missions: An Asian Case Study.* Pasadena, CA: William Carey Library Publications, 1976.

Wagner, C. Peter. *On the Crest of the Wave.* Ventura, CA: Regal Books, 1983.

Wilson, J. Christy. *Today's Tent Makers.* Wheaton, IL: Tyndale House Publishers, 1979.

Wilson, Samuel, ed. *Mission Handbook: North American Protestant Ministries Overseas.* Monrovia, CA: MARC, 1980.

Winter, Ralph. *The Grounds for a New Thrust in World Mission.* Pasadena, CA: William Carey Library Publications, 1978.

————. *Penetrating the Last Frontiers.* Pasadena, CA: William Carey Library Publications, 1978.

————. *The World Christian Movement: 1950-1975.* Pasadena, CA: William Carey Library Publications, 1976.

Winter, Ralph and Hawthorne, Steve. *Perspectives on a World Christian Movement.* Pasadena, CA: William Carey Library Publications, 1982.

World Evangelical Fellowship. *I Will Build My Church.* Papers Presented at Wheaton 1983 International Consultation. Monrovia, CA: MARC, 1983.

## Prospects

Anderson, Norman. *Issues of Life and Death.* Downers Grove, IL: Inter-Varsity Press, n.d.

Beachey, Duane. *Faith in a Nuclear Age.* Scottdale, PA: Herald Press, 1983.

Bernbaum, John A. *Perspectives on Peacemaking: Biblical Options in the Nuclear Age.* Ventura, CA: Regal Books, 1984.

Broek, C.M. and Webb, John W. *A Geography of Mankind.* New York: McGraw-Hill Publication Co.

Clouse, Robert, ed. War: *Four Christian Views.* Downers Grove, IL: Inter-Varsity Press, 1981.

Dayton, Edward and Wagner, C. Peter. *Unreached Peoples.* Unreached Peoples Series, 1970 through 1984. Elgin, IL: David C. Cook Publishing Co.

Elsdon, Ronald. *Bent World.* Downers Grove, IL: Inter-Varsity Press, 1981.

Graham, Billy. *Approaching Hoofbeats.* Waco, TX: Word, Inc. 1983.

Griffiths, Brian. *Is Revolution Change?* Downers Grove, IL: Inter-Varsity Press, n.d.

Guiness, Os. *Dust of Death.* Downers Grove, IL: Inter-Varsity Press, 1973.

Hubbard, David A. *Right Living in a World Gone Wrong.* Downers Grove, IL: Inter-Varsity Press, 1981.

Malik, Charles H. *Christian Critique of the University.* Downers Grove, IL: Inter-Varsity Press, 1982.

Mooneyham, W. Stanley. *What Do You Say to a Hungry World?* Waco, TX: Word, Inc., 1975.

Murphree, Jon. *A Loving God and a Suffering World.* Downers Grove, IL: Inter-Varsity Press, 1981.

Naisbitt, John. *Megatrends: Ten New Directions Transforming Our Lives.* New York: Warner Books, Inc., 1982.

Newbigin, Lesslie. *The Other Side of 1984.* Geneva: World Council of Churches, 1983.

Ramseyer, Robert. *Mission and the Peace Witness.* Scottdale, PA: Herald Press, 1979.

Schaeffer, Francis A. *A Christian Manifesto.* Westchester, IL: Crossway Books, 1981.

_____ . *Death in the City.* Downers Grove, IL: Inter-Varsity Press, 1969.

_____ . *Pollution and the Death of Man.* Wheaton, IL: Tyndale House Publishers, 1970.

Scott, Waldron. *Bring Forth Justice.* Grand Rapids: Wm. B. Eerdmans Publishing Co., 1980.

Sider, Ronald J. *Cry Justice: The Bible on Hunger and Poverty.* Downers Grove, IL: Inter-Varsity Press, 1980.

_____ . *Rich Christians in an Age of Hunger: A Biblical Study.* Downers Grove, IL: Inter-Varsity Press, 1977.

Sider, Ronald J. and Taylor, Richard K. *Nuclear Holocaust and the Christian Hope: A Book for Christian Peacemakers*. Downers Grove, IL: Inter-Varsity Press, 1982.

Simon, Arthur. *Bread for the World*. Grand Rapids: Wm. B. Eerdmans Publishing Co., 1975.

Sine, Tom. *The Church in Response to Human Need*. Monrovia, CA: MARC, 1983.

————. *The Mustard Seed Conspiracy*. Waco, TX: Word, Inc., 1981.

Stott, John R.W., ed. *The Year Two Thousand*. Downers Grove, IL: Inter-Varsity Press, 1983.

Tonna, Benjamin. *A Gospel for the Cities*. Maryknoll, NY: Orbis books, 1982.

Ward, Barbara. *Progress for a Small Planet*. New York: W.W. Norton and Co., Inc., 1979.

*Area Handbooks*. Washington, D.C.: U.S. Printing Office.

# VIDEO TRAINING WITH THE AUTHOR

**World Christian Video Training Curriculum**
Over the past ten years, David Bryant has traveled the United States presenting his World Christian Conferences and Concerts of Prayer Seminars to thousands of Christians on campuses and in churches. Benefit from these years of experience as you interact with the author in a classroom setting or informally in your own home, through *video cassettes.*

These video conferences are useful to student groups, laypeople and local churches. Includes five hours of video cassettes for each conference, plus student workbooks/discussion guides, and leaders' guides. Many of the World Christian Handbooks, beginning with *In the Gap,* can be used to follow up the video training.

Each training experience can be pursued in a variety of ways. For example: in a one-weekend event; during six Saturday morning study breakfasts; over a series of evening sessions for six nights in ten; extended Sunday School sessions, etc. Write for the free brochure.

## RECOVERY Series: Getting Set for the Coming Global Awakening

Missions motivation by giving the biblical, theoretical, and practical *overview* of what it means to be a World Christian in this generation. Recommended for those who are ready to build a basic *framework* for personal and corporate involvement in the world mission of the Church.

## BREAKTHROUGH Series: Explorations into World Christian Discipleship

Missions motivation by giving biblical and practical experimentation with personal aspects of a World Christian life-style. Recommended for those who want to act upon personal implications of the world mission of the Church for their day-to-day life as Christ's disciples.

## CONVERGE Series: Becoming Teams of World Christians

Missions motivation by giving biblical and practical experimentation with the corporate aspects of a World Christian life-style. Recommended for those who want to act upon corporate implications of the world mission of the Church for their day-to-day life together as Christ's disciples.

Available for rent or sale from:
> Gospel Light Media
> 2300 Knoll Drive
> Ventura, CA 93003
> 1-800-4-GOSPEL